PRAISE FOR *BUSINESS ANALYSIS AND LEADERSHIP*

"The world of business analysis is about any controlled organizational changes; not just the ones we call projects. It is a structured way of identifying, formalizing and managing those changes to ensure alignment to business objectives. To do this well, the BA requires a combination of discipline skills, knowledge and behaviours.

This book provides an overview of many important characteristics of a BA as both a leader and change agent. It draws together a diverse set of sources to help a BA gain a deeper understanding of what it takes to be a change leader from any perspective, whether it is in a project (agile or traditional), waterfall, continuous improvement, or enterprise initiative. It also emphasizes that successful business analysts require an understanding not just of the scope of the challenge or opportunity, but awareness and sensitivity to the personalities, politics and environment they are operating within." **Kathleen Barret, former President and CEO, International Institute for Business Analysis**

D0140231

Business Analysis and Leadership

Business Analysis and Leadership

Influencing change

Edited by
Penny Pullan and
James Archer

KoganPage

LONDON PHILADELPHIA NEW DELHI

First published in Great Britain and the United States in 2013 by Kogan Page Limited

120 Pentonville Road	1518 Walnut Street, Suite 1100	4737/23 Ansari Road
London N1 9JN	Philadelphia PA 19102	Daryaganj
United Kingdom	USA	New Delhi 110002
www.koganpage.com		India

© Penny Pullan and James Archer 2013

The right of Penny Pullan and James Archer to be identified as the editors of this work has been asserted by them in accordance with the Copyright, Designs and Patents Act 1988.

ISBN: 978 0 7494 6862 0
E-ISBN: 978 0 7494 6863 7

British Library Cataloguing-in-Publication Data

A CIP record for this book is available from the British Library.

Library of Congress Cataloging-in-Publication Data

Business analysis and leadership : influencing change / [edited by] Penny Pullan, James Archer.
    pages cm
Includes index.
ISBN 978-0-7494-6862-0 – ISBN 978-0-7494-6863-7 (ebook)   1. Business analysts.
2. Leadership. 3. Organizational change. I. Pullan, Penny. II. Archer, James
(Business writer)
    HD69.B87B87 2013
    658.4′092–dc23
                                                2013015785

Typeset by Amnet
Printed and bound in India by Replika Press Pvt Ltd

CONTENTS

ABOUT THE EDITORS

Penny Pullan works mainly with people in large organizations who are grappling with tricky projects and programmes of change. Many of these are working in business analysis, influencing and enabling successful change in tricky situations. This means:

- changing, complex and often ambiguous requirements;
- a complex and usually culturally diverse mix of stakeholders, who need to be interested, engaged and involved;
- probably team members dispersed all over the world;
- lots of risk!

Within this context, she brings order and clarity, providing support and tools to develop the leadership skills necessary for effective business change.

She has 20 years' experience across many multinational companies and the consultancy she founded, Making Projects Work Ltd. She hosts the free, global, virtual Business Analysis Summit (**www.basummit.com**) in November each year, which is attended by thousands of business analysts, and helps to organize the annual Business Analysis Conference Europe.

She contributed chapters on facilitation, global working and virtual teams, developing thought leadership, visual thinking and dealing with uncertainty to this book. She has a PhD from Cambridge University, is a certified professional facilitator and has multiple qualifications in business analysis, and project and programme management, as well as being a chartered engineer.

Contact: e-mail: penny@makingprojectswork.co.uk; **www.baleadership .com/penny**

James Archer is a consultant and trainer working to bring about change in organizations. He specializes in:

- connecting high-level strategy to all levels of organizations and projects;
- helping people understand what the real problem they need to solve is;
- applying systemic thinking to real-life problems;
- using business analysis techniques to cut through complexity;
- understanding the implications of solutions for different stakeholders;
- providing innovative solutions to business problems.

He has helped organize the Business Analysis Conference Europe since it began, and co-founded the BCS Business Change Group. In 2009 he was voted Business Analyst of the Year.

After teaching in Darfur and programming in Cobol, he moved to the Royal Borough of Kensington and Chelsea council as a business analyst on award-winning projects. Most recently, he defined common business processes in social care across three councils as part of the ground-breaking tri-borough project in London. He is an associate partner of Perspectiv and a qualified consultant in the Volere approach to requirements.

He contributed chapters on skills, the business analyst as a facilitative leader, and ethics to this book. He is completing his Master's degree in innovation, creativity and leadership at City University, London.

Contact: e-mail: james@perspectiv.co.uk; **www.baleadership.com/james**

ABOUT THE CONTRIBUTORS

David Baskerville is a lead business analyst for a multinational financial services firm, who has had detailed experience of introducing new and re-engineering business processes and procedures. He has undertaken a business analyst role for the last 16 years, supporting the branch network as well as other non-face-to-face delivery channels. He is passionate about the business analyst role and developing others.

Dav Bisessar is a strategist and business architect in IBM's Global Business Services division. During his 20 years in the business, he has advised chief information and technology officers, and solved major issues in a range of industry sectors, including financial markets, retail, media and government. His work in the fields of technology strategy and business architecture has led to assignments across the world. He is also head of the IBM UK business analysis community of practice, and has a keen interest in photography and travel, sometimes at the same time.

Kevin Brennan, CBAP, PMP, is the chief business analyst and executive vice-president for IIBA. He led the development of Version 2.0 of *The Business Analysis Body of Knowledge*® (BABOK® Guide) and was also one of the authors of the CBAP exam. He is a frequent speaker on business analysis, project management, and software quality assurance topics at conferences. He has over a decade of experience as a business analyst and project manager across several industry sectors, including regulated professions, utilities, automobile manufacturing, courier services and mortgage banking.

Michael Brown has been a business skills trainer for over 15 years. He works with organizations of all shapes and sizes around the world, specializing in negotiations, conflict handling and leadership. Prior to that he worked in sales and marketing in the hospitality industry for 15 years. Michael is a keen blogger, and posts regularly on business skills topics at **www. reallearningforachange.com**. He creates business skills videos using a 'How not to' approach: these are available at **www.hownottovideos. wordpress.com**.

Sarah Coleman is an international consultant specializing in business transformation and organizational change. She began her career in business analysis and IT, subsequently moving into project and programme management.

Sarah founded Business Evolution (**www.businessevolution.co**) to help organizations across the public and private sectors bring about significant shifts in direction, shape, culture and performance. She is a visiting senior fellow at Lincoln University, a guest speaker and the author of blogs, books and articles on the subject of project leadership.

Joseph da Silva is currently head of service design at British Gas and over the last 12 years has held senior roles within business analysis for organizations including Virgin Media, IBM and Skandia. He is also currently the president of the UK Chapter of the IIBA and the author of *What Is a Business Analyst... and Why Do I Need One?* As a founder member of pragnalysis.com, a website offering entirely free business analysis resources, templates and tools, he is passionate about the free exchange of ideas and knowledge across the business analysis community. He is currently writing his second book, entitled *Business Analysis in Practice*, and in his spare time he is a keen musician, photographer and runner.

Nick de Voil is a certified management consultant with over 20 years' experience. He is the founder and managing director of De Voil Consulting, a UK-based consultancy that helps organizations to design and build platforms for outstanding customer experience. He is also a director of the IIBA's UK chapter.

Simon Edwards has 20 years' experience working in change in international banks in London. He has worked as a business analyst and project and programme manager, including building a global team of business analysts and programme managers.

Tamsin Fulton, MA (RCA) is a service design consultant working with colleagues in local and national government to deliver complex change projects. Through applying the principles of design she models new services and new ways of working, while embedding innovative thinking to find new routes to better services.

Allan Kelly works for Software Strategy, where he provides training and consulting in software development, business strategy and agile practices. He is the author of *Business Patterns for Software Developers* (2012) and *Changing Software Development: Learning to become agile* (2008). Find out more about him at **www.allankelly.net** and on Twitter as @allankellynet.

Andrew Kendall is a consultant and trainer, currently managing a creative problem-solving hub for the New South Wales government in Sydney, Australia. He holds an MBA with a major in strategic information technology from the Graduate School of Business at the University of Technology,

Sydney. When not consulting, he runs a social enterprise designing play pro-grammes for children's hospitals, having previously led a team at London's Great Ormond Street Hospital for Children.

Emma Langman specializes in using systems thinking approaches for help-ing her clients to lead change through her company Progression Partner-ship Ltd (**www.progressionpartnership.com**). Her projects range from large multinationals wanting to improve their structures, processes and practices, through to local authorities, charities and small and medium-sized enter-prises. She has been a fan of these ways of thinking for 15 years, and is delighted to have the opportunity to share these ideas through her consul-tancy work, keynote speeches and this book.

Jake Markham is a director at Credit Suisse, and EMEA lead for Client Technology Solutions, a horizontal group responsible for client technology. He started his career as a graphic designer, and specializes in user experi-ence and business engineering. He organizes Credit Suisse's business analysis community events and training opportunities, and plays a key role in Credit Suisse's relationship with industry groups like the IIBA UK chapter.

Chris Matts is a consultant who specializes in building risk management and trading systems for investment banks. He favours practical approaches that work over theory that sounds good. He is writing a graphic novel on project risk management using real options. He blogs his random musings at **www.decision-coach.com** and **www.theitriskmanager.wordpress.com**.

Roger Mawle is a consultant business analyst working for a large commer-cial broadcaster in London.

Kent J McDonald is an author and consultant who helps organizations under-stand and solve the problems they face. He is active in the business analysis and agile software development communities, helping people share stories about what does and does not work. He shares those stories through **www.beyondrequirements.com**, **www.techwell.com** and **www.projectconnections.com** in addition to presentations at various conferences and local user groups.

Ruth Murray-Webster is a leading organizational change consultant, man-aging partner of Lucidus Consulting Ltd, and a visiting fellow at Cranfield School of Management. She's written several books on the human side of risk and was the lead author for the 2010 update of *Management of Risk: Guidance for practitioners* (M_o_R).

John Niland is best known as a conference speaker and coach with VCO Global (**www.vco-global.com**), focusing on creating opportunity via better dialogue with customers and the marketplace. He is one of the co-founders of the European Forum of Independent Professionals, following 12 years of coaching more than 500 professionals to create more value in their work. His book *The Courage to Ask* is co-authored with Kate Daly.

Vanessa Randle is a top UK graphic recorder, working through her company thinkingvisually Ltd. Together with Penny Pullan she founded Graphics Made Easy, which provides resources and courses for business analysts and others who would like to add more visuals to their work, especially with groups. You can find out more and sign up for a free e-course at **www.graphicsmadeeasy.co.uk**

Adrian Reed is a consultant, trainer and speaker who is passionate about the analysis profession. He is principal consultant and director of Blackmetric Business Solutions, a niche business analyst consulting firm. Additionally, he holds the position of marketing director of the UK Chapter of the IIBA and is constantly looking for ways of promoting the value that good-quality business analysis can bring. You can contact him, and read his blog, by visiting **www.adrianreed.co.uk**

James Robertson of the Atlantic Systems Guild is a consultant, teacher, author and project leader, whose area of concern is the requirements for products, and the contribution that good requirements make to successful projects. He is a leading proponent of the principle of introducing creativity into the requirements process. He is co-author of *Mastering the Requirements Process: Getting requirements right* (2012), *Requirements-Led Project Management: Discovering David's slingshot* (2005), the Volere approach to requirements engineering, and *Complete Systems Analysis: The workbook, the textbook, the answers* (1994), a two-volume text and case study that teaches the craft of systems analysis.

Suzanne Robertson is a principal and founder of the Atlantic Systems Guild. She is co-author of *Mastering the Requirements Process*, which is a guide for practitioners on finding requirements and writing them so that all stakeholders can understand them. Her current work includes research and consulting on the management, sociological and innovative aspects of requirements. The product of this research is Volere, a requirements process, template and techniques for assessing requirements quality and for specifying requirements. Her other interests include a passion for the opera, cooking, skiing and finding out about curious things.

Melanie Rose is the business analyst team lead at Totaljobs Group (TJG) and has over 10 years' experience in delivering projects across print and digital media using both waterfall (Prince 2) and agile (Scrum) methodologies. She steered TJG's business analysis team through the choppy waters of the company's transition from Prince 2 to Scrum delivery at the start of 2009. As the company seeks to improve and mature its agile delivery model, she works within TJG's technology management team to drive process improvement, delivery efficiency and iterative thinking across the business.

Kate Stuart-Cox is a founding partner of Perspectiv. Before founding Perspectiv, she acquired over 20 years of management and leadership experience in new product development and new business development within the publishing and media arena, integrating creative problem solving, and training and development initiatives to enhance performance and innovation.

Corrine Thomas has over 20 years of experience as an analyst across a range of industry sectors including local government, healthcare, telecommunications and financial services. She is currently the lead business analysis practice manager with Virgin Media and is a certified trainer and master practitioner of NLP. She is passionate about developing the business analysis profession and combines her experience of analysis with her NLP expertise to create and deliver soft skills training tailored to the challenges faced by busy business analysis professionals.

Andy Wilkins is an honorary senior visiting fellow at Cass Business School and is part of the team delivering the new Master's course in innovation, creativity and leadership at City University, London. He is also a founding partner of the UK-based professional services firm Perspectiv and works to enable organizations to improve performance. He has experience working with clients in the United States, Europe and Asia across a wide spectrum of businesses, functions and needs.

ACKNOWLEDGEMENTS

This book embodies the friendly and collaborative nature of the business analysis community. Our very first thank-you must go to all the authors who have contributed chapters. They are exceptional people, and we are very pleased to share them with the wider world. We editors are delighted that we didn't have to take on the huge task of editing alone, but were able to share this, bouncing ideas off each other and holding each other to account (and sometimes jointly letting each other off the hook of over-enthusiastic deadlines!).

This book would not have seen the light of day without our commissioning editor, Julia Swales. She spotted a gap in the market and went on the hunt for possible authors, meeting us at a packed business analysis event in the City of London. She quickly embraced the concept of a multi-author book and has been very supportive throughout.

Vanessa Randle has come up trumps with the illustrations in this book, magically bringing concepts to life. Thank you, Vanessa! Claire Smith and Malcolm Pullan have supported us, carefully read through many chapters and given thoughtful suggestions for improvements along the way, for which we are truly grateful.

Penny would particularly like to thank her family for their support once again during her seemingly-endless writing and editing of chapters. James would like to thank colleagues for their inspiration. Over the years, James and Suzanne Robertson have provided friendship and wonderful opportunities for collaboration. Andy Wilkins was an inspiring lecturer on the inaugural Master's course in innovation, creativity and leadership at City University, London and is now a business partner. Andy, Nick De Voil and Jake Markham have provided invaluable feedback on chapters.

Finally, we come to dedications:

Penny: I would like to dedicate this book to the memory of my mother, Cristabel Urry. While she never was a business analyst, she displayed many of the leadership skills described in this book. She was an inspiration to me, no stranger to stepping up with courage, whether in MI5, in the soup kitchens of Crossroads squatter camp or crossing the Atlantic several times in a sailing boat. She proved a model to me in the way that I hope this book will be a model to business analysts and consultants all over the world. Thanks, Mum!

James: To my dad, who would have loved this book, and to Claire for not only being supportive but challenging me all the way.

FOREWORD

Debra Paul
Managing Director, Assist Knowledge Development

The organizations of the 21st century, across all sectors and of all types, have to cope with an international marketplace where change is frequent and customer expectations continue to rise. However, business change initiatives and information systems projects have a chequered history, with many resulting in limited success or failure. Within this context, the work of business change professionals is of paramount importance if organizations are to succeed and grow. Given the prevailing economic situation, it is vital that these programmes are based upon a rigorous case for investment that ensures the fundamental issues are addressed and the most pertinent changes are recommended. In short, organizations need to do the right things rather than adopt those actions that are expedient.

And this is where business analysis has so much to contribute. Activities such as stakeholder engagement and situation analysis are vital if change programmes are to be successful. If an organization wants to resolve a problem then a thorough investigation of the issues followed by a creative approach to generate feasible options is required. If a great opportunity is to be grasped, the business needs must be examined and defined holistically so that they can be addressed in their entirety. If a new policy or law is to be introduced, then it is important to conduct an accurate impact analysis and consider all of the possible implications. A quick examination of many problems experienced by organizations exposes how some of the key skills, techniques and frameworks of business analysis could at best ensure such problems are avoided or, at the very least, help to diminish their impact.

To achieve this though, senior business analysts have to display competence in a range of areas, not least of which include the ability to challenge, lead and influence. Technical proficiency and business knowledge, while vital, are not enough. Business analysts have to gain credibility and respect at an early stage in a business change project if they are to deliver the beneficial impact needed by their organizations. For this, the skills of leadership are vital.

This book was written to help business analysts develop leadership skills and to enable them to understand leadership across different contexts. Four different perspectives on business analysis and leadership are explored: leadership of self, leadership within your project, leadership within your organization and leadership in the wider world.

Understanding of self has to be the starting point for success in any profession. This is assuredly the case for business analysis, so the chapters in this section provide insights into some key personal competencies. Communication skills such as listening and building rapport are fundamental building blocks if business analysis is to be conducted effectively. To really understand business needs, a business analyst has to be curious about the business and work environment and has to be prepared to challenge and highlight potential impacts and inconsistencies; passive responses are simply not acceptable.

The second section of this book looks at leadership in projects. A key topic covers engagement with those who have some involvement with the project or are affected by the outcome. Whether this concerns working with one of the business analyst's closest colleagues – the project manager – or with the wider stakeholder community, building relationships underpins the work of a business analyst and failure to do so can lead to serious problems, if not disaster. We are also given guidance for running successful meetings or workshops, where the business analyst has to be able to demonstrate authority, focus, organization and the ability to keep everyone engaged. Within projects there may be occasions when dealing with actual or potential conflict situations, and understanding strategies to address them, is essential, requiring business analysts to demonstrate leadership in order to navigate towards a positive outcome. The book provides invaluable insights to help business analysts should a conflict arise.

One of the great challenges for business analysts is the ubiquitous issue of 'solutionizing'. OK, this is a made-up word, but most business analysts will find this syndrome all too familiar. Handling situations where the solution has already been identified before the analysts come on board demands strong leadership skills. Business analysis work, at its essence, is about problem-solving, and just accepting pre-defined solutions requires acquiescence rather than analysis. This book explores the use of abstraction and viewpoint analysis in order to gain a clear view of the real problem before solving it, and also asks us to consider some key questions including 'is this a problem worth solving?' and 'is this a "tame" or "wicked" problem?'; vital questions when time and budgets are constrained. One of the features of this book is the excellent quotations supplied throughout and, to my mind, Chapter 9 contains one of the most thought-provoking (JK Galbraith's comment on mental models).

If there is a role that has 'agile' written into its manifesto, it is unquestionably that of the business analyst. The overriding focus for business analysis has to be on achieving the best possible outcome for the organization, and several chapters in the 'projects' section provide insights in support of this. We are reminded that collaboration is key, as is doing what is right for the situation, and that handling the variety of uncertain and ambiguous situations that business analysts face requires the ability to understand which approach will work best for the situation, which techniques need to be applied and how the ever-present risks are managed. Following an approach or method unthinkingly is not good enough. Delivering business agility is the essence of agile and to achieve this, business analysts need to lead by example.

Beyond the project, all business analysts have to operate within the rules, procedures and goals of the organization. At this level, the analysts need to be aware of the culture and climate, the constraints of global working – often with virtual teams, the internal politics and the levers of power within the organization. Understanding the organizational context is critical and this book provides a variety of tools and thinking frameworks that help business analysts in their endeavours. For example, we have a discourse on systems thinking – arguably one of the most useful philosophies available to business analysts. We are also given insights into working with partners and strategic thinking – again vital elements of the analyst toolkit.

Business analysis has developed and matured over the last two decades. The term 'BA profession' is now mentioned far more frequently than ever before. There are conferences dedicated to business analysis. Ultimately, some business analysts may wish to become thought leaders, raising the standards, extending the boundaries and enabling the development of the business analysis community. Penny Pullan offers some perceptive insights on this in Chapter 24. While this is not for everyone, it is still imperative to recognize the importance of continuous development whether through reading, studying or learning through experience. The prospects for business analysts have grown as the role becomes more accepted and understood in the wider world. But with recognition brings responsibility. Leadership in the areas of ethics and professionalism is something to which all analysts should aspire. As James Archer suggests in Chapter 25, developing an 'ethical radar' is vital for the professional business analyst.

This book has been written with the leadership role of the business analyst in mind. It explores many perspectives on leadership and reflects a wealth of experience from its contributors. It is vital that business analysts adopt a leadership role and this book will provide a valuable resource to enable them to do so. Some people aim for the horizon while others are examining the ground; I know which is more desirable for anyone wishing to succeed as a business analyst.

Introduction

Business analysis is the key to successful business change. The purpose of this book is to inspire all those involved in business analysis to develop into leaders, in order to meet the needs of today's and tomorrow's world.

Who is this book for?

Do you work with business change? Do you strive to understand organizations undergoing change, define what's needed and deliver value for people? Do you work towards the delivery of real and lasting benefits for your organization? If so, this book is written for you.

We call this work 'business analysis', and we will refer to those who carry it out as 'business analysts' throughout this book. For us, a business analyst is a catalyst for change, taking organizations from analysis of the present situation to innovation for the future, while adding value at every step.

This book is written for all who practise business analysis, whatever their job title. Business analysis is developing rapidly, yet the terms 'business analysis' and 'business analyst' are not universally recognized, even by many of those who practise the discipline. So, even if you don't call yourself a business analyst, this book is written for you if you manage the delivery of change in organizations. Process and business improvement specialists will benefit, as well as other internal and external consultants. Change, project, programme and portfolio managers should find it useful too, as will business architects. The contents of this book will apply whether people work in the private sector, in the public sector or for non-governmental organizations.

This book is designed to help you gain practical advice and ideas on how to develop your leadership of change, starting with self-leadership and moving on to leadership of your project, your organization and the wider world. With a set of world-class authors drawing from their years of experience, you will find plenty to help you reflect on your current skills and develop further.

What does a business analyst do?

'So what exactly do you do?' This is a question that people regularly ask business analysts. Unfortunately, many seem to find it difficult to answer this question and articulate their own worth, leading to misunderstandings about the role and the value it can bring.

Business analysis involves both understanding and responding to a business situation. It is therefore carried out knowingly or unknowingly in every business and organization in the world. It is a role whose purpose is to turn strategic goals and visions into reality while adding value. The role begins with understanding challenges and problems, and discovering new opportunities that help the business meet its vision and goals. The business analyst's role shouldn't end until the identified benefits and value to the organization have been realized. This is the ideal; the reality can be different.

Meeting the demands of rapid and constant change is not easy. It requires an inclusive leadership style, thinking innovatively, working collaboratively and acting strategically. By applying these approaches the best business analysts increase their credibility and show the strategic value of business analysis to organizations. They help their organizations to learn more about themselves as well as how to use that knowledge to solve problems and take advantage of new opportunities.

To operate at this high level, business analysts need to act as leaders within their project and organization. To be effective, they will need strong self-leadership skills to build upon.

A systemic and holistic approach

Business analysts achieve better results by paying attention to all the different elements that have an impact on change. They need to look across organizations' processes, people and culture. This helps them to understand the context for the change, in addition to any technology and infrastructure that could enable the change to happen.

This book is divided into four parts: self, project, organization and wider world. Each part looks at how the different elements of change interact and how the business analyst can deal with each element, as well as the system as a whole.

Why this book?

The editors have spent years working with thousands of business analysts around the world. During this time, we have noticed a huge variation in their capability, from very poor to excellent. We have met outstanding business analysts, who are real assets to their organizations. They create value, save money, build relationships and influence leaders. They are real agents for change, and their organizations value them as trusted advisers. At the other end of the spectrum are those who restrict the role (or are restricted) to acting as 'order takers', missing opportunities to make a difference at every turn. Too often they write down what people in the business say they need, rather than working with the business to draw out what is really needed.

What is it that makes the difference between outstanding and adequate business analysts? Could it be that outstanding business analysts have a much deeper knowledge of business analysis tools and techniques? Perhaps many years of experience? Perhaps they have attended a large number of training courses or have multiple certifications? Many of these are indeed helpful. However, the strongest indicator of an outstanding business analyst we have found is something extra. It is leadership. This provides a strong and committed mindset, the willingness to step up and take on a leading role, the courage to challenge appropriately and respectfully at all levels of the organization, and the drive to make a difference. Those we've interviewed in preparation for this book agree.

While there are many excellent books on the market covering tools and techniques for effective business analysis and change, we noticed a lack of books focusing on leadership and developing excellence specifically aimed at business analysis. That's where the idea for this book began. We noticed too a growing interest in leadership topics both in our work worldwide and in the conferences that we organize and attend. Penny Pullan's annual business analysis virtual summits have focused on leadership and have grown year on year (with over 1,500 participants in 2012). All of this reinforces the interest in the subject of leadership for change.

With stagnant economies around the globe, failing projects are no longer acceptable, if they ever were. Organizations realize that business analysis has a big part to play in preventing failure and providing better solutions. As a consequence, business analysis is booming around the world.

What will you get out of this book?

- *Self.* Leadership comes at different levels, and this book reflects that reality. First of all, we focus on leadership of self. Before people can lead others effectively, they need to develop a leadership mindset, becoming aware of their own strengths and weaknesses, building up the courage to act and honing communication and relationship skills.

- *Project.* Most business analysts work within projects and programmes of change. It is in the context of their project that business analysts lead, through their work with stakeholders as they build understanding of what's needed, and look to future. We explore how business analysts can lead through their relationships with stakeholders and in a variety of project settings.

FIGURE I.1 The different levels of leadership

- *Organization.* While many business analysts see no need to look beyond their immediate project, outstanding ones will always have one eye on the organization they work within. They realize that, in order to make change stick, they need to understand and engage widely across their whole organization. This requires an understanding of the entire system, the ability to deal with power and politics, skills in working across boundaries of culture, and an understanding of both strategy and commercial realities.

- *The wider world.* The very best business analysts realize that they have a lot to give to the wider world, starting with their own professional colleagues. From writing articles to presenting at conferences, they give back to their profession and, in the process, may be recognized as thought leaders. Others serve on professional associations such as the International Institute of Business Analysis (IIBA) around the world, supporting new analysts and developing the profession in many ways. Still more engage with others through networks, within and across companies and on social media, grappling with dilemmas and solving problems together.

This book, along with many supplementary resources at **www.baleadership. com**, aims to shine a light on all these areas, providing practical tips that can be applied straight away to make a difference.

Who are the authors and why were they selected?

In choosing the individual contributors to this book, the editors searched for people who were already recognized as outstanding business analysts, displaying the qualities described above. They have developed their skills through years of experience working in organizations and are living examples of business analysis leadership. Some of the authors now focus on supporting business analysts to develop leadership to the highest levels.

In addition to the chapters covering aspects of business analysis leadership, we have four opinion pieces. These are written by leading practitioners across a range of industries, from investment banking to television and recruitment. They bring their own personal views and stories on leadership.

A key to business analysis is to be broad-minded, to be able to see from a wide range of perspectives and enable others to do so. This book seeks to bring together and blend a wide range of perspectives and styles in order to model this.

We're delighted with the range of authors who have come together to create this book. They are inspiring people, and we hope that you enjoy their input as much as the editors have enjoyed working with them.

To support the book, we've created a website, **www.baleadership.com**. There you can access a wide range of resources for business analysis leadership, as well as finding out more about the book, the topics, the authors and their work. We hope that you will find it useful and that you'll join in the conversation there.

We wish you all the best as you explore how business analysis leadership can be the catalyst for successful change.

PART I
Leadership of self

Introduction to Part I

Leadership comes at different levels, and this book reflects that reality. First of all, in Part I, we focus on leadership of self. Before people can influence, inspire and lead others effectively, they need to develop a leadership mindset. This means becoming aware of their own strengths and weaknesses, building up the courage to challenge, and honing communication and relationship skills.

What do we mean by leadership of self?

A historical view of leadership is that of a general leading troops into battle from the front, with followers who have to obey whatever the cost. While this view might have made sense in 19th-century battles, it is of limited use in the complex world of 21st-century organizations. The leadership described in this book is much less about formal power and authority. Instead, it is much more about making a difference through shared vision and understanding, influencing and inspiring others to enable effective change.

Part I focuses on the inner work that's needed to build the foundations to become great at business analysis. To do so you'll need to develop self-awareness, understanding your strengths and weaknesses, as well as the values you hold dear. From there, you can build on your strengths and find ways to cover for your weaknesses. Knowing your own values will help you to see how they relate to the values of the other people you work with and those of your organization. Leadership of self also needs a positive mindset that takes responsibility and is proactive, even when this means challenging the status quo. For all of this, you'll need credibility, not on the basis of your professional competence alone, but also by paying attention to how others see you. Leaders are seen as honest, forward-looking and inspiring. Are you?

What does Part I cover?

Part I starts off in Chapter 1 by looking at the three sets of skills that business analysts need – professional, business and interpersonal skills – and how developing these is a never-ending job! It touches on the value of reflection in the life of a business analyst and how we most effectively learn by revisiting our basic assumptions rather than just polishing what we do.

Moving on, Chapter 2 looks at the imperative for those in business analysis to be able to challenge people, many of whom may be very senior inside organizations. It goes on to explore seven different ways build courage for these challenging situations.

'The business analyst as a facilitative leader' (Chapter 3) introduces the idea of facilitation being core to business analysis. This will appear again and again throughout this book. By offering process and structure, rather than the more traditional leadership of direction and answers, business analysis really encourages others to think and to find their own answers. The chapter works through a real example of how this inclusive leadership can work out in practice.

The rest of Part I looks at honing communication skills. Chapter 4 introduces a range of techniques from neurolinguistic programming (NLP) to support key aspects of communication, from building rapport to listening well and influencing. A positive mindset and a positive emotional state will help too.

Part I concludes with an opinion piece from the President of the UK Chapter of the International Institute of Business Analysis (IIBA). He asks if business analysts are waiting to be anointed as leaders, and encourages you to make the decision to step up to leadership now.

You can find additional resources for leadership of self at **www.baleadership.com**. These include an ongoing study on the subject of credibility, contrasting results for leaders in general with business analysts in particular, and an article on negotiation, which looks at five questions that can make the process of negotiating much smoother.

How does Part I relate to leadership in your project?

Part I forms the building blocks for the business analyst who wishes to work effectively within a project. Part II provides a whole range of ways to develop further in a project context.

Skills for business analysis

01

JAMES ARCHER AND KATE STUART-COX

There are three broad sets of skills and knowledge needed for business analysis: the technical skills of the profession, business knowledge, and a range of personal and interpersonal skills. This chapter concentrates on some of the key personal skills and developing approaches that pull together the three sets of skills and knowledge.

The role of a business analyst is to provide help to individuals and organizations. Edgar Schein first wrote about types of helping in *Process Consultation*, published in 1969. His distinction between 'expert' and 'process' consultant types of help, most recently articulated in his book *Helping* (Schein, 2010), indicates two very different approaches to business analysis. This chapter starts by explaining the differences from the perspective of business analysis and argues that business analysts should aim to be process consultants. The concept of process consultancy is particularly useful, as it describes the type of inclusive or facilitative leadership that we have in mind when we mention business analysis and leadership in the same breath.

The business analyst acting as a process consultant requires many different skills in order to provide help and leadership. Building on the concept of 'T-shaped skills', we propose the 'T-shaped business analyst' (see Figure 1.1) to show how even the biggest and baddest business analysis toolkit full of tools, techniques, models and methodologies is useless without the ability to work with people.

Business analysis involves listening to multiple voices, viewpoints and perspectives, analysing multiple situations, reflecting on all those voices, synthesizing them and pulling it all together into a proposed way (or ways) forward that meets both strategic needs and the needs of those on the ground.

This chapter covers a number of skills, approaches and ways of thinking. The three core skills of listening, reflecting and providing feedback are all explored. These skills are essential in being able to provide help, which ultimately is what business analysis is all about. Two different types of help and two types of learning are compared and contrasted. We conclude with a case study to show how the theory works in practice.

Providing help – expert versus process consultant

The consultant or business analyst can operate in one of two modes when helping people: as the 'expert', who provides information, diagnoses the problem and comes up with the solution, or as the 'process consultant', who works with the client to jointly understand problems and co-create solutions.

Business analysis can fall into either category. It is important to recognize which type of help is being provided. Most business analysts would like to think they are being the process consultant when often they are being the expert, a situation that may be caused by the actions of either the business analyst or the client. It may be explicit, for example clients may say they do not have the time to be involved, or it may just be the way things are done in that organization.

The term 'client' is one that is not used often enough by business analysts, who will frequently say they are working for 'the business'. The term 'client' means a person or organization using the services of a professional. It is critical that on any piece of work the business analyst is crystal clear who the client or clients are that he or she helping.

Expert help

There is always a tension between the amount of time the business analyst wants the client and people working for the client to give to a project and the amount they actually give (see Chapter 11). This can increase the pressure on business analysts to become experts. The following situations need to be true for the expert role to be successful:

1 The problem has been correctly diagnosed (see Chapter 8).

2 The problem is straightforward, tame or simple (see Chapter 9).

3 The client has effectively communicated exactly what they are expecting.

4 The client has thought through the consequences of the business analyst gathering the information. This means the client must be prepared to give access to the relevant people and knowledge. The client must also ensure the people being asked for information are clear about why they are being consulted.

5 The business analyst has the skills to discover and provide the information (see Chapter 26).

There are not many situations where the first four assumptions will be true. This means the expert role is usually extremely unhelpful, particularly at the beginning of a helping situation. There are further things to be careful of. First, the temptation is for business analysts to use their technical and business knowledge to assume that they understand the problem and potential solution better than the business, resulting in the conclusion that it is easier for the business analyst just to get on with it on the basis that he or she knows all the answers. Second, if the client loses interest or does not have time to be involved in the piece of work, one of the following may happen:

- The advice or solution can seem irrelevant to the business and is not acted on.
- Advice is pleasantly accepted and ignored.
- A defensive reaction may result and the proposal is opposed.

Process consultant help

The process consultant works on the assumption that the client remains fully involved in both understanding the real problem and identifying the proposed solution. The following guidelines will help you encourage collaboration and adopt a modest approach, demystifying the art and science of business analysis in the process:

1 You do not own the problem; the client does.

2 The client understands the business better than you do.

3 You are working jointly with the client to identify what to improve and how to improve it.

4 You use process and techniques to help the client to understand the problem and to develop and communicate potential solutions.

5 Always try to be helpful: business analysis is an overhead, and the client is the one directly creating value!

6 Only the client will know what will work in the particular situation. However, the business analyst should look for and propose a variety of potential solutions that are well thought through for the client to consider.

7 When clients learn to see the cause of the problem and how to come up with the solution themselves, the solution is far more likely to be successful.

8 It is your objective to leave clients better able to diagnose future problems and come up with their own solutions.

What type of help are you providing?

Whenever you have difficult situations in a piece of business analysis work, reflect on the type of help you are providing. Using these guidelines for process consultancy, can you readjust your thinking and behaviour? In stressful times it is easy to fall back into your comfort zone and to start behaving like the expert. The most important lesson from the process consultant approach for business analysts is to use models, tools, techniques and methodologies to help clients better understand their problem and the potential solutions. To achieve this requires the many skills of the T-shaped business analyst.

The T-shaped business analyst

Business analysis involves understanding how people, processes and technology combine with the various cultures and contexts within and sometimes outside an organization to create value of some description.

FIGURE 1.1   The T-shaped business analyst

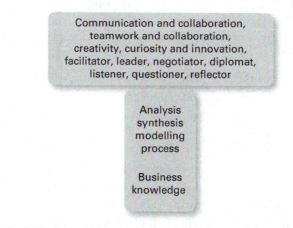

NOTE: Hard skills shown on the vertical axis and soft skills on the horizontal axis.

This holistic approach requires a fusing of technical and sociological skills. The vertical or 'north–south' axis of the T-shaped business analyst model shows the key technical skills and knowledge required, also described as 'hard skills' or content. Business knowledge does not mean being an expert in everything an organization does. It is about having enough knowledge to be taken seriously within an organization and to be able to make sense of things. The horizontal or 'east–west' axis represents transferable skills and knowledge, also described as 'soft skills' or process.

The power within business analysis lies in the potential to blend hard skills with soft skills, a fusion that can be used to great effect. 'People possessing these skills are able to shape their knowledge to fit the problem at hand rather than insist that their problems appear in a particular, recognizable form. Given their wide experience in applying functional knowledge, they are capable of convergent, synergistic thinking' (Leonard-Barton, 1995: 75).

The terms used to describe the skills and knowledge in Figure 1.1 are open to debate. What is not open to debate is that the most successful business analysis is carried out when those skills are combined.

Business analysis technical skills serve to share a common understanding of how aspects of a business function and to show different viewpoints and perspectives of organizations. The purpose of all tools is to shed light on situations and explain potential ways forward.

Challenging yourself and your beliefs

You have to learn from what you and others do, learning from what works and what doesn't work. Learning means being prepared to challenge yourself and your beliefs. Chris Argyris provides the single- and double-loop learning model in 'Teaching smart people how to learn' (Harvard Business Review, 2011). Becoming a T-shaped business analyst acting as a process consultant does not happen automatically; single-loop and double-loop learning provides an invaluable framework in which to develop your practice.

Single-loop and double-loop learning

Single-loop learning is improving what we already do. Double-loop learning means questioning the underlying assumptions behind what we do.

FIGURE 1.2 Single-loop and double-loop learning

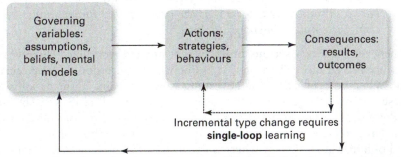

- *Governing variables:* the beliefs, mental models or assumptions that people want to keep intact and undamaged and use to solve problems. For example: *Business analysts believe that their organization doesn't appreciate business analysis.*

- *Action strategies:* the governing variables will determine the patterns of actions one takes, using those beliefs to solve problems. For example: *This business analysis function works on IT projects after the organization decides what its priorities are.*

- *Consequences:* the repercussions of solving the problem in the way that you did, getting the result you wanted or didn't want.

For example: *The organization is dissatisfied with the results of IT projects because their main problems do not seem to be resolved.*

- *Single-loop learning:* this is when the consequences are not quite what you expected or wanted (the less serious or severe the consequences the more likely you are to need single-loop learning), but instead of altering your governing variable you keep the governing variable the same and just alter or check over your action strategy. For example: *The business analysts continue to complain that the organization doesn't involve them early enough*; or *The organization has no trust in the business analysis function and brings in external consultants.*

- *Double-loop learning:* this is when, after the consequences show a wrong answer or an undesired result (the more serious or severe the consequences the more likely you are to need — double-loop learning), you alter the fundamental governing variables used to solve the problem. This type of learning requires you to reflect on your beliefs to check whether they are still relevant and to expand your knowledge to solve the problem in a way that results in more of what you want. For example: *A business analyst in the organization reads the opinion piece by Joseph da Silva at the end of Part I and realizes that his or her feeling of entitlement to be involved in projects earlier is misplaced*; or *The business analysis function now understands it has to promote the role so that the organization understands the strategic value of business analysis.*

Whenever there is a serious problem that appears very hard to solve or has been fixed more than once it is likely to require double-loop learning. When you reflect on the governing variables being applied, some of these trickier problems become easier to understand. However, sharing and getting common agreement of that understanding are another matter. It is hard to challenge and change the governing variables of individuals and organizations. This is where the skills of listening, feedback and acting as a process consultant and a T-shaped business analyst become even more relevant.

A further challenge arises where management or part of an organization has adopted new assumptions, beliefs or values. This means the new system, product or structure is designed with one set of beliefs, but used by people with another set of beliefs. This mismatch is so often missed but is where business analysis can provide a new level of value and importance.

The concepts outlined above of being a process consultant and a T-shaped business analyst who undertakes double-loop learning rely on the core personal skills of reflection, listening and feedback, at which we'll now take a closer look.

What is reflection and why is it important?

What is reflection? Reflection means 'drawing from the past that which helps you grow as you move forward'. It is a process of enquiry about the past in order to learn or better understand something that can help us in the future. It means reviewing an event, an interaction or a behaviour in order to discover something we may not have known before. When we reflect we seek to search deeply rather than accept the surface view, the first impression. Reflection is a wisdom-building tool, and we can use it in a group or alone.

Reflection is a voyage of discovery, a lifelong detective game! A detective studies a crime scene deeply, asks questions, never assumes or judges prematurely, but looks beyond the obvious and from many angles before taking action. Detectives use all their senses, including intuition or 'gut feeling'. They switch from soaking in the whole picture to detailed examination of minutiae. A detective is always enquiring: what else, why else, how else, what could have happened, what other reasons could there be…?

Self-reflection is still about being a detective, but the subject of enquiry is you: discovering things about yourself you didn't know, opening your eyes to your potential strengths and weaknesses, seeing yourself as others see you. The aim of any reflection should be to come out of the reflection a more knowledgeable person than when you went in. It should be enlightening. The reflective process enables you to:

- *Ask valuable questions* rather than move to action. See the value in the questions themselves. This enables you to ask better questions of others.

- *See the value of slowing down your actions.* Pause. Stop. Listen well to your many voices, to the diversity of thoughts. Hold the thought and start to see the pause as valuable, rather than frustrating! Reflection does not demand that you must come up with the right thought now!

- *Understand the 'truth'.* Reflection urges us to want to seek verification from others, rather than fearing it. Once you really start to discover something, you will want to know if it is true! This kick starts the process of asking for feedback from friends and colleagues: 'Do I really do…?' 'I was thinking to myself that maybe I… You know me well. What do you think?' However, you control the questions and the way you accept and manage feedback. Reflection makes you well prepared for feedback and helps you see it positively.

- *Build on your strengths.* Understand what you are good at, what your skills are, what you do well and what motivates you.

- *Confront your fears.* We tend to bury deep fears. Fear is good for us: it's a valuable protective mechanism to keep us from harm, to alert us to danger, but fear can take over and sabotage our efforts. Reflective practice and getting used to exploring ourselves are immensely helpful. Naming fears and asking 'Why do I feel scared of this? Where is this fear coming from?' help us diffuse them.

- *Do something based on your insights to improve yourself*, to change, to develop and to grow as a person, which in turn has an impact on the lives of others.

What is listening and why is it important?

Listening matters because communication matters. Communication inefficiencies or breakdowns cost. Successful communication depends on being able to send and interpret messages skilfully. When that communication occurs through language, the best interactions happen when both the sender (speaker) and the receiver (listener) have an effective relationship.

Good listeners are not just good communicators; they make well-informed judgements and decisions, build engaging relationships, solve problems, encourage knowledge and idea sharing and uncover critical information. Skilled listeners listen for both:

- *the what:* listening for content (a factual/task orientation)
  - to gain information (to find out facts, to learn, to collect data, to check information),
  - to evaluate (to interpret, to analyse what has been said in order to respond appropriately, to make a decision); and
- *the why:* listening to fully understand (an emotional/people orientation)
  - to understand (to make sense of something, to determine why something is happening),
  - to empathize with the person (to make a connection, to understand the feelings of another person, to find the meaning behind the words).

In business it is often assumed that listening for facts and information is the only orientation required, that communication for empathy and understanding is something that should happen outside the workplace, reserved for home or even seen as the domain of counsellors. If listening is a 'relationship', for business, understanding both the person and the facts is essential.

Active listening enables us to balance both the what and the why. Active listening is about enquiry, finding out, uncovering what is hidden, fully understanding, not accepting the surface of things. It's about asking questions, not giving immediate answers that are based on your first (and therefore probably inaccurate) impressions. It needs your eyes as well as ears, for you to observe acutely, to tune into and sense what is not visible or audible.

Developing a mindset for listening

1 *Get into the mindset for listening.* Be the reflective detective (but not an interrogator!).

2 *Pay focused attention.* Concentrate on *them*. Avoid other internal or external distractions.

3 *Be interested, not interesting!* Switch from 'me' ('I am more interesting') to 'you' ('I am more interested in you').

4 *Manage the listening gap.* Our brain processes what we hear approximately four times faster than a person can speak (Carver, Johnson & Friedman, 1970). Listeners are always ahead of speakers. Use this gap to fully understand the speaker, not prepare what you want to say next!

FIGURE 1.3 The biggest barrier to listening

5 *Actively listen.*

- Pay attention to tone of voice and body language (yours and the other person's), encourage, and have patience.

- Use silence. Shut up! Slow down your thinking. Give the person time to speak.

- Use open questions. Enable the speaker to reflect and work out the solutions for him- or herself.

– Reflect back. Show you've understood the person's feelings.

– Clarify and check your perceptions.

– Summarize and synthesize.

What is feedback and why is it important?

Effective feedback builds trust in relationships, prevents problems escalating into conflict, motivates individuals and promotes personal growth. Sadly, it more typically evokes memories of aggressive criticism and is generally perceived as something to be avoided.

Feedback: 1) is a way to let people know how effective they are in what they are trying to accomplish, so they can become more effective in the future; and 2) enables us to learn things about ourselves that we couldn't learn otherwise. There are three types of feedback:

- *Positive feedback* encourages, promotes strengths, improves morale, and ensures the person can repeat the things that work well. (Receiving only positive feedback creates a skewed reality. People are left with false impressions of their effectiveness.)

- *Negative feedback*, if given well, provides insights, increases self-awareness and is a springboard for development. (Receiving only negative feedback can be ultimately demoralizing, knocks self-esteem and creates a distorted reality.)

- *No feedback at all* is easiest, but potentially most damaging. No progress is made, no learning acquired. For good or bad, people continue to do what they have always done.

Developing a mindset for feedback

If feedback is something given to you to enable your development, it helps to think of it as a gift. What is the process you go through to give a gift?

- *Ensure the gift is appropriate.* What is the value to the receiver? Will the receiver gain learning to improve performance? Are you doing this for the receiver's benefit or to 'get something off your chest'?

- *Choose it carefully.* Have you thought it through with the needs of the receiver in mind? Have you accurate observations to support your feedback?

- *Give the gift at the right time.* Is the receiver ready, willing and able to accept feedback now? Or is the timing just to suit you?

- *Give the gift graciously.* Are you mentally prepared to give feedback (not angry or upset)?

- *Take responsibility.* You gave it! If it's not right, be willing to make it right.

Improve your feedback capabilities

1 *Check perceptions first.* Watch for assumptions. We see things from different perspectives. Ask the person what was his or her understanding. Check what happened, not what you think happened.

2 *Watch your tone, facial expressions and body language.* It's not what you say but how you say it!

3 *Change the negative into positive.* Negative feedback can be dispiriting. Changing the problem into a question shifts the person to use these as a springboard for ideas and solutions. Use the 'How to…?', 'How do…?' and 'How might…?' Instead of saying 'You're consistently late for meetings', ask 'How might you ensure you're on time for the next meeting?' Instead of 'You go into so much detail about what you've done it's hard to find your proposal', try 'How do you ensure your proposals are clear and easy to find?'

4 *Find three positives before you share one negative.* Searching for three things done well, three positive behaviours, before you share even one negative point is a powerful habit to acquire.

Thinking it all through

This chapter has covered a lot of ground, discussing skills and approaches that are never totally mastered and can always be built on. It is important to be able to relate these skills to your own circumstances. The following case study, written by James Archer, shows how you put the theory into practice. Once you have read it, try reflecting on a situation, work or otherwise, and apply the concepts of this chapter to it.

My decorator painted one wall of my new home office with Smart Wall Paint, a paint that forms a whiteboard surface on any wall. The decorator was nervous because he'd never used it before and the paint was expensive. The instructions were followed and the paint applied and left to dry for five days. It looked brilliant, and as I write this chapter I have a mind map of this story written on my wall.

Unfortunately there was a small patch of less than 10 square centimetres that was partly missed, leaving a smeared black mess. I immediately took on the role of the well-meaning self-proclaimed expert, the type of client business analysts frequently have to work with! From my perspective, I had employed a professional decorator to apply the paint. We both read the instructions and followed them to the letter. We checked the wall when he finished and it looked great. I diagnosed the problem as being the difficulty in applying the paint to fully cover all 60,000 square centimetres, and calculated that we had achieved an accuracy level of 99.98 per cent. After a friendly discussion with Smart Wall Paint, they sent me a new small tin (for 2 square metres) of the paint to cover up the missed area. This reinforced my single-loop learning that I had done everything I should have and that the fault lay in the product. Next I imagined a solution, which was for Smart Wall Paint to include a miniature tin of paint with every new Smart Wall Paint kit, to be used to cover up any small missed patches evident after the wall had been used.

Smart Wall Paint drew different conclusions. In the expert role they had total confidence in the product. At some point they challenged their own belief (reflection) that the problem was poor application by their customers and decided to examine their instructions on how to use the paint. This double-loop learning led to the discovery of the root problem and the rewriting of the instructions. Smart Wall Paint acted as expert in diagnosing the problem and finding the solution. Their solution was far superior to mine, which was simply addressing a symptom of the problem.

As the customer I only discovered the solution (feedback) when I received my free tin of paint. The instructions had been totally redesigned. Smart Paint had added a new section stating: 'VERY IMPORTANT! The roller must pass over each section of the wall at least 5 TIMES'. Later on, a further section stated 'After you have finished painting ensure to inspect the painted area from every angle ensuring there are no missed spots or pinholes on the surface make sure to repaint any patchy areas.' I felt vindicated, because they had finally recognized there was a problem. I was convinced if I'd had those instructions the wall would have been perfect first time. However, I did not feel satisfied, as I did not feel appreciated as a customer trying to resolve a problem.

The double-loop learning was only done within the organization because Smart Wall Paint had helped me by using the expert model of helping. Smart Wall Paint challenged their belief that the instructions were clear – double-loop learning – but they did not tell me (feedback) it wasn't my fault. So when a business analyst creates a solution that changes a belief or mental model that the client or organization holds, there is a real risk the solution will not be adopted if the business analyst has not shared the double-loop learning with the client or organization. For the solution to be successfully implemented and used there may be a need for the organization to change its belief or mental model. This requires the business analyst to act as a process consultant.

The process consultant approach

Imagine that Smart Wall Paint customer service had responded to my issue by listening to me, then asking meaningful questions, and followed this by appreciating my situation (reflection). The company would have understood that I had followed the instructions, that the patches were not obvious and that I was disappointed by being let down. They could have asked me to check for other patches, which would have led me to see several half-covered areas. They could have asked how many times we covered each part with the roller and discovered we never paid attention to this.

They may even have discovered that my decorator felt nervous, as he'd never used such paint before and didn't know he had to treat this paint differently (listening and feedback).

This would have been joint problem solving. It would have required double-loop learning as a partnership. I would have had to confront my belief that we applied the paint as well as it could be applied (reflection), and Smart Wall Paint would have admitted their instructions were poor (reflection). My status and face as a customer would have been maintained.

The final word must be about Smart Wall Paint. Not only has it provided a great case study, but having a whiteboard on a wall in my office is fantastic!

Conclusion

It is not possible to learn the skills of listening, feedback and reflection in depth just by reading the introductions provided here. The intention is more to stimulate your thinking on how these are relevant to and would be valuable in your role. To further your reflection, ponder on the following questions. As a business analyst:

1 How would you benefit from self-reflection? If you were more skilful at reflection, what impact would it have on your work? What stops you reflecting?

2 How well do you listen? Would your clients describe you as a good listener, and why or why not? Could interactions with clients that did not go as well as you expected have had anything to do with how you listened? In what way could the quality of your listening have affected outcomes? In interactions do you tend to speak (tell) more than you listen (ask)? What are the consequences of this?

3 Are you comfortable with giving and receiving feedback? Is it different depending on the person, whether peer or client? Why might it be important in your role to develop these skills? Are there situations where feedback was appropriate but you weren't able to provide it? Why was that?

About the authors

Kate Stuart-Cox is a founding partner of Perspectiv, a consulting and training company.

James Archer is co-editor of this book, a business analyst, consultant, trainer and associate partner at Perspectiv.

References and further reading

Carver, R, Johnson, R and Friedman, H (1970), Factor analysis of the ability to comprehend time-compressed speech, *Final report for the National Institute for Health*, American Institute for Research, Washington DC

Charan, R (2012) The discipline of listening, *Harvard Business Review Blog Network*, 21 June

Collins, J (2005) My golden rule, *Business 2.0*, 1 December

Ferrari, BT (2012) The executives' guide to better listening, *McKinsey's Quarterly*, February

Ferrari, BT (2012) *Power Listening: Mastering the most critical business skill of all*, Penguin, New York

Goulston, M (2010) *Just Listen: Discover the secret to getting through to absolutely anyone*, Amacom, New York

Grimsley, A (2010) *Vital Conversations*, Barnes Holland Publishing, Princes Risborough

Harvard Business Review (2011) *HBR's 10 Must Reads on Managing People*, Harvard Business School Publishing, Boston, MA

International Listening Organization [accessed 20 April 2013] [Online] www .listen.org

Leonard-Barton, D (1995) *Wellsprings of Knowledge: Building and sustaining the sources of innovation*, Harvard Business School Press, Boston, MA

Schein, EH (1969) *Process Consultation: Its role in organization development*, Addison-Wesley, Reading, MA

Schein, EH (2010) *Helping: How to offer, give, and receive help*, ReadHowYouWant, Sydney

Schön, Donald A (1983) *The Reflective Practitioner*, Basic Books, New York

The courage to ask

02

JOHN NILAND

When change happens slowly, it's easy to miss. Whether it's the growth of a child, the extra kilo acquired each year or the evolution of a job, it's often only when we take a step back and measure that we find that change is happening at all.

The role of the business analyst has certainly changed. If we go back a decade or two, we find the traditional analyst focused on 'requirements gathering', as if the requirements were already hanging from the trees and just needed to be picked and gathered, like ripe fruit. Today the fruit has to be cultivated. Current business analysts are more active 'cultivators' of the agenda. They no longer just gather requirements and document needs; they actively shape the agenda with project stakeholders. They draw out the (often conflicting) needs implicit in the business, operational and technical dimensions of a project.

It's hardly a surprise therefore that the personal characteristics of business analysts have also evolved. The 'hunter-gatherer business analyst' needed an eye for detail, good analytical ability and enough communication skills to make sure the scope was clear to everyone. Today's 'cultivator business analysts' certainly need all of those qualities, but they also go further:

- challenging some of the requirements set by operational managers, eg 'Why are we putting so much effort into managing exceptions?';
- teasing out the issues that need consensus at senior level, such as resolving conflicting priorities, particularly use of resources;
- anticipating changes in the organization and in the marketplace, eg 'What will our competitors be doing two years from now?';
- overcoming resistance and anticipating obstacles to change, if only because there are always obstacles and roadblocks.

In short, 'cultivator business analysts' need a lot more courage than their 'hunter-gatherer' predecessors. They frequently debate sensitive subjects at senior level. They probe current functionality and infrastructure, asking lots of 'Why?' questions. They actively listen for what's *not* being said, as much as for what they are being told.

All of this takes courage. Churchill famously remarked that 'Courage is rightly esteemed the first of human qualities... because it is the quality which guarantees all others.' Without courage, business analysts may well be in possession of lots of great questions and tools, but on the day they are up against a harried and hurried chief operating officer will they have the courage to use them?

So what do we mean by courage? Whatever courage is about in the military or in sports, in professional life courage is the ability to deal with uncertainty, risk or change. Courage is not so much the absence of fear as the ability to persist in the face of fear. For example, it is reasonable to be apprehensive before a meeting in which we might have to deliver some bad news. These are the moments however in which courage develops.

It takes courage to obtain senior-level meetings, to set the agenda, to probe conflicting requirements and to question the obvious. It also takes courage to know when to depart from the agenda and take the discussion off-piste. It takes courage to face up to impossible deadlines, whether in working towards them wholeheartedly or in getting consensus to be more realistic.

So how can a business analyst develop this vital quality of courage? Is courage just a 'given': either you have it or you do not? What are the specific ways in which it can be developed?

This chapter focuses on the development of courage: how a business analyst can develop this vital quality. We outline seven 'gateways' via which professionals can access courage, and explore these gateways from the perspective of professionals seeking to develop their career and add value to the organization they serve.

In summary, here are the gateways:

- connection to others;
- purpose and meaning;
- influence and communication skills;
- self-awareness;
- self-discipline;
- curiosity and creativity;
- physical stamina.

Connection to others is particularly important for people who are extroverts and who are naturally friendly people. It may be less significant for some introverts, or those who are guided by duty, correctness or conscientiousness, though even these professionals often take pleasure in collaborating with others who have the same mindset as they have.

When business analysts are looking at this gateway to courage, they will probably be thinking of being close to top colleagues in their field who are also spearheading best practice in the profession. They may also be thinking of a coach or mentor who believes in their potential. Still others find that staying connected to former clients and colleagues helps them to maintain perspective and to believe in themselves.

When business analysts fail to connect to others, what happens? Some become rigidly attached to a single methodology. Others find themselves isolated and shut off from new developments, not hearing about useful events or publications. Many become reactive without realizing it, so they are no longer setting the agenda, but just reacting to the demands of others.

Purpose and meaning are a gateway for those who think a lot about why they do what they do. They derive courage from being inspired and excited by the end result. This result may be a reflection of their personal ambition or an agreed target (purpose), or it may be more connected to deeper values (meaning).

Business analysts who are motivated by purpose and meaning will be looking for projects that excite them. They will probably be seeking to do something more than reduce the cost per order or streamline a process; they will probably be encouraged by projects that create some economic or social opportunity or advantage. They will be excited about the end result, and emboldened to work for this.

In fairness, it's worth noting that purpose and meaning are two different things. A purpose can be a simple aim or objective, such as hitting a deadline or resolving a specific problem. It may also be a larger purpose, eg improving customer service. Meaning on the other hand is about significance: the reason *why* this project is important to its stakeholders. This might be some contribution to society, a belief in excellence, or a wish to add value in a new sector.

In short, not all purposes have meaning, and not everyone cares about meaning either. But, for those stakeholders and collaborators for whom meaning is important, a meaningful project is likely to inspire courageous action and heroic levels of achievement.

Influence and communication skills have a direct bearing on courage: they equip professionals to have more influence and power in the world around them. This is particularly significant to business analysts who, more than ever before, have to deal with leaders in senior positions.

To take one simple example, a business analyst who can co-create the agenda for a meeting has an immediate advantage over one who either sets the agenda in advance (as many traditional business analysts sought to do) or simply responds to an agenda imposed by a senior executive. Business analysts who co-create an agenda are usually perceived as collaborative, but also as people who have something to contribute. They are neither reacting nor imposing. In the act of agreeing the agenda, they are communicating that they are 'working with you, not for you'. As they build credibility in this way, their courage naturally grows.

This is just one example for business analysts, but the list could be extended. Powerful questioning, reframing requirements, dealing with difficult stakeholders, active listening, facilitation skills: these are all cognitive skills that empower and encourage a business analyst. They widen this gateway to courage.

Given the evolution of the profession, this is an area worth looking at for many business analysts. Many are still hamstrung by outmoded communication styles, eg slogging through the actions from the last meeting, long wordy presentations of content, over-engineered task lists and project charts. What they gain by being organized and reliable, they may lose in terms of impact and influence.

Self-awareness is an important gateway to courage for the simple reason that, without it, people can rarely develop the other gateways. You can certainly learn technical skill without self-awareness, but it's practically impossible to learn leadership or facilitation skills if one is blind to one's tendency to react angrily or to interrupt others.

However, for courage to develop, it's even more important to develop self-awareness around one's strengths. In our professional culture, people tend to associate self-awareness with what they are *not* so good at. For example, a business analyst might conclude that he or she is not so good at handling conflict, or presentation skills, and therefore spend a lot of time and effort in filling these gaps. But business analysts might develop more courage by focusing instead on their strengths, eg talent for coordination (instead of handling conflict) or facilitation skills (instead of presentation skills). When people focus on strengths instead of weaknesses, their levels of courage seem to grow more readily, and therefore they are willing to challenge and 'go further' in dialogue.

Of course, this does not mean that every moment spent in self-awareness will be an encouraging one! To take the example above, when a business analyst first discovers that he or she communicates irritation when someone wants to change the agenda, this moment of self-awareness may be initially a discouraging one. However, if the business analyst goes on to deal with it constructively, this reinforces the person's knowledge of his or her own capacity and strength. Knowing that we can take feedback and learn from it enhances our access to courage.

Self-discipline is an oft-neglected gateway to courage. For many years, courage and boldness seem to have been linked to envisioning, raising the bar and dreaming of new heights. When we thought of professional courage, perhaps we thought of the speaker in front of thousands or the director in charge of millions, but even for them the more daily exercise of courage consists of doing the next task in front of them.

In this context, we define self-discipline as the ability to bridge the gap from thought to action. In professional life, this usually takes the form of doing the next thing on the to-do list, irrespective of how we might be feeling about it. This may be a task, a phone call, an e-mail or a question to be asked. Whatever it is, it's often accompanied by an equal and opposite force of procrastination and/or dread. The ability to do it anyway is an important gateway to courage.

The big problem that usually surfaces around this gateway is the issue of procrastination. This is quite a complicated phenomenon, with different roots (or causes) for different people. For example, an analyst who is quite rigorous and organized may also be a strong 'completer' or 'finisher' and hence prone to perfectionism. Hence the analyst puts off finishing a document or a presentation (or even starting it!) for the simple reason that it's never good enough. For someone who is easy-going and spontaneous, however, procrastination is more likely to be linked to distraction and problems of focus.

Curiosity and creativity are a particularly important gateway to courage for a business analyst. Indeed, cultivating the 'right to be curious' has proved to be a crucial development milestone for many of the business analysts we know. If one is hamstrung by 'I should know already' or 'I don't feel entitled to ask this person', this sets a glass ceiling over the head of the business analyst and limits his or her career.

Nor is this confined to the hours of professional activity. For many talented people, work life has become a treadmill of e-mails, processes and tasks. Without doubt, there is always some heavy lifting to be done; indeed this is essential if self-discipline is to develop. But most business analysts also need mental challenge and stimulation, and simply being stuck in 'task mode' certainly does not develop courage.

Physical stamina is the seventh gateway and, as with all of the others, some people relate to this more easily than others. Yet the courageous role of today's business analyst requires energy, and there is an important physical dimension to energy and stamina. If we spend our days in meetings or in front of a screen, then 96 per cent of our body mass is just wasting away, while 4 per cent of us (the head) does all the work.

It takes courage to get up earlier, to go for a run or even to leave the office. Yet this is precisely the quality that we seek to develop: the determination to overcome resistance and procrastination and to 'do it anyway'.

For a business analyst to adapt to today's world, the dimension of courage is likely to be just as crucial as the dimension of skill. Without courage:

1 Business analysts are unlikely to achieve as much as they wish:
   - Professionals cannot even use the skills they already have, eg giving difficult feedback to a client or colleague. This is like the farmer who said to the adviser 'Please don't tell me how to farm any better; I'm not even farming as well as I know how already.'
   - Vital decisions get postponed, and procrastination takes over. To cover up, business analysts call for more information and consultation, often making unnecessary work for others to disguise their own fear of making vital decisions.

2 They cannot open doors:
   - They cannot initiate those meetings that are vital for getting jobs, presenting new propositions, opening doors or reaching decision makers. They will prepare for the meeting, but will baulk at making the call to ask for it.
   - They cannot follow up the new contacts they have made, or the people with whom they are being connected by others.

- They cannot stay in touch, not even with the people they already know, far less those whom they would like to meet. As a result, their reputation diminishes as time goes by; they simply get forgotten.

3 They cannot manage themselves:

- They cannot deal with setbacks and disappointments. As the salesperson said to the trainee, 'If you are afraid of risk, stay in the car.'
- They have difficulty dealing with uncertainty and lack of control, yet opportunity is rarely controlled by any one person. For people who need control, opportunity creation can therefore be a scary space, and scary spaces require courage.
- They cannot learn, because learning requires making the mistakes of a student, and many don't have the courage to do that. In the same vein, self-awareness also takes courage to develop and, as outlined above, courage also involves a degree of self-awareness.

4 Their focus is distracted:

- They are likely to put more energy into Plan B than wholeheartedly tackling the challenge of Plan A.
- They react to whatever comes up (e-mails, requests, tasks) because they don't have the courage to push back and make space for themselves and their priorities.
- They suffer from 'hurry sickness', constantly rushing from one thing to the next, often because this is preferable to confronting the reality of their situation, which takes courage and honesty.

We could extend this list for many pages. The point we are making is that skill development alone – *without a corresponding shift in courage* – is unlikely to overcome many of the issues in leadership, business analysis or business development.

On the other hand, when courage is present, analysts are motivated to challenge, initiate and probe. They are ready, willing and able to bring experience from one project to another. They can present their point of view and defend it. This makes them valued assets to the organizations they serve.

About the author

John Niland is the co-author of *The Courage to Ask*, written with Kate Daly, and is a conference speaker and coach with VCO Global.

Further reading

Niland, J and Daly, K (2012) *The Courage to Ask: Cultivating opportunity in the new economy*, VCO Global, Brussels

The business analyst as a facilitative leader

03

JAMES ARCHER

Business analysts are often in a position to work on projects that can make a real positive difference. In this chapter I have applied my thinking about the centrality of leadership to business analysis by reflecting on my role as business analyst in developing and implementing a system used by social workers that was judged to have made just such a positive difference, winning a UK national award and judged to be 'the one that broke the mould'.

On this project, I played the role of a facilitative leader. The following quote beautifully describes my view of how business analysis should be carried out: 'The defining feature of facilitative leaders is that they offer process and structure rather than directions and answers. In every situation, they know how to design discussions that enable group members to find their own answers' (Bens, 2006).

This book contains a number of different definitions and interpretations of what leadership means in the context of business analysis. The concept of facilitative leadership is one that every business analyst can aspire to, regardless of seniority or experience. Facilitative leadership, also known as inclusive leadership, is what the process consultant as discussed in Chapter 1 provides.

Five exemplary practices of leadership are identified by James Kouzes and Barry Posner in their valuable book *The Leadership Challenge* (2012). I will examine in turn how the five practices were key both to informing my facilitative leadership as a business analyst and to enhancing my ability to contribute to the success of the in-house Kensington and Chelsea Integrated Children's System (KCics). The five practices are:

1 *Model the way:* how you can set an example.
2 *Inspire a shared vision:* helping people decide on what should be done.
3 *Challenge the process:* getting to the essence of problems and articulating ways forward.

4 *Enable others to act:* building collaboration.

5 *Encourage the heart:* recognizing contributions and celebrating success.

First the story of the KCics project needs to be told. The purpose of telling this story is to encourage you to reflect on the best projects you have been involved in, thinking about the extent to which you exemplified the five practices and how you can apply them now and in the future.

The Integrated Children's System

In 2005 the British government announced that all local councils in England and Wales were required to implement the Integrated Children's System (ICS). ICS was designed as a framework for working with children in need and their families. The practice and case record keeping would be 'supported by information technology that is designed to handle a large amount of information on individual children' (Department for Children, Schools and Families, 2005).

The ICS gained national notoriety in the United Kingdom after the death of a 17-month-old boy known only as Baby P, later named as Peter Connelly. Peter suffered from over 50 injuries over an eight-month period leading up to his brutal death in 2007.

Nearly all the 160 councils affected used one of six social care software suppliers to provide the IT system. Kensington and Chelsea council decided that none of these systems would meet its business requirements and developed its own solution, the KCics.

The tragic tale

To set the scene I quote extensively from a report into the ICS, which has taken its place in a shamefully long list of disastrous change projects. In contrast to the national project, a holistic and systemic approach to business analysis was adopted in Kensington and Chelsea that sought to understand not just the objectives and the processes required to meet them but also the people involved and affected. Thorough consideration was given to the context, climate and cultures being worked with.

The 'tragic tale' of the ICS is told in the report (White *et al*, 2010), which shows how:

> the Integrated Children's System (ICS), by attempting to micro-
> manage work through a rigid performance management regime, and a
> centrally prescribed practice model, has disrupted the professional task,
> engendering a range of unsafe practices and provoking a gathering storm
> of user resistance.

With multiple design deficiencies, it has been rolled out in an escalating fervour of commitment by policymakers, who are distanced practically and intellectually from the realities of practice. As the story unfolds, parallels with the dynamics of Greek tragedy naturally suggest themselves.

The report, by lecturers from four universities, was based on extensive research over nearly two years in five councils and stated:

It is no exaggeration to report that across our sites we found not one social worker, or manager, who was happy with the system. All were negative, not necessarily about the *idea* and the aspirations associated with electronic recording, in which many could see great potential; rather, the contours of this particular model were ubiquitously a source of immense frustration.

Across our sites, social workers report spending between 60% and 80% of their available time (that is time when they were not travelling, or in meetings) at the computer and this was borne out by our observations.

The result, according to the report, was that:

Dissatisfaction with the ICS has been so extreme as to prompt some local authorities to declare independence. The Royal Borough of Kensington and Chelsea, having decided some years earlier to develop an in-house system (KCics), withdrew from the ICS compliance regime in late 2008, losing around £150,000 of funding. The sense of frustration at the repeated failure of attempts at constructive dialogue comes over strongly in the following Council minute recording its decision to withdraw:

'[the] Borough's approach differed from the Government's specification in the Council's emphasis on the family unit and an avoidance of a simple tick box approach to assessment. Throughout this time the Council has continued to engage, inviting government officials to see demonstrations [of the system]... contributing to reviews of the national ICS project and feeding back comments.'

The decision of the above-mentioned London borough to develop an in-house system was motivated by the need to involve practitioners. The soundness of this approach is attested by the confidently made claim which recorded the Borough's divorce from the national project:

'The system has been extremely well received by practitioners and many new social work recruits from other London boroughs have commented favourably on KCics in comparison with those systems used elsewhere... [which are] difficult to use, time consuming and overly prescriptive.'

Creating an alternative

Before he retired, my manager Ian Swanson had worked closely with social workers at the Royal Borough of Kensington and Chelsea to create the first electronic recording system for social workers in the UK to carry out their statutory case recording for children in need. This began by the trialling of Word templates and the creation of a workflow system within which social workers recorded all their detailed work with children and their families using Lotus Notes.

Richard Holden was the social work manager who designed the forms social workers used on this system. He was consulted – and ignored – by the government when he raised concerns that the extremely long and complex new 'exemplar' forms being created for ICS would not work. We started to understand the challenge of having to introduce new ways of recording case work. The challenge was made even greater because Kensington and Chelsea social workers loved the system they already had. It was the start of a long two and a half years.

The role of the five leadership practices

Model the way

The first of the leadership practices is to model the way by aligning actions with shared values. This immediately catapults many business analysts out of their comfort zone. How is it possible to discover what the shared values are, let alone align action with them? The starting point has to be to understand yourself. When you understand your own values, you start being able to understand other people as well. When we judge other people, we tend to judge them on the basis of our own values rather than theirs. And if we don't understand our own values then how can we understand other people? A good way to start exploring your values is just to go on the internet, search for a list of core values and then start thinking about which ones are important to you, that is, those values that are important at all times in your life. Once you start, you spend the rest of your life trying to understand them!

As business analyst, my job was to understand the values and ethos of children's social services in Kensington and Chelsea. A strong tradition of managers recognizing the professionalism of the social work staff existed. Social workers' role was seen as one of not just analysing a situation, but coming up with a way forward for the child and the family the child lived in by synthesizing that information. The service had repeatedly been rated by inspectors as one of the best in the country, and its electronic recording system was viewed as key to that success.

The academics who created the underlying objective for the government project started from the lowest common denominator, that is, with the assumption that poor social work practice was the biggest issue that had to be tackled. Recording was patchy and largely held as paper records in many councils, and this made services hard to manage effectively. Therefore, in a top-down approach, it was stipulated that social workers had to be given all the questions they might possibly need to ask for each piece of work they undertook with children. It quickly became clear that adopting the government approach was not only incompatible with the way Kensington and Chelsea carried out social work but could undermine the service and ultimately put vulnerable young people at risk.

The principle demonstrated here is the importance of understanding the connection between values and actions. The values inherent in the government project were a lack of trust in the social work profession and a belief in the need to instruct social workers how to carry out their work. Kensington and Chelsea's values were respect for social workers as professionals and an expectation of high-quality work. Those values were the starting point in articulating the business requirements for Kensington and Chelsea. We aimed to adopt as much of the government specification as possible without compromising social workers' professional approach.

A core principle was adopted that KCics, the in-house-built case recording system, would have the minimum possible number of questions and fields on each form. The slogan was 'Every field must be a wanted field!' The unwanted fields were combined into a series of prompts to encourage social workers to think through what might be relevant in this case.

At the heart of the national proposal was the requirement for each individual child in a family to have his or her own record. The Kensington and Chelsea approach was and still is to understand the individual needs of children within a family context. Child protection hearings are held for families where the children are at risk of neglect or abuse. ICS stipulated a lengthy separate report for each child where much of the information was the same for each child. Professionals and parents attending a child protection conference for a family of four children would be presented with over a hundred pages of reports to read, with much of the same information being repeated four times. KCics created one form for the whole family, incorporating sufficient space to address the needs of each individual child, which was simpler both for professionals and for parents, especially when working with a large family. The centrality of this approach was later formalized by the director with the strap line 'Strong families at the heart of strong communities'.

My underlying principle in business analysis has always been to understand what is in the interest of each different group of people who will be affected by the chosen solution. That approach allowed me to understand the shared values of the Children's Service and articulate a way forward that represented those values, the alignment of values with action.

Questions

- What are your core values?
- What are the shared values on a project you are or have been involved in?
- How are or were shared values aligned with action, or how could they be?

Inspire a shared vision

Any proposed solution should relate to moving towards the future, even if that means preserving what you already have. The more a project can be linked to strategy and visions for the future, the more useful the project can become. The tools of the business analysis profession help us turn the ideas and visions of others into practical solutions.

We worked to take what was best out of the proposals for a national framework for working with vulnerable children and create a solution that would help social workers deliver a better service for those children and their families. The business case articulated a vision built around the importance of giving social workers the tools and conditions to be effective.

A good business case tells a story and clearly spells out the potential consequences of different solutions. The Kensington and Chelsea business case spelt out the fear that the national ICS specification would prove unworkable and that it was incompatible with the way that Kensington and Chelsea wanted its social workers to work. It also spelt out the danger that the proposed solution of a system designed by social workers for social workers would risk the council not being compliant with government standards, with potentially serious financial and other consequences.

A shared vision was key to the KCics project. It was used to ensure that all parts of the solution were compatible with the vision. When the going got tough, we related the issues to the shared vision, which helped decision making. Over two and a half years there were a number of changes in the senior stakeholders. The shared vision, connected to the values of the service, helped manage those transitions. The Royal Borough of Kensington and Chelsea had a reputation amongst staff for being risk averse. However, our shared vision made the case clear, thus helping senior managers and councillors to accept the identified risks.

The vision articulated in that business case was realized. Firstly, the national ICS proved to be unworkable. The report's most damning indictment was its declaration that 'transformational government does not guarantee a thing of beauty; as we have seen, metamorphosis may beget a cockroach'. The current national recording requirements have been totally rewritten and the original specification scrapped. Secondly, Kensington and Chelsea council formally withdrew from the compliance regime, and did indeed lose its grant of £150,000.

At the same time KCics was a resounding success. It was an in-house-built system designed by social workers for social workers. A year after its introduction job adverts for children's social workers in Kensington and Chelsea sold the KCics as a reason to work there. It described the benefit of having an IT system that really helped social workers do a difficult and stressful job.

Questions

- What approaches could you use to help your organization imagine more exciting possibilities?
- How could you involve others in creating and sharing a common vision?

Challenge the process

Kouzes and Posner (2012) describe a set of essential behaviours that leaders use to make extraordinary things happen. Key among these are 'Search for opportunities by seizing the initiative and looking outward for innovative ways to improve' and the need to 'Experiment and take risks by constantly generating small wins and learning from experience.' In my view, these two concepts are absolutely central to effective business analysis.

Encouraging fresh thinking and creating space to consider ideas from outside the organization or from other professions and industries are just some of the ways to challenge the process. There is a common complaint from organizations that business analysts don't come up with interesting options. As more organizations see the need to innovate, business analysts should be part of any innovation process. Most innovations come from people closest to the work. Business analysts should be listening for and welcoming innovative suggestions rather than seeing them as a threat or being out of the scope of a project.

KCics was only created because the business was prepared to challenge the process. The starting point was to look for all the strengths. This took the best principles behind the national ICS, the strong professional social work practice in Kensington and Chelsea and a much loved recording system; although a sensible approach, it could be arrived at only through being prepared to challenge the process.

Innovation is not about invention; it's about implementing something that is new and useful. KCics had to be innovative to make complex processes intuitive for social workers to use. For example, one of the main software suppliers used a traffic light system to alert people to new work. Social workers were worried this feature would bombard people with alerts. By taking this concept from outside and experimenting with it, we were able to allay concerns and make it something really useful that helped social workers plan their work.

People will only have the confidence to challenge the process if the culture and climate are conducive. All the indicators for a productive climate (see Chapter 17) were kept strong throughout the project. The confidence people had in being able to challenge the process meant that not only was a good system created but the chief information officer, David Tidey (current member of the BCS professionalism board), described it as the smoothest implementation of a project he had seen in 20 years.

Questions

- How could you create time to search for alternative solutions?
- How can you build experimentation and taking risks into projects?

Enable others to act

Nearly any solution a business analyst proposes involves change. The success of that change usually depends on how well the change is adopted. While that depends partly on the solution, the wider implications and the impact the solution will have on the people who use it are elements that are equally important.

It is vital to share knowledge and to facilitate relationships. Business analysts are often in the privileged position of being able to see how different parts, or silos, of an organization really operate. This means new connections can be made. Information gleaned from business analysis can have uses that go beyond the original objective. The simple act of sharing how two parts of an organization have different ways of dealing with similar issues may be outside the formal scope of a piece of work, but can be incredibly useful. Firstly you are sharing knowledge that could result in a quick and easy change; secondly you are being seen as someone who is collaborative and helping build a useful network of relationships.

One of the best ways of ensuring success for new solutions is giving a key role to local experts or champions. In KCics two social workers, Suzy Mullaly and Sarah Sansbury, were seconded to the project team to ensure the purpose of the project was perceived by all as changing the way social work practice was carried out rather than as the introduction of an IT system separate from their practice. They created a network of champions who ensured successful and rapid adoption of the new ways of working. The earlier these people become engaged with the process of change, the greater involvement, understanding and ownership they have of the solution. The result is a greater knowledge of how the solution is likely to be received and of the steps that can be taken early and cheaply to remove barriers.

As stated at the start of the chapter, the practice of facilitative leadership proved to be critical. A common issue for business analysts can be influencing a development team over whom they have no formal management control. In this case the team had to learn new skills and were often out of their depth, but were given encouragement, praised when things went well and given the space to try things out. The social workers on the team were supported when they drew a line in the sand over the battle for 'stretchy text boxes', as described below.

The original Lotus Notes system they used had a feature where a text box expanded as each line was added. The developers could produce only fixed-size text boxes. Each assessment may have 10 or 20 of these boxes, and there was no way of knowing which ones had capacity for only a few words and which ones could accommodate 20 lines of text. A solution was found that helped make it an intuitive and user-friendly system designed to help. Not only did those social workers own part of the project in their role as champions, but they resolved problems and contributed to the efficiency of the system.

A striking feature of the project was a strong climate that supported the project. All nine dimensions of climate as described in Chapter 17 were extremely positive.

In short, the business analyst needs to behave like Google Earth, zooming straight into the detail, right down to street level, looking at the work from different viewpoints, layering on the terrain and then taking it off. This is what business analysis skills give us, the understanding that enables the business to look at its work from different viewpoints. From being right into the detail, you can then go whoosh, straight out, and you're looking at the whole planet. I think that is how business analysis enables others to act, by understanding individual perspectives and giving them the information and tools they need.

Questions

- How have you built trust and fostered collaboration?
- How could you build your reputation for enabling others to act?
- How could you deliver not just a solution but a more competent organization?

Encourage the heart

Most of the people in the business we collaborate with have a busy day job. It is very easy to 'encourage the heart' by recognizing the contributions that people make, but also easy to forget the simple, human act of thanking people. Bringing a cake to a workshop from a genuine desire to show appreciation can transform the atmosphere. Publicly thanking contributors to your work has an important part to play in developing respect and credibility and creating a more enjoyable atmosphere in the workplace.

This was a stressful project. There was a spirit of community that built on the shared vision that was important to everyone on the project. The business analyst is in a unique position of being able to see the real impact a solution can have on people. Playing the facilitative leadership role means paying attention to the contributions people make and challenges they face and sharing that knowledge with a wider leadership.

Questions

- How do you recognize individual contributions from people who help you do your job?
- How do you celebrate the values of teams you work in and the victories you achieve?

All too good to be true?

There is also a salutary lesson. I was not only the business analyst but the project manager for KCics. At the lessons learnt review we agreed that formally the project was a failure. It was over budget and over time. I learnt I am a better business analyst than project manager and that it is hard to retain your sanity when performing two very different roles (see Chapter 5).

Developing exemplary leadership practices

This story is not unique. There are countless examples of business analysts being facilitative leaders and demonstrating the strategic value of business analysis. Recognizing, understanding and developing facilitative leadership skills are key to developing the business analysis profession.

The framework of the five practices of exemplary leadership is evidence based. The Leadership Practices Inventory (LPI) has been taken by nearly 2 million people. It is a 360-degree instrument that assesses how frequently leaders engage in the five practices. James Kouzes and Parry Posner (2012) have compiled evidence that shows that leaders who more frequently use the five practices are considerably more effective than those who use them infrequently. As a business analyst you do not have to be on a big project to reap the rewards from practising the five practices and be part of the growing recognition of the strategic importance of the business analysis profession.

About the author

James Archer is co-editor of this book, a business analyst, consultant, trainer and associate partner at Perspectiv.

References and further reading

Bens, I (2006) *Facilitating to Lead! Leadership strategies for a networked world,* Jossey-Bass, San Francisco

Department for Children, Schools and Families (2005) [accessed 19 December 2012] Integrated Children's System [Online] http://webarchive. nationalarchives.gov.uk/20090617172700/http://dcsf.gov.uk/everychildmatters/safeguardingandsocialcare/integratedchildrenssystem/ics/

Kouzes, J and Posner, B (2012) *The Leadership Challenge*, Jossey-Bass, San Francisco

White, S *et al* (2010) When policy o'erleaps itself: the 'tragic tale' of the Integrated Children's System, *Critical Social Policy*, 30 (3), pp 405–29

Communication for success

CORRINE THOMAS

Becoming successful at business analysis depends on much more than your qualifications, experience and job-related skills. These are all important things to have, but to become excellent at analysis and add maximum value to your organization you need exceptional communication skills and the ability to flex and change continually. This chapter is about how to be a successful communicator and will focus on using tools and techniques to enable you to become more self-aware and confident in working with other people. You will learn how to lead and communicate with others more effectively through being flexible, influential and maintaining a positive outlook for yourself.

Good leadership starts with an understanding of self. This is then built on to understand others and find ways of working together to achieve great results. Business analysts by nature are curious about the world and discovering how things work, what people want and how to find options for implementing goals. Paying close attention to yourself does not initially come easily to many people; however, it is all about noticing what patterns or programmes you run, ie your default way of thinking and behaving. By becoming aware of your patterns you can notice those times when habitual thinking and responses may not be useful to you and may stop you achieving a successful outcome. Once you become aware of these habitual responses, you have the choice to change the way you run the patterns.

To be really successful as a business analyst you have to work well with others, for example other members of your project team, your stakeholders, your sponsor and your peers. Understanding what makes others tick can make a huge difference to the result you get in your communication with them; being curious is crucial. When you start to be curious about other people and what leads them to speak and act as they do, you can be far more understanding and flexible when working with them.

It is possible to use some tools from neurolinguistic programming (NLP) to assist you in becoming an effective communicator. NLP enables you to understand what makes you tick, how you think, how you feel and how you make sense of everyday life in the world around you. At the heart of NLP is the idea that, if you continually try different things and seek new choices, you achieve what you want.

Neurolinguistic programming is quite a lot to say, and it starts to become clearer when you break the name down into its components:

- *Neuro:* this relates to your brain and things that go on in your mind. It also includes how you use your senses both to experience the world outside and to form internal representations of the world through memories and visualizing.

- *Linguistic:* this relates to the language you use, both spoken and non-spoken, to make sense of your experiences, to talk to yourself and to communicate with others.

- *Programming:* this is all about behaviour and thinking patterns. A computer program is a succession of steps designed to achieve a particular result, and your personal patterns are like programs that you run to get results.

NLP is all about studying very precisely what human beings think, say and do. It gives you a tool to study how others achieve great results and then to form your own model of this to enable you to enjoy increased effectiveness at achieving results.

NLP is used a lot by sportspeople to improve their skills in their sport and also to maintain a positive mindset when in competition. We all naturally studied and modelled the behaviour of others when we were children. My daughter has recently learnt to drive, and her instructor noticed that she held the wheel and flicked on the indicator in exactly the same way as me. I'd not consciously taught her this; she had watched and modelled me from an early age.

Self-awareness – discovering your personal style

We all have senses that we use to interact with the world around us; each of us filters many pieces of information that reach us. Through use of your senses you capture information about what is going on around you and form your own internal representation of what you have experienced. Each of us is able to use all of the senses, but few people use them all equally; most people favour one or two over the others. Over time the one preferred most can be seen in personality traits, behaviour and choice of language. The senses are:

- *Sight/visual.* Some indicators for visual thinking may be:
  - talking quickly;
  - a short attention span;
  - noticing how things look and commenting on it;
  - liking diagrams, charts and pictures;
  - drawing diagrams to help explain one's thinking.

This may be associated with eyes looking upwards and use of phrases such as 'I see what you are saying', 'I get the picture' and 'It looks good to me'.

- *Sound/auditory.* Some indicators of auditory thinking may be:
  - measured pace of speaking and activity;
  - being distracted by background noises;
  - liking to discuss ideas and plans;
  - talking to oneself out loud;
  - being a good mimic of accents and voices.

  This may be associated with eyes looking to either side of the head and use of phrases such as 'I hear what you are saying' and 'It sounds good to me.'

- *Feelings/kinaesthetic.* Some indicators of auditory thinking may be:
  - taking time and moving deliberately;
  - speaking slowly;
  - being distracted by physical discomfort – temperature, hard chairs, etc;
  - walking around to think clearly;
  - liking demonstration and interaction;
  - trusting gut feeling.

  This may be associated with eyes looking downwards and use of phrases such as 'It feels about right.' Many people regard businesslike behaviour as non-emotional, so people with a high kinaesthetic preference may detach from it while in the work environment in order to appear more professional.

- *Digital/non-sensory thinking such as facts, figures and concepts.* If it is not obvious how someone is thinking it may be that they have a strong digital preference. This is also the conventional mode of communication in business, so someone may appear to prefer the digital mode but may have detached him- or herself from the preferred system while at work. Some indicators are:
  - low sensory awareness, finding it easy to concentrate;
  - having a large vocabulary;
  - choosing words carefully;
  - liking facts and figures;
  - often pausing in the middle of a sentence, to allow time to think through how to express thoughts;
  - rarely showing emotion.

  This may be associated with the use of phrases including words of logic such as 'think', 'know', 'calculate' and 'deduce'.

These are the senses that are most commonly indicated in a business situation. There are also the sense of smell (olfactory) and sense of taste (gustatory). While these are powerful and useful senses they are seldom used when considering building relationships at work. Over the next few weeks, as you go about your daily activities, start noticing which senses you prefer to use and what comes most naturally to you. When you have run a workshop or meeting and are preparing to write up the output, notice how you remember what went on in the session and how you are representing it within your mind. What comes to you first? Is it a picture of what happened? Do you remember the sounds of people talking to each other? Or do you predominantly have a feel for how things went? Once you become aware of which senses you prefer to use, develop flexibility by practising using one of your less preferred senses in various situations and notice what difference this makes.

People tend to use language that relates to the senses they prefer to use as they speak. By listening carefully, you can work out what sense someone prefers and start adapting your communication to suit those preferences.

There are many occasions where as a business analyst you may need to prepare a presentation or e-mail to a group of people where you don't know their preferences or the room may be full of people who cover all the preferences. In this case it is worth preparing the presentation to include language that will appeal to all the main representational systems. That way you are more likely to engage with the group and hold their attention.

Building rapport

Rapport is an essential building block for people to build good relationships with each other and underlies all good communication. When people are relating well they trust, respect and understand each other even unconsciously. In any interaction, wherever you encounter resistance, it is a sign of a lack of rapport.

As a business analyst in businesses today you need to be creative and prepared to take risks, try new angles and guide people towards new ways of thinking. To be able to influence others in this way requires good levels of rapport through taking a real interest in what others are doing and saying and an ability to really understand how they build their own views of the world. People will allow themselves to be influenced by people they trust and will rarely buy from somebody they do not trust. Business decisions are often made as a result of good rapport rather than just on the merits of an idea or proposal. Rapport is built over time through ongoing relationship building, although we often don't realize when we have rapport with others, as it is such an unconscious and instinctive state. When you feel easy with someone it is very likely that you are in rapport with that person, and when rapport exists you probably notice how much smoother and more straightforward discussion and decision making are. When starting to understand

FIGURE 4.1 Two people matching each other with posture

and work with rapport it is often easier to spot when others are in rapport. Here are some of the signs when two people are in rapport:

- matching body posture and movements;
- similar facial expressions;
- good eye contact;
- similar voice pitch, tone, volume and speed;
- identical words and phrases.

To create good rapport with people at work with whom you don't obviously have anything in common it is important to notice their behaviour and subtle changes in this. It is often the subtle changes that give most clues to a person's thought processes. By focusing completely on the other person and showing an interest in what he or she is saying, you can notice changes in the person's behaviour from cues such as posture, breathing, skin tone, expression and voice qualities. Rapport can be developed by simply pacing various physical conditions, for example pacing someone's breathing or matching and mirroring body language. The intention of matching and mirroring is to communicate to a person's unconscious mind that you are on his or her wavelength.

Building rapport with a group is more complex than developing individual rapport, yet it is particularly useful in long and drawn-out meetings. Some tips to use when you want to have more influence in a meeting are:

- Greet everyone in the group at the start, making sure to use names where possible.
- Match and then pace any dominant style of the meeting, for example its formality, humour, level of detail, etc.
- Make eye contact with each member of the group at several points during the meeting.
- Use key words, phrases or metaphors that others express.

Listening

Listening is one of the most important skills in being an effective and successful communicator. How well you listen has a major impact on how effective you are as a business analyst and your relationships with others. Listening is a skill we could all benefit from improving, and through becoming a better listener you will improve your productivity and ability to influence and negotiate with others. Without the ability to listen effectively messages are easily misunderstood, communication breaks down and the sender of the message can easily become frustrated or irritated.

In order to become a better listener you need to pay very close attention to the person you are having a conversation with. Our listening changes with the amount of focused effort we direct towards the other person. As our level of listening deepens, so does our focus and attention on the person we are listening to.

When you are listening well to someone, then you are actively seeking to understand what the person is telling you. In this situation you will be using more effort to listen and process information than speaking yourself and you will continually be confirming to the other person that you are listening by making appropriate sounds, gestures or expressions. To demonstrate that you have understood the person you will ask clarifying questions and summarize back to the speaker, offering observation and maybe conclusions. Here are some tips and suggestions on things to do to become a better listener:

- Pay attention: give the speaker your undivided attention and acknowledge the message you are being given. To do this you need to listen to the words being said and be very aware of the body language you are seeing.

- The human mind is easily distracted by other thoughts, for example what's for lunch, what time you need to leave to catch your train, or whether it is going to rain. Try to put other thoughts out of your mind and concentrate on the messages that are being communicated.

- Demonstrate that you are listening by creating good rapport through the use of an open and inviting posture, and use small verbal comments to acknowledge what you are being told.

- Seek to understand the other person's point of view and let go of your own preconceived ideas. By having an open mind you can more fully empathize with the speaker. If the speaker says something with which you disagree then wait and construct an argument to counter what is said, but keep an open mind to the views and opinions of others.

- Gestures, facial expressions and eye movements made by the speaker can all be important. We don't listen just with our ears but also with our eyes – watch and pick up the additional information being transmitted via non-verbal communication.

● Do not jump to conclusions about what you see and hear. You should always seek clarification to ensure that your understanding is correct.

It takes a lot of determination and concentration to become an excellent listener and requires a lot of practice to break old habits and put all your attention on the other person in the conversation rather than focus on what you want to say next. By focusing on the other person and showing real interest in him or her, you will find that the questions you need to ask will come to you naturally. You will also be able to put your point across in a manner that is respectful and means you in turn will be listened to.

Influencing

Through a combination of understanding self, listening well and raising an awareness of how others are forming views of the world it is possible to gain buy-in to your ideas and proposals through influence. To influence someone to your way of thinking you need to initially be clear on what outcome you want from the conversation and then consider the other person and how you want him or her to behave at the conclusion of your interaction. When doing this it can be helpful to use a technique known as different perspectives. By using this you can rehearse and prepare for how you would like the conversation to go through considering various viewpoints:

1 The first viewpoint is from self. Ask yourself: What do I want to achieve from this conversation? How do I feel about the other person? What do I know about him or her already?

2 The second viewpoint is through putting yourself in the other person's place. Think about how the person is feeling. What is important to him or her? How is the person filtering and forming views of what is going on around him or her?

3 The third viewpoint is imagining you are observing the conversation from a distance. Think about what an observer may see when watching the conversation. How are the two people getting along? How balanced is the conversation?

Having looked at each of the viewpoints, you then need to work out how to communicate to the person in order to build rapport. This involves planning the language you will use and what senses the other person prefers to use. The aim here is to speak to the person in a way that enables him or her to easily form his or her own internal representation of what you are saying. Building rapport and using language the person is comfortable with lead to

FIGURE 4.2 Three viewpoints: self, other and observer

good inner feelings in the other person, which finally enable him or her to respond to you in the way you would like.

Managing your emotions and developing a positive mindset

Leading starts with the ability to lead ourselves. To do this we need first and most importantly to be able to manage our emotional state. The word 'state' is used to describe something's condition; it may also be used to describe people, for example 'in a bad state' or 'in the right state of mind'. When using the word 'state' to describe people you are describing their whole condition, ie how they are thinking and feeling in body and mind.

Have you ever got up on the morning of a very important meeting or workshop and felt tired, moody and lifeless? It happens to us all, and often when we have an important event coming up we can experience higher-than-normal levels of stress and challenge, which leave us feeling drained and not at the top of our game. This less-than-resourceful state could lead to a dip in performance and achieving less than desired in the meeting or workshop.

Emotions can become infectious, and at times a whole group of people can share the same or similar feelings. To become a good communicator and stay engaged positively with other people it is helpful to be able to manage your emotions and remain in a positive state. This can be achieved through using a technique known as creating anchors. Good leaders know how to anchor the emotions and confidence in themselves that they need to be able to stand firm when everything around them appears to be challenged. To build credibility as a business analyst and maintain strong relationships with others you need to be able to present a professional and positive image to others.

An anchor is an external stimulus that leads to a response; we all naturally create representations of our experiences as we lead our lives, and we store them away as memories. These memories often have things associated with them, for example a sound, a smell, a feeling or a place. When you come across something similar in the future it may trigger the memory to come into your conscious mind; this is an anchor. How many times have you found yourself remembering something that has happened to you a long time ago and you were bemused as to why you have started thinking about it? For example, have you ever heard a tune on the radio and found that you are thinking about something that happened in the past that is associated with that piece of music, such as the music played at your wedding or perhaps something from a disco or hymn you sang at school? You may also find that you start to get the same feeling as the one you had during the experience you are remembering.

To manage your emotions and build a positive state while working, it is possible to create a set of useful anchors for yourself, the ones that can help you perform at your best. This is done by deciding on what state you want to have, for example calm, confident or assertive, and then practising recalling times in your life when you were in that state. You need to take time to bring the memory back into your conscious mind as fully as possible by considering in detail all aspects of that memory, such as what you were doing, what you were seeing, what you were hearing and how you were feeling. As the memory becomes strong you can anchor it by attaching it to a small gesture you make for yourself, such as pressing your thumb and index finger together. By practising this over a number of days you will gradually find that when you stop and press your thumb and index finger together you recall the state of being calm or confident and you begin to feel this within your body.

By learning to create anchors it is possible to change feelings in challenging situations to more positive and helpful ones. Think about some situations that you currently find challenging and for which you would like to have a different emotion. Here are some suggestions:

- presenting to a large group;
- facilitating a workshop where you know there will be lots of conflict;
- talking to someone who is very senior;
- negotiating an agreement on requirements prioritization.

As you think of the situations that you currently find difficult, consider what emotions you would like to have instead of the ones that you experience currently. Then practise setting up some anchors that you can use time and time again in very specific situations.

About the author

Corrine Thomas is the lead business analysis practice manager with Virgin Media and is a certified trainer and master practitioner of NLP.

Further reading

Cooper, L (2008) *Business NLP for Dummies*, John Wiley & Sons, Chichester

Knight, S (2002) *NLP at Work: The difference that makes a difference in business*, 2nd edn, Nicholas Brealey, London

Lowther, D (2012) *Introducing NLP for Work*, Icon Books, London

Molden, D (2011) *How to Manage with NLP*, 3rd edn, Pearson Education, Harlow

Opinion piece
Are you waiting to be anointed?

JOSEPH DA SILVA

Business analysts have an ongoing leadership role within their organizations. In my opinion, the real value of the business analyst is in providing an independent, unbiased focus on determining the real business need. In my view, however, this skill is often not taken advantage of. The skills of business analysts in offering independent, analytical thought and their unique position in offering a holistic view across both business and technology change is something that, on paper, most organizations would highly value.

But they don't.

As I see it, there are multiple reasons for this. For one, while organizations as a whole may want an independent, challenging view, certain individuals in that organization may not. There may be individuals whose objectives are directly threatened by such a viewpoint. These individuals often bring in external consultants, ostensibly to provide an independent view, but in many cases they are used to reinforce a decision that has already been made. The use of consultancies helps prop up egos; it's much more flattering to one's self-importance to have engaged a highly paid, well-known consultancy rather than use an internal team to do the same job for less.

This is an inherent contradiction that exists within organizations: while a single organizational strategy may be clearly articulated, you can't run an organization without people – and people have their own agendas that conflict with the organizational strategy. It's sometimes not even that simple – often senior managers are set conflicting objectives, so that one part of the organization is measured on one target that, if met, would mean that another part of the organization couldn't meet its objectives. Arguably many projects display this contradiction; a project manager who is targeted on delivering to time (but not quality) is much more likely to cut corners on quality than one who is targeted on outstanding defects. Sadly it's rare to see projects or project managers that are targeted on any aspect of supportability after going live, so again this is an area that often gets missed. But organizationally this is critical – and one of the biggest drivers of cost in many cases; and business analysts can do something about it.

As well as having the same skills, business analysts offer something in addition with which external consultants will never be able to compete: organizational context. Business analysts occupy a unique position within the organization, having cross-functional visibility of change and an understanding of how the organization works. This is related not just to the processes and technology in use, but also to the people – who the key decision makers are, who the influencers are and how the internal networks of people operate. In short, business analysts de-risk business change in a way that external consultants can never replicate. Having this knowledge of the business means business analysts can add extra value, for example by identifying opportunities to share resources across similar initiatives, whether people or funding. They also bring knowledge of what's been tried before, what has and hasn't worked. Furthermore, they may bring relevant knowledge of other industries or even competitors.

Another reason why business analysts aren't utilized to their full potential within organizations is that they don't make enough noise. Part of this is marketing the role more, part of it is measuring and demonstrating the benefit we bring, and part of it is forming more alliances. In my experience, too many business analysis functions either wait to be anointed or have a misplaced sense of entitlement or expectation that they should be being used because it's the 'right thing to do'. Many business analysts complain about the organization 'not doing things properly', but how many try to change things or find ways of working within those constraints? It's often easier just to feel bitter and moan that 'This organization doesn't appreciate business analysis' or 'This organization doesn't know how to run projects properly.' It may be enjoyable in the short term to have a bit of a moan, but it's much more enjoyable to make things better for the long term and improve the overall success of your organization. It's harder, definitely, but much more rewarding to push for change in a positive way, and at the very least it's a great thing for the CV to have made the effort to make a change rather than just accept the status quo.

Promoting the role needs to be done through several mechanisms. There is above-the-line activity, which can involve producing posters or holding roadshows. There is targeting of specific stakeholders and actively selling the value of the role to them. There is the production and distribution of thought leadership material such as white papers – why more business analysts don't do this (and why more business analyst managers don't encourage it) is beyond me, as every consultancy has proven it's an excellent way of getting attention.

But more than this are alliances – business analysis cannot rely on convincing the organization of its value based solely on marketing. We all know that recommendations are among the most effective forms of promotion, and mutually beneficial partnerships should be formed internally in the way that they are externally. Complementary organizations partner all the time, but you rarely see this internally. Recommendations can work on an individual basis as well as the overall function; if you have particular business analysts within your function who are consistently getting great feedback then you should use that – getting recognition and engagement isn't an overnight thing.

Leaders in business analysis should identify other leaders within their organizations with whom to form alliances and partnerships. Obvious functions to consider include test, quality assurance, project management and development, but it's also worth looking wider: legal and compliance teams, finance teams and marketing teams can all be valuable advocates of the business analysis capability. Anyone with an analytical mindset or who deals in risk will be supportive of the need for the role if it is explained to them, regardless of where they sit in the organization, and those who are influential will be invaluable in helping promote the business analysis cause.

The business analysis community as a whole is growing in maturity; however, I feel there is a need for a step change. We've been too internally focused, for good reason, as we needed to professionalize the role, build a community of like-minded individuals and share knowledge and experience. This activity has got us to a certain level of maturity, but now we need to look externally. We need to form relationships with other communities; we need to promote the value of the role outside our own function, outside projects and outside IT. Recently, the International Institute of Business Analysis (IIBA) UK Chapter has been lobbying the UK government for explicit recognition of the business analysis role in its Major Project Authority guidelines. We need to do more of this, not just through government but also through non-project and non-IT industry bodies.

As leaders within our own organizations we also need to do more; we need to engage with other leaders and identify common goals. We need to be able to express the benefits of our role to them in a way to which they can easily relate in order to promote our value. And we need to be more flexible in how we work with the constraints within our organizations, rather than focusing energy on complaining about the lack of a perfect state.

Business analysis has the potential to be a vital source of leadership within an organization, but it's up to us to make it so.

About the author

Joseph da Silva is the head of service design for British Gas and president of the IIBA UK chapter.

PART II
Leadership within your project

Introduction to Part II

Part I covered leadership of self, giving a foundation for business analysts who wish to work effectively. Part II provides a whole range of ways to develop further when working with others in the context of your project.

What do we mean by leadership within your project?

Formal authority within a project is likely to reside with others: the project manager, programme manager, project sponsor and/or project board. Business analysts work alongside those with formal authority, challenging where necessary. They display leadership by taking responsibility, proactively working with others to understand what's needed and to inspire and influence others towards a common goal.

What does Part II cover?

Part II starts off by exploring the critical relationship of the business analyst and the project manager in Chapter 5. Displaying leadership within a project does not mean taking over from the project manager, but working alongside him or her, bringing complementary skills to the project and, together, aiming for successful change.

Moving on, Chapter 6 takes a light-hearted, but at the same time powerful, look at how to work with difficult stakeholders. It explores a variety of different responses to conflict and how each has its place.

Almost all of the work of business analysis involves facilitating groups and individuals. Chapter 7 sets out different ways of making meetings and workshops as productive as possible, even difficult ones.

The next two chapters focus on problems. Chapter 8 explores how to find the right problem to solve. Chapter 9 looks at the mental models used when dealing with problems. It looks at tame problems – those with optimal solutions – and contrasts these with wicked problems, which may not have any solutions at all.

Visual thinking can help people to 'see what they mean', and this is particularly useful in business analysis. Chapter 10 explains why this is so, and introduces several different ways to use visuals. Chapter 11 builds on this, including 'visualizing insights and ideas' as a key step in design thinking, which should be applied to business analysis. The other useful design steps include spending time with people, co-design or collaboration, and prototyping ideas.

Methodologies for running projects are important, and Chapters 12 and 13 explore the role business analysts can play in helping organizations adopt more agile and iterative approaches. These chapters are full of real-life lessons learnt, practical suggestions and share a common goal of delivering value to customers at frequent intervals.

Business patterns are the focus of Chapter 14. These ideas initially came out of construction and architecture, moved into software engineering and are now being applied within businesses as a whole. The chapter explores how to notice patterns and then to use them for knowledge sharing and analysis. Whatever patterns are involved, the only certainty of change projects is uncertainty! Chapter 15 looks at how business analysts can deal with the risks their projects face, outlining a simple but effective risk management process. It introduces risk facilitation as a role where business analysts can add a great deal of value. Part II is rounded off by an opinion piece by a banker on creativity.

On the website **www.baleadership.com**, you will find further resources for leadership within your project, including an article on people-oriented design. This restates the importance of having people at the very centre of design in business analysis and explores what this means in practice.

How does Part II relate to leadership within your organization?

Most projects operate within the context of at least one organization. Part III provides a wider view, looking at a whole range of ways that business analysts need to look outside their project to provide leadership for effective change.

Working with the project manager

SUZANNE ROBERTSON

How does the work of business analysis connect to that of project management? How can business analysts and project managers help each other? Who should do what? How do the tasks overlap? Should we have both roles? This chapter addresses these and other questions about the benefits of successful collaboration between business analysts and project managers.

Guiding the work

The job of a business analyst is to identify what people need so that they can improve the way that they do their work and to communicate those needs to people who can implement solutions. In theory the needers and the implementers could communicate directly. In practice there are many reasons why an intermediary, translator or facilitator is necessary:

- The needers usually do not know what they need.
- The implementers do not understand the needers' business.
- The implementers and needers talk different languages.
- The needers and implementers have different goals.
- There is a high rate of change in the needers' and the implementers' worlds.
- The needers and implementers are often in different locations.

The job of the business analyst is to discover the real needs of the work and to communicate them to the implementers. The business analyst digs behind how the work is done and makes the abstractions necessary to discover the real purpose or essence of the work.

Another part of the business analyst's job is being an innovator, which includes questioning and suggesting new and changed business policy to better meet the organization's goals. An understanding of the essential business

FIGURE 5.1 The business analyst acts as the communication bridge between the needers and the implementers

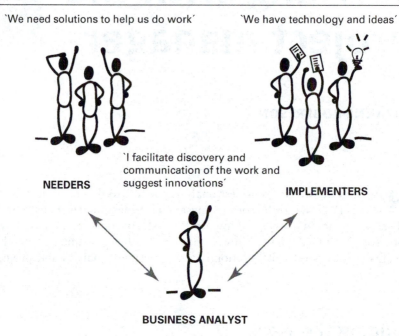

`We need solutions to help us do work´                `We have technology and ideas´

`I facilitate discovery and
communication of the work and
suggest innovations´

NEEDERS   **IMPLEMENTERS**

BUSINESS ANALYST

data often leads to ideas for how the business can take advantage of data that they already have to make better business decisions. Exposure to new implementation technology will often trigger the business analyst to talk to the implementers and identify new ways that the business can benefit from the use of the technology.

The business analyst coordinates the skills and special interests of many stakeholders, always with the intention of helping the business to make improvements to the work and the way that it is done.

Managing the project

A project is a dynamic mixture of wants, needs, technology, politics, facts, opinions, feelings and people. Very quickly this conglomeration acquires a life force of its own and can easily stray from the original intention. The project manager is responsible for getting to know and monitoring interactions and changes between these diverse elements and ensuring that the project stays on track and meets its goals as well as possible within the constraints.

The project manager plans and monitors the tasks that must be carried out. This involves allocating responsibilities, estimating, supervising, motivating and ensuring that the project team have the facilities that they need in order to do the project. Looking outward, the manager is concerned with identifying and managing risk and responding to changes that have an effect on the project.

To do all of this effectively the project manager needs, above all, to know what is really happening on the project and to be aware of the skills and personalities of the project team.

The ideal alliance

The concerns and responsibilities of the business analyst and the project manager are different. The project manager is primarily concerned with facilitating the activities necessary to get the project done. The business analyst's primary concern is to understand and communicate the work of the business and to make recommendations for improving that work. On the surface the two roles are very different, but the most successful projects recognize that there is a lot of important overlap.

The project manager and the business analyst are concerned with different perspectives of the same knowledge. For example, to plan the project schedule and allocate tasks, the project manager needs to know the organization's goal – its reason for investing in the project – so that the schedule and priorities are congruent with that goal. The business analyst also needs to understand the same goal, but for different reasons. The business analyst uses the goal as the basis for prioritizing needs, identifying the real requirements, making decisions about scope and driving relevant suggestions about improvements.

As well as the project's goals, stakeholders, scope of investigation, scope of solution, business use cases, product use cases, atomic requirements, data definitions and implementation modules are other classes of knowledge that are interesting to both the project manager and the business analyst. However, each party is interested in this knowledge for different reasons. The business analyst is concerned with discovering and communicating the knowledge so that the eventual solution fits the real needs. The project manager uses the knowledge as input to making project management decisions.

The business analyst is rather like the detective inspector in a police investigation. The business analyst investigates the crime, interviews the suspects, witnesses and subject matter experts and reviews the facts with the objective of solving the crime. The project manager plays a role more like that of the chief superintendent of police. He or she is concerned with understanding the progress towards solving the crime and needs to address questions like: what are the indicators of progress, what resources have we used, how can we best use the resources available, are the members of the team working effectively, have we assigned the responsibilities to the right people, and how can I summarize progress in order to keep the commissioner informed? The communication between the detective inspector and the project manager is facilitated by them (and the whole team) sharing a common vocabulary for communicating knowledge about the investigation of a crime.

Similarly, if the project manager (PM) and the business analyst (BA) share a common vocabulary they will be able to collaborate and take individual actions that contribute to the overall project goals:

PM: Have you been able to identify the scope of the work you need to investigate?

BA: Yes. There's the model on the wall. From that we estimate there will be 50 business use cases. We've prioritized their value according to the project goal.

PM: Ah – I see that you have classified number 20 as the highest priority. But in today's management meeting there was a change in the supplier policy; would it be possible to do the first iteration for number 15 instead? It would help if we can show some progress in that area first.

BA: I think it will be OK given our understanding of the dependencies – yes, I think we'll be able to present a prototype of number 15 at the review meeting next week.

PM: Based on our current rate of progress I see that one business use case takes a pair of analysts around a week to investigate and come up with the first-cut product use case prototype and its requirements. I'm using this metric to help plan task assignments and I'm keeping track of variations. Let me know if there are any changes in the work scope. I want to be sure to keep the schedule congruent with what is happening on the project.

BA: OK, we'll do that. I can also give you a relative weighting of the business use cases to help with the scheduling. Something else you should know is that together with the implementers we have done some experimentation with the new web interface implementation unit and we did not have the problems we anticipated with that new technology.

PM: Ah, so something that was potentially high-risk looks easier than we thought. Thanks. I'll look at your notes and make the appropriate adjustments to my risk management models.

A common knowledge model

A requirements knowledge model provides a common language for people with different concerns to be able to talk about project progress and strategies. Figure 5.2 is an example of a knowledge model. The knowledge model

FIGURE 5.2 A requirements knowledge model illustrating the concept of having a common language that can be used by the business analyst, the project manager and other members of the team

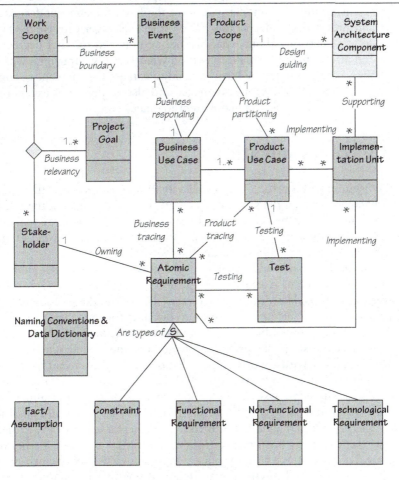

KEY A rectangle represents a *class* of knowledge, and the name of the class is written in the rectangle. A line represents a *relationship* between two or more classes.
Multiplicity is represented by 1 (one) and * (many).
NOTE For more details of this model refer to Robertson and Robertson (2012).

identifies the classes of knowledge concerned with requirements and the relationships between them.

A description, and attributes of what the team means by each of the classes and relationships, is recorded in a dictionary. For example, the team might define work scope as: 'The boundary of the investigation of the work.

Defined by input flows, output flows and the adjacent systems that they come from and go to. Used to guide the investigation and as the traceable basis for partitioning the work into smaller pieces.'

Bear in mind that your own knowledge model might contain different classes of knowledge and different relationships. Provided everyone on your project is using the same model, you have the basis for effective feedback loops and productive conversations. The project manager can use the language to ask questions about what has been completed to what degree of detail and also to make estimates based on what is really happening within the project team. Similarly the business analyst can use the language to communicate progress to the project manager and also to point out exceptions and difficulties in a precise and consistent manner.

Early communication

At the beginning of a project the business analyst is concerned with achieving a balance between the scope of the work to be investigated, the stakeholders who need to be involved and the project goal. Given this balance the business analyst can partition the investigation, prioritize the pieces and start doing some detailed business analysis work.

The project manager also wants to pin down the scope, stakeholders and goals for different reasons. Early project management questions need answers: how big is the work to be investigated, how will the investigation be partitioned, what is the estimated amount of effort for each task, how does the budget compare with the estimate, and have we defined the constraints?

If, at this early stage, the project manager and the business analyst can sit down together with a work scope, a list of the business events, a stakeholder map or list, and a measurable goal then the project is off to a flying start. The business analyst can give the project manager input about the business value and priority of the different business use cases and possible risks. The project manager can inform the business analyst of the project management strategy with respect to a sequential or iterative methodology, involvement of external suppliers, quality review checkpoints, mandated documents and anything else that pertains to the conduct of the project.

Most of all they are using their common language (as illustrated earlier with the knowledge model) to establish a partnership and to plan strategy and identify useful feedback points to keep the project on track.

Iterative collaboration

The business analyst investigates the work of the business with the objective of discovering the real business needs. Provided the analyst continues to use a consistent language to capture knowledge about the business needs, then the

FIGURE 5.3 The project manager and business analyst have different but overlapping perspectives

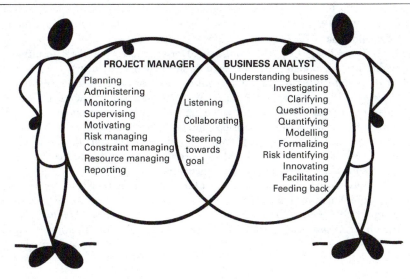

project manager can continue to use that knowledge as input to making management decisions. For example, if the business analyst discovers additional interfaces around the scope of the work to be investigated, then the project manager knows how many interfaces there were originally and how many extra ones have been discovered. The manager understands what has changed and can make the appropriate management decisions necessary to adjust the schedule, estimates, priorities and task assignments in line with reality.

There are connections between the responsibilities of a business analyst and a project manager, but each role has different and complementary (and overlapping) perspectives. The business analyst is concerned with investigating the work to understand the business needs and facilitating iterative feedback loops between the business people and the implementers. The project manager is concerned with monitoring the results of the investigation, allocating resources, planning and replanning, and keeping higher management informed.

First, the project manager and the business analyst need to understand the advantages of iterative collaboration. Then, with the help of a consistent language, they can jointly steer the project towards success.

About the author

Suzanne Robertson is a principal and founder of the Atlantic Systems Guild and co-author of *Mastering the Requirements Process*.

References and further reading

Atlantic Systems Guild, http://www.systemsguild.com (systems engineering topics)

Bolton, R (1996) *People Skills*, Touchstone, New York (invaluable communication skills handbook)

DeMarco, T and Lister, L (1999) *Peopleware*, Dorset House, New York (inspiring insights into the human issues surrounding software development)

Robertson, S and Robertson, J (2005) *Requirements-Led Project Management: Discovering David's slingshot*, Addison-Wesley, Boston, MA (how the project manager can progressively use the emerging requirements artefacts to make relevant project management decisions and provide feedback loops)

Robertson, S and Robertson, J (2012) *Mastering the Requirements Process*, 3rd edn, Addison-Wesley, Boston, MA (coherent techniques for addressing the socio-technical issues in getting requirements right)

Volere, http://www.volere.co.uk (the home of the Volere requirements template and other requirements techniques)

Weinberg, J (1992) *Quality Software Management*, vol 1: *Systems Thinking*, vol 2: *First-Order Measurement*, vol 3: *Congruent Action*, vol 4: *Anticipating Change*: *An integrated guide for a modern software manager*, Dorset House, New York

Dealing with difficult stakeholders

MICHAEL BROWN

Introduction

And now for something, to coin a phrase, 'completely different'. So far this book has been principally concerned with the profession of business analysis. We are now going to talk about something much more riveting: a subject that you find fascinating above all others. We are going to talk about *you*!

Let's start with some news. The bad news is that you cannot change the other person. The good news is that you can change the way the person responds to you, and that is through you changing your behaviour.

We are going to have difficult stakeholders in the front of our mind as we go through the chapter, but in fact, between you and me, this material works anywhere with anyone. Try it out at home, with your boss and your next-door neighbour.

One word of reassurance: you're not alone! A survey by the Centre for Effective Dispute Resolution called *Tough Times Tough Talk* revealed that two-thirds of managers feel that their biggest challenge is holding difficult conversations, and that only 44 per cent feel they are effective at managing conflict (CEDR, 2010).

It's all your fault!

Before we get started I'd like to make an outrageous proposition. Let's start as we mean to go on: this is a chapter about conflict, after all. *There is no such thing as a difficult stakeholder.* Difficult stakeholders are created, not born. They don't carry a business card saying 'Difficult

Stakeholder'. In my experience of over 30 years of working in business, stakeholders do not start off as 'difficult'. I suggest that they *become* difficult, usually as a result of what the person engaging with them does (or doesn't do).

Perhaps I can go a little further with this. *You get the difficult stakeholder you deserve.* Not convinced? Let me ask you to visualize for a moment a stakeholder who fits the description of 'difficult'. If you can't think of one, well done, go to the next chapter. Or stay with us and think of a 'difficult' business colleague. Think a bit about the sort of behaviour that this person displays that you find difficult. Make a few notes about it if you like.

Note how you feel when you've done that, by the way. Any increase in body heat? Sweaty hands? How's your heart rate?

Now I have a further tricky question for you: does this 'difficult stakeholder' behave the same way towards everyone? If not, why might that be? Could it be that you bring out this particular response? And if so, let's remember, this is good news, because you can make a change, and if you do it may well change the person's response to you.

Do you think everyone else in the business thinks this person is 'difficult'? Could it be that you are telling yourself that he or she is 'difficult': that it exists in your mind more than in reality? How much might you be exaggerating? How many assumptions are you making? How much of this is subjective and emotional rather than based on logic and facts? Feel free to pause and scribble down a few more thoughts here.

Your personal conflict handling preferences influence the outcome

I wonder whether you'd agree that you are at least half the problem when you deal with 'difficult' stakeholders? That the way you approach people like this often makes things worse? That somehow every time you get involved it seems to become more problematic?

We are going to explore a model that will help you to pinpoint this, and also to analyse the other person through a new lens. Before we do so, let me invite you to carry out a short exercise. I am not going to say anything about why we're doing it, as that might influence your response. Please take a metaphorical 'honesty tablet' so that you respond to what comes next *completely* as yourself (not a version of yourself that you wish you were).

When you have taken the tablet, please carry out the exercise. You will need a pencil (not a pen) and paper.

Write down the least lawful thing you have ever done. Note: Speeding fines and parking tickets do not qualify.

Thank you. We will refer back to how you responded as we go through the next model.

The way you just responded to my instruction might be a useful indicator as to how you prefer to deal with conflict. The question I asked was a cheeky one, to say the least. Some might say inappropriate, rude, intrusive, risky. How did you respond?

Let's get the model on to the table. It is the world's most widely used conflict preferences model, known as the Thomas–Kilmann Conflict Mode Instrument (TKI for short). The model is based on the premise that we all have a personal preference for how we respond in a conflict situation. We are able to use our non-preferred response, but under pressure and in the heat of the moment our preferred response is the most likely to present itself.

FIGURE 6.1 Conflict preferences

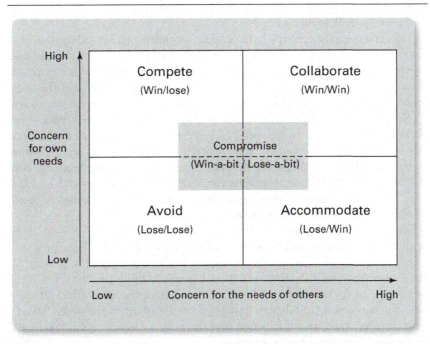

Adapted from Thomas, K (1976) Conflict and conflict management, *Handbook of Industrial and Organizational Psychology* ed MD Dunnette, p 900. Used with permission.

The model shows five conflict modes, each of which will vary based on the extent to which, when under pressure, you are concerned with what other people need (what Kilmann calls cooperativeness) or how much you are concerned with your own needs (what he calls assertiveness).

Your preferences are organic: they evolve. You learn how to deal with conflict, from others around you, where you work, the nature of your work, and so on. Maybe your boss encourages a certain style, or other styles are frowned on in your organization. The chances are these might influence your personal 'defaults' when there is conflict around.

Let's first try to work out what your preference is.

Remember the exercise we did five minutes ago? Let's see if it was your preference in action.

Accommodators might have done as instructed, but not felt very comfortable about it, maybe wrote down a truthful answer that was in fact the least lawful thing they have ever done, and felt glad they used a pencil so they could rub it out (because it's incriminating evidence!). They perhaps complied with my request because I issued it and I'm in charge here. Was that how you responded?

What about Avoiders? Maybe they didn't do it at all, hoping that wouldn't spoil their understanding. Maybe they wrote down something that wasn't true, or something that was unlawful but not the most unlawful thing they had ever done. Was this you?

Competers might perhaps have proudly written down something that was true (maybe rather pleased with it, as it was very naughty at the time, but no one found out and they got away with it), but knowing that under no circumstances are they going to share what they wrote down. They met the challenge from me, but had a plan as to how to get the better of me if necessary.

Compromisers are those who like to find workable solutions when there is conflict around, but won't spend all night over it. 'It'll do: it's not perfect, but let's move on.' They might have written something a bit illegal – something that might go along with the exercise in order to get the learning from it – but shying away from revealing the truly illegal thing they did 10 years ago. They will have worked with me, but not revealed their complete hand. Might this have been your response?

And finally we come to the Collaborators. They might have gone along with the exercise despite feeling uncomfortable, because they were prepared to take a risk in order to get the maximum return from their investment. So they might have written down the truth but would draw the line if I said the next stage of the exercise would be to e-mail me what they wrote. If we'd been face to face, a Collaborator would have asked questions of the 'What's in it for me?' type, and if satisfied that there was a benefit from taking the risk would have been happy to do so.

It may or may not be the case that there is a link from this exercise to your conflict profile. Only you can answer that. If you think it helps you to assess what you think your profile is, that will be very helpful to us as we talk about the model in more detail.

FIGURE 6.2 A time and place for all styles

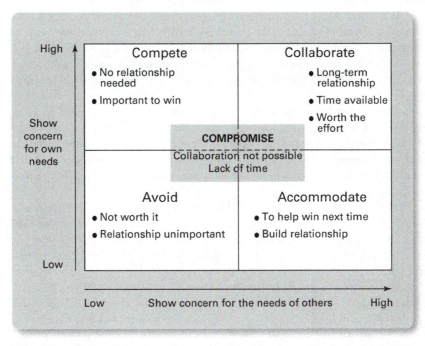

Adapted from Thomas, K (1976) Conflict and conflict management, *Handbook of Industrial and Organizational Psychology* ed MD Dunnette, p 900. Used with permission.

Research has shown that, as people develop and climb the corporate ladder, conflict preferences tend to climb up the model as well. In other words, people tend to become more comfortable with competing and collaborating over time. No real surprise: business leaders need to be able to take unpopular decisions at times (competing) and need to be able to sit down and work out win/win solutions when the stakes are high and they need a long-term solution (collaborating).

Collaborating is found in equal measure across both genders. However, males are significantly more competitive at all ages than females. (Dare I suggest no surprises there either?)

A time and a place for each conflict preference

Consciously choosing which mode to be in for a given situation can be a great time saver, as well as helping to gear you up for dealing with conflicts that really do need to be resolved. We can make conscious choices about which mode to be in. Which one should we use when?

It is a good idea to compete when you don't ever need to talk to the person again or don't need to care about them. Bad salespeople tend to bring out the competer in me, especially if they ring me at home on a Friday evening! This might also apply if it is high stakes and I need to win. I might go competitive if the house is on fire or if someone is threatening my daughter.

Collaborating is a good idea when the stakes are high, we need to work together in the future, and I have the time to do so. One of the big downsides of collaborating is that it takes time and energy. I probably won't bother to collaborate when we are trying to agree which TV programme to watch. I should try to collaborate when you, a key stakeholder, keep cancelling meetings at short notice.

This raises an important point about timing. If you need to have a collaborative outcome on a high-stakes issue, start early. Allow plenty of time for it. It is very hard to collaborate when you are pushed for time, and you may find you have to slip back to the next best thing, which is a compromise outcome.

Compromise is a good choice when there is not enough time to do a collaborative deal, or where perhaps it is not worth the effort. Meeting someone halfway can leave a slightly bad taste in the mouth, but it is better than no deal, and we live to work together another day. Go for compromise if you want to show that you are flexible as a means of building trust, but do it on issues where a real win/win is not crucial.

Accommodate when you want to build the relationship and it is low stakes. Let the other person have his or her way on something you don't need to worry about, so that you can build your bank of points up and cash them in later on high-stakes collaborative issues. I would recommend that you sit down and work out which issues do not matter to you and you can use to build up this reserve of good will. The best issues to pick, of course, are the ones that have low cost to you and high perceived value to the other party. When you put them on the table, of course, you are going to make them look high cost to you, so that they are valued more highly by the other party. This is all basic negotiations stuff, and no rocket science is involved. Use the appropriate body language to make it look painful. (Let your eyes fill with tears, wince a bit, sigh maybe. At times it's an act, especially if you are dealing with a cynical stakeholder who is doing the same to you.)

On this point, let me suggest the idea of the Considered Response. When your stakeholder asks for a concession, slow down your response. Allow a bit of silence; do a few calculations; check your project plan. Then respond. This technique has three advantages:

1 It allows you to think (it is very difficult to think and talk at the same time).

2 It adds weight to your response. It feels less easy to bat it away, because you appear to have weighed it up carefully.

3 It shows that you are listening and considering what has been said to you. This in itself is a form of respect, which in turn means that it will often (not always; there are some plain nasty people out there) be reciprocated.

A word of warning on the Accommodator response. Use it sparingly. If you do it too often it tends to make the other party think that you are going to accommodate on everything, which can lead to the person asking for more. Be a little unpredictable, and make sure the other party realizes this is a one-off.

When is Avoiding a good choice? Not often. It does work in a couple of situations:

- When you need more information ('Let me come back to you').

- When emotions are running high ('Let's take a break and talk again after lunch').

- When you know you can't win and can't afford to let someone else win. If you see no prospect of getting what you want, try to make the issue go away entirely (by being creative) so that no one ends up with it.

Summary

We all have our own preferences for how we deal with conflict. These are particularly relevant when we deal with a difficult stakeholder. Building your flexibility and the skill of making conscious choices about how to respond will help you to get more of what you want from others. It's easier said than done, but it will become more fluent with practice. If you would like to complete your Thomas–Kilmann profile and receive some guidance on it, contact me by e-mail at michaelbrowntraining@ live.co.uk.

Good luck with your difficult stakeholders!

About the author

Michael Brown has been a business skills trainer for over 15 years.

References

Centre for Effective Dispute Resolution (CEDR) (2010) *Tough Times Tough Talk: A guide to working life conflicts*, http://www.cedr.com/about_us/toughtalk

Thomas, K (1976) conflict and conflict management, *Handbook of Industrial and Organizational Psychology*, ed MD Dunnette, p 900

Facilitating groups and individuals

PENNY PULLAN

In this chapter, we focus on facilitating groups and individuals. We ask what facilitation means and why it is important for business analysis. What exactly needs facilitating and how should this be carried out? We look at the preparation required before a facilitated meeting, how to get the best out of everyone during meetings (including the facilitator) and how to make actions happen as a result. We'll also explore how the ideas we present will be useful for those working one to one with individuals, as well as those working with groups.

What is facilitation?

Business analysis involves working with people, both in groups and dealing with individuals in one-to-one situations. Facilitation of this work aims to make things easy for participants, allowing them to achieve their goals as effectively as possible. Indeed, the Latin origins of the word 'facilitate' mean 'to make easy'.

Let's look at definitions from two different facilitation experts. Roger Schwarz (2002) describes group facilitation as 'a process in which a person whose selection is acceptable to all the members of the group, who is substantively neutral and who has no substantive decision-making authority diagnoses and intervenes to help a group improve how it identifies and solves problems, and makes decisions, to increase the group's effectiveness'. David Sibbet's (2003) definition brings in ideas around creativity and ownership. He describes facilitation as 'the art of leading people through processes toward agreed-upon objectives in a manner that encourages participation, ownership and creativity from all involved'. Both authors describe the use of facilitation within business analysis, although there is a caveat.

While facilitation is easiest when the facilitator is 'substantively neutral', business analysts are unlikely to be 'substantively neutral' all of the time. They will have their own views as members of the project team, as well as wanting the group to be effective and come to their own decisions.

Business analysts will need to manage a couple of metaphorical hats when working with groups: their hat as the neutral facilitator of the group; and their hat as a valuable project team member. It is best for analysts to wear one hat at a time, being really clear at each moment whether they are playing a neutral facilitator or a project team member with valuable information to share. This complex role mixing is often known as facilitative leadership.

Why is facilitation important for business analysis?

Business analysts work with groups that are usually mixed in a whole variety of different ways, including:

- *hierarchy:* from different levels of the organization;
- *functions:* from across different parts of the organization and different jobs;
- *cultures:* from diverse country cultures in global teams to different cultures across organizational boundaries.

In addition, analysts are likely to work virtually as well as with face-to-face groups and individuals. In all of these situations, they need to work without much formal authority. They do not line-manage the groups they work with but, despite this, need to help the group to come to the right solution for a range of stakeholders. While doing this, they need to engage people, encouraging ownership and participation throughout. Facilitation provides the tools and techniques to do this.

Business analysis is normally carried out within the context of a project and involves a range of people and cultures. Every person will have his or her own individual perspective, and it is part of the business analyst's job to ensure that each perspective is heard and understood by the others. This leads to a shared understanding and true consensus as to how to proceed. Without this common understanding, there will be many conflicting views and, unfortunately, too often projects suffer from the resulting disagreements, misunderstandings and confusion.

A parable from India illustrates this well (see page 94 for a poem containing this parable). There are six blind men, who know nothing about elephants. In the room, there is an elephant. Each goes up to the elephant in turn. The first blind man feels the elephant's side and thinks that an elephant is like a wall, the second thinks the elephant is like a spear (he felt the tusk), the third thinks that an elephant is like a snake (he felt the trunk), the fourth thinks an elephant is like a tree trunk (he felt the leg), the fifth thinks that an elephant is like a large fan (he felt the ear) and the final blind man thinks that an elephant is like a rope (he felt the tail). In the story, they argue for the rest of eternity. That's what projects can feel like. Many start off this way. Part of the role of the business analyst is to facilitate a shared understanding of the problem to be solved and the way forward, taking into account the views of all the members of the group.

What needs facilitation?

Facilitation is very helpful for project meetings and workshops, where particular objectives need to be achieved. These can range from project kick-off meetings to make sure everyone is clear about the vision for the project, through to the final project reviews to ensure that benefits were delivered and that the solution is working well. Facilitation skills can also help interviews with individuals to be more productive.

Facilitation is useful to help people handle change and carry it out. For humans, resistance to change is a normal reaction, and many will need support to be able to grapple with change and eventually work well in a new way.

How to facilitate meetings and workshops

We will look at the practical steps a facilitator can do before, during and after a meeting or workshop to make success more likely.

Before the meeting

In my experience, careful preparation makes meetings run much more smoothly. While it is possible to spend huge amounts of time in preparation, agonizing over all the possible ways that a meeting could go wrong, it's better to focus on just a few things. Several of these are illustrated in Figure 7.1, which shows the key steps in starting up a meeting. If you use these in your preparation, you'll be ready to start up your meeting effectively.

It's really important to be clear about what the purpose of the meeting is ('We are here to…'). Without a clear purpose, the meeting is likely to lose focus and drift off course. A clear purpose will make it much easier to work out who should attend and to encourage them to do so.

'Today we will…' in Figure 7.1 outlines five objectives for the meeting. Ensure that you know what the objectives are and how you will know when you have achieved them. Four or five objectives are plenty for most meetings. Any more will make it more likely that your meeting will overrun and/ or lose focus.

FIGURE 7.1 Steps to start up a meeting

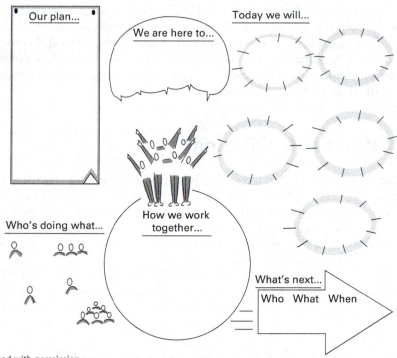

Used with permission.

Make the timing clear with a plan showing what's going to happen when. Perhaps some people can come in just for parts of the meeting rather than attending throughout and wasting their time.

'Who's doing what?' The purpose will help you work out what roles are needed for the meeting. Typical roles might include a timekeeper, a facilitator and a scribe to write down actions and decisions.

The most crucial step for nipping problems in the bud is 'How we work together', sometimes referred to as 'ground rules'. These rules, which are developed with the group, explain how the group will work together throughout the meeting. While best developed at the start of the meeting, it's good to have some prepared for discussion. Topics might include confidentiality, use of mobile devices, and only one person speaking at any one time. By anticipating problems up front and agreeing ground rules as a group, it's possible to avoid much conflict later on. I like to include a ground rule 'Spelling dusn't mater', which allows those with dyslexia or anxiety to take part fully, and generally raises a laugh!

In addition to these start-up steps, consider any risks to your meeting. Are there any known issues? If you are likely to have a mixture of hierarchy in the meeting, plan your process so that it allows for anonymous input. An example of this is generating ideas by writing on sticky notes and sticking them in clusters on a wall. In this way, the group build up their work together, regardless of seniority or who has come up with each idea.

At senior levels and where office politics is key, it's helpful to meet each meeting participant beforehand. This can lay the foundation for a very effective meeting. If some individuals are missed out, this can lay the seeds for future problems, so it's usually best to speak to everyone.

During a meeting

Start by using the meeting start-up steps outlined above. Make sure that the purpose is clear. When this is written up and displayed for all to see, it helps people to focus.

Your state and theirs

It is important for you, as the facilitator, to be in a productive energy state. A nervous or anxious facilitator will not be much help to the group. It can be helpful to anchor back to previous successful meetings, focusing on what you could see, hear and feel at that time. See Chapter 4 for more on this and other NLP techniques.

The state of the group as a whole is important too. Are they productive, ready to work hard and eager to solve problems and take decisions? Or are they looking tired and uninterested? As a facilitator, you need to be able to diagnose the energy state of the room as a whole and take steps to change it where necessary.

The spotlight and being transparent

A question to ask yourself is 'Where is my spotlight?' Where do you feel that the focus of the meeting is? Is it on the group or on the facilitator? Many facilitators find that the pressure they experience diminishes when they keep this spotlight firmly on the group, focusing all their attention and energy on the group rather than themselves.

With the spotlight on the group, the facilitator can be transparent about problems encountered. For example, if someone has been speaking without pause for 10 minutes and others have been raising their hands to make points but have given up, it is tempting just to call for a new speaker. Another facilitator might feel that the speaker is being domineering and wants to block others. Another might ask the person to be quiet! Instead, it's more helpful to reflect back what you see. 'I've noticed that x has been speaking for 10 minutes and others have been raising their hands, sometimes several times. What shall we do about that?' In this case, most speakers will back down, having not realized that they'd been speaking for so long! This reply has kept the focus on the group and also avoided labelling any motivations behind the speaker's actions.

FIGURE 7.2 The ladder of inference

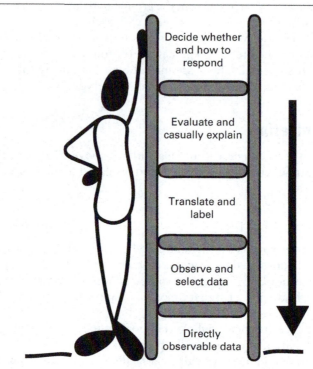

A tool to help you stay away from inferring motivations and more is the ladder of inference, shown in Figure 7.2, which is adapted from Schwarz (2002) and others. In a possible conflict situation, check that you are going to intervene based on the data that you observe, without labelling, evaluating or explaining it. Stay down the ladder and, if you notice that you have moved up the ladder, come back down.

This all relates back to the metaphorical spotlight. With the spotlight focused on ourselves, as facilitators, we are far more likely to seek to maintain control of the group, seeking to cover up any weakness and not exposing any vulnerability. When the spotlight is focused on our groups, we will be concentrating on getting the best result for the group members and serving them well.

Sustaining participation

The best facilitators keep participants engaged and interested throughout the process. The worst meetings are likely to have lost people's interest, and the participants may be on the point of leaving or going to sleep!

How can we engage people in our meetings? Involving people helps, as does inviting only people who really need to be there. Visual prompts help too. In my own practice, I use graphics throughout meetings so that people can 'see what they mean'.

Use people's senses to keep them engaged. Think of sight (provide plenty of natural daylight), sound (turn off any buzzing air-conditioning or projectors if possible), smell (open the windows in a stale room) and touch (comfortable chairs to sit on).

Dealing with conflict

During business analysis meetings, you are likely to come across conflict. Why? Perhaps it is because people care about the work. Remember that most conflict arises only because people care so much about the outcomes of the project and their own perspective.

Much conflict can be avoided by anticipating what might happen up front and preparing for it. Remember the blind men and the elephant? Most conflict is due to differences in perspective and understanding. This is natural, especially at the early stages of a project. In these cases, it makes sense to listen to each perspective carefully before designing your meeting to build a common understanding.

Many business analysts fear that conflict will break out in the middle of a session they are running. If this happens, don't panic. It's usually possible to have a short break while the issue is sorted out. Remember that most of the models of team development include a storming or conflict stage, and so this is a natural step in the development of a group and should be expected.

There is one type of conflict that needs to be sorted quickly and that's where two or more people have a poor relationship that is affecting the group. This is different from the task conflict described so far and should be sorted out carefully before proceeding.

Making sure actions happen after meetings

Too many meetings result in no action. Sometimes this was a deliberate choice, but more often actions had been planned, but were never carried out. Perhaps the actions were unclear? Perhaps people didn't take notes of their actions and were not sent a reminder? Perhaps they had no intention of acting? Perhaps no one followed up on actions?

To ensure that actions happen as a result of your meetings there are a few steps to take:

- Write down actions publicly during your meeting, stating who will do what by when.
- Ensure actions are clear and unambiguous.
- Gain agreement on the actions before the end of the meeting.

- Ensure that everyone has a copy of the actions.
- Follow up to check that actions are completed.

It can be useful to check that people intend to carry out their actions by asking them how sure they are they'll be able to carry them out. I find a scale from 1 (not at all sure) to 10 (certain) works well. If people's intent is lower than 10, why not amend the action to make it more likely to happen? Surely it's better to have an imperfect action carried out than a perfect action that never happens.

Working with individuals

While most people would not think of one-to-one interviews and meetings as facilitated sessions, these too will benefit from many of the techniques and ideas presented so far. Prepare carefully, anticipating problems as you design your questions. Use the meeting start-up steps in Figure 7.1 to make sure you are both really clear on what you are doing and how. Even individuals benefit from engaging meetings and having their actions followed up.

About the author

Penny Pullan is the co-editor of this book and develops facilitation skills in business analysts and other project professionals through her company, Making Projects Work Ltd.

References and further reading

Hunter, D (2007) *The Art of Facilitation: The essentials for leading great meetings and creating group synergy*, 2nd edn, Random House, Auckland

Pullan, P and Murray-Webster, R (2011) *A Short Guide to Facilitating Risk Management: Engaging people to identify, own and manage risk*, Gower, Aldershot

Schwarz, R (2002) *The Skilled Facilitator*, Jossey-Bass, San Francisco

Sibbet, D (2003) *Principles of Facilitation*, Grove Consultants International, San Francisco

Discovering the essence of the problem

08

JAMES ROBERTSON

W e can solve almost any problem using software – the problem is that we don't always know what the problem is.

Every year software projects all over the world produce tens of millions of lines of new code; not all of it is used. A lot of it is quietly discarded by its intended users who, after patiently bearing the strain of the development activity, either ask for heavy modifications or return to doing their work in the same way as they had done before the attempt to develop new software for them.

Why does this happen? There are many reasons, but the one that I am concerned with here is distressingly common – the development team has not understood the real needs for the software. In other words, the real problem has not been discovered.

Finding the real problem to solve – that is, the *essence* of the problem – usually takes more than just insight or a flash of brilliance. Usually it takes a little effort (not a lot, but some), and that effort has to be expended on several things, without which it is almost impossible to find the real problem:

- *Scope:* the first thing to understand is the scope of the problem. More projects fail from having too narrow a scope than fail because the scope is too large. The scope of the problem is larger, significantly larger, than the software.

- *Essence:* being able to see past the implementation and the technology and discover the underlying concepts and policies – in other words, the real problem.

- *Viewpoints:* being able to see the problem space from a number of viewpoints, and being clear as to which viewpoint is being used at any given time.

- *Not rushing into a solution:* 'If I had one hour to save the world, I would spend 59 minutes defining the problem' (Albert Einstein).

- *Behaviour:* as Donella Meadows (2008) points out, a system shows its goals by its behaviour, not from rhetoric or stated goals. So the business analyst must spend some time studying and observing the problem space.

There are other things that business analysts must do if they are to ensure that the correct product is built, but this list is enough for us at the moment. Let's look at them, but not in the order shown above.

Solutions versus requirements

Many business analysts report that, when they ask their stakeholders for the requirements, they are told how the stakeholders think the problem should be solved, and not the problem itself. This approach means that the business analyst must rely on the stakeholder's technological expertise (not always guaranteed) and that the stakeholder has a complete and accurate grasp of the problem, that the proposed solution does in fact solve the problem, is the optimal solution, and that the stakeholder understands how his or her solution will affect the rest of the organization (mostly unlikely).

We also have to take into account that stakeholders are often speaking from their own perspective; this might well colour their view of the problem to be solved, or skew the problem so that they get the solution they want, but not necessarily what the organization needs. For example, you often hear something like this: 'I need a new screen to show me all unfulfilled orders for the week.' This is a solution, but the business analyst has no way of knowing whether it solves the right problem, nor has the business analyst yet heard what the real problem is. He or she might rightly assume that the business user may also not know what the problem is.

So let's look at this fairly typical request. The user has asked for a screen; this is a piece of technology and is therefore a solution. (Technology is rarely the problem; it is almost always part of the solution.) So what is the screen for? Why does this user think that he or she needs a screen? The answer *appears* to be to provide the user with a list of unfulfilled orders. The business analyst's next question must be 'What are you doing with that information?'

Ask 'What do you do?' not 'What do you want?'

Suppose the business user tells the business analyst that he or she looks at the list of unfulfilled orders, and uses the list to assess whether or not the fulfilment people in the warehouse are able to ship the goods quickly enough to keep up with demand. The real need now appears to be the ability to monitor the fulfilment process. But is it? What is this business stakeholder going to do if the list of unfulfilled orders becomes, in his or her estimation, too long? Presumably the stakeholder would hire extra workers, or at least go and talk to the warehouse and see if there are any problems that could be solved some other way. So the real need seems to be to manage the fulfilment process.

Taking that on board, it becomes apparent that there is a need to know whether or not fulfilment is keeping up with orders, but a list of individual unfulfilled orders seems to be a very cack-handed way of doing it.

The business analyst now knows that there is a need to alert the user if the rate of fulfilment drops below the volume of orders, but now the analyst thinks about this a little further. Fulfilment is directly related to orders – that is, there must be the same number of orders fulfilled as there are orders taken. It now appears that, if the user is to manage the fulfilment process correctly, then he or she should be monitoring incoming orders so as to be able to adjust the fulfilment process in a timely manner to keep pace.

Note what happened here. By questioning (in reality ignoring) the suggested solution, the business analyst was able to uncover the real nature of the problem. This technique of ignoring implementation – that is, making an *abstraction* – will work in any situation. Let's talk about abstraction.

Abstraction

Abstraction is seeing the basis of something without its concrete implementation: the idea, not the mechanics it uses to carry out the idea; or the concept, not the technology that makes the concept work. Of course, most things can't exist in our physical world without some kind of device to make them work, but if you can step back for a moment and look at the underlying abstraction – the essence – you will see, with greater clarity, the real problem you are trying to solve.

This means ignoring any current implementation and technology that exists at the moment, and ignoring any proposed future implementation. Your only interest at the moment is the underlying essence of the problem.

> Perfection is reached, not when there is nothing more to add, but when there is nothing left to take away.
>
> (Antoine de Saint-Exupéry)

For example, if you look at how music has been sold over the past couple of decades, you see that abstraction has been taking place. We used to buy CDs to listen to music (and vinyl and cassettes before that) until the music industry made the abstraction that what we really want to do is simply listen to music. By abstracting away the implementation – the silver disc – we were left with digital music that could be downloaded directly to a computer, from where it could be played. However, by abstracting a little more, you can say that the computer is part of a solution, and the abstraction is that we want to listen to music wherever we happen to be. Rather than being tied to a desk-bound computer, we wanted portable music, and that brought us devices such as iPods and smartphones.

Abstracting further tells you that we want to listen to music as soon as we find it, so paying for each new album is an implementation detail and not part of the real problem. This has given rise to the music subscription services such as Spotify, Rdio, Rhapsody and so on, where for a monthly fee you play your chosen music (usually by streaming) as soon as you find it. Further abstracting will mean that the device you use becomes irrelevant, and the ultimate abstraction would connect your ears directly to the source of the music.

Perhaps the last one is going a little far, but many projects do not go nearly far enough when it comes to making abstractions.

The reason for making abstractions is that there is a difference between a suggested solution, which must of course be a technological solution, and the underlying problem it is meant to solve. By abstracting away the technology, you are left with only the problem. Now it becomes easier to see if this is indeed the right problem to solve.

Once you have the right problem, given the technology you have at your disposal today, it is a straightforward matter of finding the optimally valuable solution.

Viewpoints

Let us turn to why we want to make abstractions, and why it is useful to have several different abstractions. To put that another way, we can see the same piece of work using different abstractions or, as I shall call them here, different *viewpoints*. Each viewpoint plays its part in helping the analyst to see the work more clearly and, most importantly, helping the stakeholders understand and communicate about their work.

This brings us to the brown cow model as a way of organizing the viewpoints. The brown cow model, shown in Figure 8.1, has four viewpoints of the work being studied, each of which provides different and useful information to the business analyst and stakeholders studying the work. It has two axes, the horizontal one separates *what* from *how*, and the vertical axis separates *now* from the *future*.

The lower left quadrant, how–now, is usually, but not always, the starting point for modelling a piece of work. The how–now view shows the current incarnation of the work, including its technology, people and other devices used by the previous development team to make it function in our technological world.

Now move clockwise around the model. The next quadrant, what–now, is above the horizontal line, and it shows what the work is doing and ignores how it is doing it. Or, to use my terminology, this is the current *essence* of the work.

Then we move into the future; there is always a difference between now and the future; otherwise the project would not be worthwhile. This next quadrant shows the future–what view of the work, or what the essential

FIGURE 8.1 The brown cow model

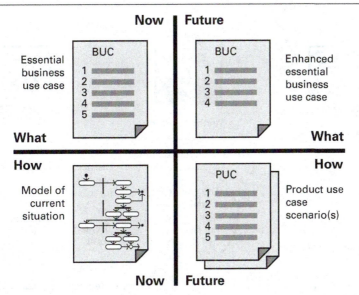

policy is meant to be – what the owner of the work desires it to be in the future. There is – at least there should be – some change to the fundamental processing policy of the work. This is the real problem to be solved by some technological solution.

The technological solution resides in the fourth quadrant – the future–how. This quadrant shows the technological implementation needed to bring the essential policy into the real world.

There is a tendency in many projects to jump directly to the future–how view, but this is rushing into a solution without bothering to find out what the real problem is. If you find that your project is beginning with the future–how, then it is necessary to do a little spadework and shift the emphasis back to the third quadrant, future–what. As I already have mentioned, if you are to find the correct solution to the problem then you have to find the correct problem to solve. The problem does not exist in the future–how quadrant; it can only be found above the horizontal line. In other words, the problem is what we want to do, *not* how we want to do it.

Scope – it's usually not wide enough

Quite a few projects fail to discover the real problem because they have concentrated their efforts on looking only at solutions and ignoring the work that surrounds these solutions. At the outset of a project, scope must

FIGURE 8.2 A context diagram showing the scope of a piece of work

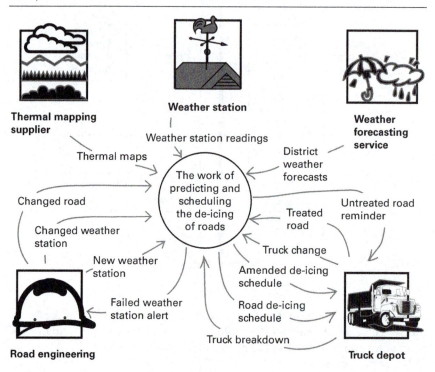

always be considered to be the scope of the work. It is all too tempting to consider only the scope of the software solution, but this almost invariably means that you're ignoring the work that the software is meant to improve.

The most reliable way of defining the scope of a piece of work is to build a context diagram; an example is shown in Figure 8.2. The central circle represents the work, and the named arrows are flows of data to and from the work. Any piece of work you study can be represented by this kind of diagram. Here we see the work contained in the central circle; the named arrows running to and from it are the flows of data provided to or by the outside world. The outside world is represented by the squares, correctly called *adjacent systems*, that surround the work.

Any piece of work looks like this – the names of course will be different, but the representation is the same. Every piece of work is connected to some other piece of work (the adjacent systems) by flows of data. There is no such thing as a self-contained piece of work – any such work would be useless, as it would have no outputs. Equally it could not function, as it has no inputs.

The context diagram demonstrates to the business stakeholders that you are looking at a piece of work – their work – so that you can understand it and in turn find the optimal solution for it. By studying the work you are looking at the problem and not just the perceived proposed solution.

User stories

User stories, used by most agile practices, are often solutions rather than requirements and, I suggest, often fail to reveal the real problem, which in turn means that they might well be solving the wrong problem. I can illustrate this better by using some examples.

> AS A BANK CUSTOMER I WANT ONLINE ACCESS TO MY ACCOUNT SO THAT I CAN SEE MY BALANCE 24/7.

The reference to 'online access' is clearly a solution to a problem. Whoever wrote this story feels that online access is the only way to solve the problem, but the problem itself is as yet unknown.

Let's ask the question 'Why would a customer want access to his or her bank balance 24/7?' Does the account holder want to gloat about the amount of money there is in the account? Or does the account holder need to know the balance for some other reason? I suggest people do not need access to their bank balance unless there is some unusual circumstance – usually they are concerned about whether they can meet a payment or whether they can afford to buy an unusual item this month. Normally bank customers would look at the balance in the account, make allowances for the regular monthly payments – mortgage, food, credit card, electricity and so on – and then calculate whether or not they will become overdrawn if they go ahead and buy whatever it is.

So the real problem, which this story card is not addressing, is that the customer needs to see his or her discretionary balance – what will be left after deducting all the usual monthly payments and any unusual non-discretionary payments that have to be made in the current salary month (tax payment, annual car insurance, etc).

If we are to solve the real problem – the one that the bank customer wants solved – then the story has to change to something like this:

> AS A BANK CUSTOMER I WANT TO SEE WHAT MY DISCRETIONARY BALANCE WILL BE AT THE END OF THE CURRENT SALARY MONTH.

By solving the right problem and thereby providing a better service to its customers, the bank now has an additional opportunity – offering an overdraft to customers who are projecting a negative balance at the end of their salary month.

Examine your story cards. Any that contain some element of technology – a screen, online access, smartphone-enabled, and so on – are solutions. Make an abstraction and find the essence of the problem, and do it as the first step of the development conversation with the business stakeholders.

And finally...

At the end of the day, if the software doesn't meet the user's needs, it is still lousy software regardless of how it was created.

(Pete McBreen)

There is no substitute for solving the right problem. It does not matter if your project comes in under budget or ahead of time, or you have used a state-of-the-art development method, or you have outsourced or used some free, open-source software; if you have solved the wrong problem, you have just wasted everybody's time – and money.

Solving the right problem is easy; knowing and understanding the right problem are a little more difficult – more difficult but not impossible.

Finding the right problem means firstly that you have enough of a playing field to inspect; this means establishing a scope to your study that is large enough to include not just the anticipated software product, but also the work in which it is intended the software should be deployed. It also means that you must resist the siren call to rush into the proposed technological solution, with its glittering technology and apparent ease of installation. You cannot expect to solve the right problem simply by buying some new hardware and software.

Finding the right problem to solve – you have to find it, as it is rarely apparent – means making abstractions and filtering out the technological solutions until you have the underlying, basic problem to be solved. In other words, you find the essence of the problem.

About the author

James Robertson of the Atlantic Systems Guild is a consultant, teacher, project leader and co-author of *Mastering the Requirements Process*.

References and further reading

Gause, D and Weinberg, G (2009) *Are Your Lights On? How to figure out what the problem really is*, Dorset House, New York

Meadows, D (2008) *Thinking in Systems: A primer*, Chelsea Green Publishing, White River Junction, VT

Robertson, J and Robertson, S (1994) *Complete Systems Analysis: The workbook, the textbook, the answers*, Dorset House, New York

Robertson, J and Robertson, S (2005) *Requirements-Led Project Management: Discovering David's slingshot*, Addison-Wesley, Boston, MA

Robertson, J and Robertson, S (2012) *Mastering the Requirements Process: Getting requirements right*, 3rd edn, Addison-Wesley, Boston, MA

Volere, http://www.volere.co.uk

Wiegers, K (2006) *More about Software Requirements: Thorny issues and practical advice*, Microsoft Press, Redmond, WA

09 Dealing with problems

ANDY WILKINS

Introduction

If business analysts are interested in 'leadership for change' or, as mentioned in the Introduction, 'turn[ing] strategic goals and visions into reality while adding value', then by definition they must be interested in problems. There is an integral relationship between business analysis, dealing with problems and leadership for change. This chapter represents our exploration towards a better understanding and articulation of the relationship between the three.

Through our work with organizations, we have come to the conclusion that developing a better grasp of how we approach problems is essential to leadership for change and therefore to business analysis itself – especially if business analysis is to realize its potential.

Our approach to dealing with problems pushes the boundaries on business analysts' everyday current mental models, their understanding of the term 'problem', and also to some degree the very paradigms of business analysis. In particular, business analysis needs to become better acquainted with the nature of wicked problems: they are pervasive, and they present many new challenges.

Our journey as authors, change leaders and fellow 'insiders' has led us to examine some of the productive practices that emerge by studying the links between leadership for change, how people deal with problems, and business analysis. We offer our insights in the hope that they will enable you to be a better business analyst and a more effective leader of change, and to provide an improved service to your clients. We also hope that it will lead to more dialogue, out of which all of us will hopefully become wiser.

Why do all of us – including business analysts – stumble with problems?

We are all experiencing the effects of an accelerated pace of change, intensified competition, and increasingly demanding customers – what has been referred to as 'vucasity on speed', where v is volatility, u is uncertainty, c is complexity and a is ambiguity. So it is unsurprising that there is often a tendency, when faced with such unsettled times, to respond with ideas and actions rather than asking, for example:

- 'Are we dealing with the right problem(s)?'
- 'Are we aware of all the problems or are some of them hidden?'
- 'Are the problems worth addressing?'
- 'What type of problem is it overall?'
- 'What sort of problem are the component parts of the overall problem?'
- 'What are our personal governing variables that are affecting the frames by which we perceive the problem(s)?'
- 'Is our approach to addressing the problem part of the problem?'

Simply asking these questions could be seen by others as purely semantics, unhelpful, undermining, wasting valuable time, a deflection from getting on with it, or even inflammatory to a situation. But the global marketplace is a veritable graveyard of initiatives that didn't meet expectations relating to growth, innovation, improvement, excellence, IT/IS and engagement. So why is our batting average so low? Surely we can do better – and surely it is not just a case of doing it the way we currently do it better: what is referred to as 'single-loop learning' in Chapter 1.

There are reasons why we stumble, and this chapter focuses on these. They will probably require you to do some double-loop learning and to deeply reflect on what your own underlying 'governing variables' currently are in relation to problem solving. They will probably require you to ask yourself if you need to be open to adding some new mental models and maybe even to consider letting go of some of your existing ones because they are past their 'use-by' dates.

Governing variables: mindsets, mental models, and frames that drive our behaviour

We are all prisoners of the current mental models we are carrying around in our heads or, as an Indian proverb put it, 'The eyes do not see what the mind does not want.' In Chapter 1 James Archer and Kate Stuart-Cox shared the single-loop and double-loop learning model to help in understanding the influence of these frames on our behaviours, and in this chapter we share with you some specific frames or mental models relating to how we conceive problems and how we behave as a result.

How we view a problem greatly determines how and if we will solve it. Mental models are the filters through which we interpret the world and subsequently define the 'reality' around us. Mental models act as frames and are really useful because they provide a mental structure to simplify and guide our understanding of complex realities as well as focusing what we pay attention to. However, these frames can also become out of date as the world evolves, possibly even making some of what we know and use no longer true. They also distort or limit what we 'see': we may be missing very useful and important information that is outside our frame, a bit like the detail missed in peripheral vision.

The good news is that we can adjust our frames to see as much as we want to see. The bad news is that we seem to be quite wedded to our existing ones. As JK Galbraith (1971) wrote, 'Faced with the choice between changing one's mind and proving that there is no need to do so, almost everyone gets busy on the proof.'

For business analysts, lots of these frames will be connected to how you see, for example the technical skills of the profession, your business knowledge and your personal and interpersonal skills. It is useful to remember that the situation to be explored is almost always more complex than the frames with which we perceive it. Remaining unaware of these mental models can limit or inhibit our thinking and lead us to miss problems and opportunities. This is why reflecting (see Chapter 1) is so important: it helps us to surface our own existing frames, mental models, assumptions and beliefs that are acting as governing variables on our behaviours.

Famously, the US poet John Godfrey Saxe (1868) based the following poem on a parable that was told in India many years ago. It's well worth reading carefully, as it beautifully illuminates the issue:

> *It was six men of Indostan*
> *To learning much inclined,*
> *Who went to see the Elephant*
> *(Though all of them were blind),*
> *That each by observation*
> *Might satisfy his mind*
>
> *The First approached the Elephant,*
> *And happening to fall*
> *Against his broad and sturdy side,*
> *At once began to bawl:*
> *God bless me! but the Elephant*
> *Is very like a wall!*
>
> *The Second, feeling of the tusk,*
> *Cried, Ho! what have we here*
> *So very round and smooth and sharp?*
> *To me 'tis mighty clear*
> *This wonder of an Elephant*
> *Is very like a spear!*
>
> *The Third approached the animal,*
> *And happening to take*

> The squirming trunk within his hands,
> Thus boldly up and spake:
> I see, quoth he, the Elephant
> Is very like a snake!

> The Fourth reached out an eager hand,
> And felt about the knee.
> What most this wondrous beast is like
> Is mighty plain, quoth he;
> 'Tis clear enough the Elephant
> Is very like a tree!

> The Fifth, who chanced to touch the ear,
> Said: E'en the blindest man
> Can tell what this resembles most;
> Deny the fact who can
> This marvel of an Elephant
> Is very like a fan!

> The Sixth no sooner had begun
> About the beast to grope,
> Than, seizing on the swinging tail
> That fell within his scope,
> I see, quoth he, the Elephant
> Is very like a rope!

> And so these men of Indostan
> Disputed loud and long,
> Each in his own opinion
> Exceeding stiff and strong,
> Though each was partly in the right,
> And all were in the wrong!

And the message of this poem?

> So oft in theologic wars,
> The disputants, I ween,
> Rail on in utter ignorance
> Of what each other mean,
> And prate about an Elephant
> Not one of them has seen!

Some new frames to enable you to deal with problems

Finding the problem is as important as finding the answer. Indeed some argue that defining the problem is more important. However, our own starting point is that not all problems can be 'solved': some problems can only be ameliorated, contained or dissolved. And the nature of the problem(s) must determine the approach.

Based on over 40 years of research, we have found the distinction between 'tame' and 'wicked' problems very useful.

Tame problems

Tame does not necessarily mean simple, but it does mean there is an answer – a solution in response to a problem.

The more we study a tame problem, the more likely we are to find an optimum solution, so tame problems tend to be solved through 'convergent', analytical methods – breaking the problem down into parts and then working on these components. We organize ourselves to solve tame problems through specialization. Indeed, isn't this why management was invented, to solve tame problems through planning, organizing, communicating, controlling and reviewing?

Culturally tame problems (organizational, professional or national) enjoy broad agreement – on the whole everybody pretty much agrees why something needs to be done (problem definition) and the way to go about doing it (solution). Some examples of what would typically be conceived as a tame problem include:

- landing someone on the moon;
- determining the source of a food contamination outbreak;
- open heart surgery;
- producing the annual company accounts;
- identifying a fault on any engineered product;
- creating process maps of the current situation for part of an organization;
- finding potential requirements that would help meet a clearly defined objective;
- creating a key stakeholder map for a project.

Unfortunately historical 'gravity' seems to pull us all to wanting to deal with many – if not all – problems as if they were tame because it involves less effort and less anxiety, and because a business analyst's typical existing toolbox and strategies are equipped to address problems as if they were tame. Using strategies and tools for dealing with tame problems is fine as long as we share an overriding social theory or approach. If we don't, we face 'wickedness'.

Wicked problems

Wicked means the problems do not have straightforward solutions. Indeed they do not even promise a solution at all in many situations. They are 'divergent' in nature so the more wicked problems are studied, the more people come to different solutions.

The more tame problems are studied over time, the more tame problems tend to converge on a solution. The more wicked problems are studied over time, the more wicked problems tend to diverge on more and more solutions.

And, just to make life more exciting, there are very real dangers in how you approach the problem. Without attending to this distinction, business analysts are likely to mistake or misrepresent wicked problems for tame problems, which in turn will almost inevitably lead one to conclude that those with different answers lack integrity, intellect or both.

As well as being more complicated, a wicked problem is more complex – that is, it cannot be removed from its environment, solved and returned without affecting the environment.

Wicked problems therefore present not just operational challenges for every organization but also thinking challenges for every professional. And it is the thinking challenges (mental models, frames, mindsets, etc) that are the more critical ones; in particular, wicked problems require people to make changes in their mindset as well as their behaviour (double-loop learning).

Trust is the key resource for collectively coping with wicked problems. Another unwanted consequence of misdiagnosing wicked for tame problems is the undermining of that trust. Since wicked problems are becoming ever more common, this means we constantly face the following choice: we can continue to misrepresent wicked problems as tame problems, hoping they will not get any worse and ideally hoping they will go away, or we can acknowledge wicked problems for what they are and try to stabilize them as 'conditions'. This is not easy, because wicked problems offend and vex our sense of logic and common organizational mantras. In today's world of work, we are obsessed with solutions and action to meet the numbers, often to the exclusion of really understanding the problem(s). And wicked problems that sometimes can only be stabilized are pretty hard to accept – a problem that has no solution seems tantamount to giving up!

Given that many people care about or have something at stake in how the problem is resolved, the process of solving a wicked problem is fundamentally a social one. Solving a wicked problem is therefore fundamentally a social process. Most wicked problems involve lots of stakeholders. For any organization, as David Hancock (2010) explains in his excellent book *Tame, Messy and Wicked Risk Leadership*, there are two compelling reasons to approach problems in the right way: 1) solving the wrong problems fails to solve the right problems; 2) by solving the wrong problems, we unwittingly undermine what it takes for us to solve the right problems. The risk is not that we fail to build our bridges across the right rivers. Rather, the greater danger is that we erode or destroy the resources we need to build our bridges across those rivers – resources that are very difficult to develop or obtain, such as resilience, engagement, collaboration and trust.

TABLE 9.1 Tame and wicked problems summary

Tame	Aspect	Wicked
• Present or past orientation • Reactive or planned • Answer known somewhere, either inside or outside your organization • Requires process, procedure or practices to fix • May be simple or extremely complex	**The nature of the problem**	• Future orientation • Anticipatory or responsive • Answer not known – tends to rely on emotional and ideological aspects • Broad in scope and complex • Questions and learning drive the work
• Management based • Creates teams, committees, task forces • Sets guidelines, milestones, and deadlines or due dates • Can be delegated • Activity based and biased	**The 'leadership' approach needed**	• Facilitative leadership based • Identifying people to involve is important • Addressed through dialogic conversation • Collaborative effort across a wide spectrum of organizations and people • Fairness of participation • Cannot be delegated – needs role modelling • Can appear inactive or passive

How to approach tame and wicked problems

Give supervisors or managers a description of a problem in their area and they will most likely come up with a solution, quickly. In the 21st century, in many organizations, that's what people believe is expected of them. But some problems – especially wicked ones – probably can't be solved quickly. That's why they remain problems.

FIGURE 9.1 Effective problem solving depends on how well the following are attended to

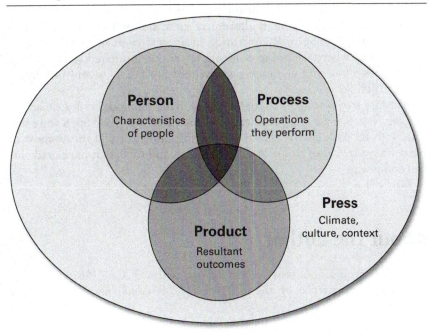

Person
Characteristics
of people

Process
Operations
they perform

Press
Climate,
culture, context

Product

Resultant
outcomes

The approach to addressing tame problems differs from strategies appropriate for wicked problems. It's worth remembering that in reality most situations involve a mixture of tame and wicked problems.

There is no shortage of tools and processes, but the key we believe is to become skilled in a system that allows for problem structuring as well as problem solving, such as Creative Problem Solving (CPS), in particular the latest version, 6.1, because it can be used for tame and wicked problems. The framework pays attention to: the context and in particular the climate; the people involved and the leadership approach required; the choice of process; and the intended outcomes.

You can view this system as a bit like an operating system that is always on, into which you can then plug applications – a bit like software for the mind. Another great advantage is that it comes with a generalizable process and bags of tools, but it can also be and has been integrated with most other tools processes, such as agile, lean and Six Sigma.

CPS combined with skilled facilitative leadership is ideal for many situations. However, additional aspects, approaches and tools are necessary for approaching wicked problems, many of which are covered in this book. After all, isn't 'leadership for change' itself a wicked problem?

To conclude

We've taken an oblique look at the topic of dealing with problems, and I hope that it will offer you an alternative view and will prompt some further thinking. Are we really operating in an environment or market that is stable and where we are in control? Or are we prepared to throw our insecurities away and embrace systems that are complex and ultimately uncontrollable.

As Margaret Wheatley (2010: 43) wrote in her fabulous book *Leadership and the New Science*, 'Any moment now, the earth will crack open and I will stare into its dark centre. Into that smoking caldera, I will throw most of what I have treasured, most of the techniques and tools that have made me feel competent.'
Wicked!

About the author

Andy Wilkins is an honorary senior visiting fellow at Cass Business School and founding partner of the UK-based professional services company Perspectiv.

References and further reading

Fairhurst, G (2005) Reframing the art of framing: problems and perspectives for leadership, *Leadership*, **1** (2), pp 165–86

Galbraith, JK (1971) *A Contemporary Guide to Economics, Peace and Laughter*, New American Library, Boston, MA

Grint, K (2005) Problems, problems, problems: the social construction of leadership, *Human Relations*, **58** (11), pp 1467–94

Grint, K (2008) Wicked problems and clumsy solutions, *Clinical Leader*, **2** (1), pp 54–68

Hancock, D (2010) *Tame, Messy and Wicked Risk Leadership*, Gower, Aldershot

Isaksen, SG and Tidd, J (2006) *Meeting the Innovation Challenge: Leadership for transformation and growth*, Wiley, Chichester

Isaksen, SG, Dorval, KB and Treffinger, DJ (2011) *Creative Approaches to Problem Solving*, Sage, Thousand Oaks, CA

Rittell, H and Webber, M (1973) Dilemmas in a general theory of planning, *Policy Sciences*, **4**, pp 155–69

Saxe, JG (1868) *The Poems of John Godfrey Saxe*, Ticknor and Fields, Boston, MA, pp 259–61

Wheatley, M (2010) *Leadership and the New Science: Discovering order in a chaotic world*, Berrett-Koehler, San Francisco

Wilkins, A and Stuart-Cox, K (2012) *An Introduction to Wicked Problem Solving*, Perspectiv, Cuddington, Bucks

Visual thinking for business analysis

PENNY PULLAN AND VANESSA RANDLE

Business analysis is not just about analysis and detail, understanding complex situations and solving problems. It has a much wider part to play in the world of change, from exploring ideas and possibilities and envisioning the future through to sharing information and building consensus across a range of perspectives. In all of these, and more, visual thinking is a key tool to support people through change. In this chapter, we'll explore why visuals are such a powerful tool for business analysis work and give a range of examples that business analysts can use for their work.

What do we mean by visual thinking? Dan Roam (2008) describes it as follows: 'Visual thinking means taking advantage of our innate ability to see – both with our eyes and our mind's eye – in order to discover ideas that are otherwise invisible, develop those ideas quickly and intuitively and then share those ideas with other people in a way that they simply "get".' It's all about using the power of visuals alongside words to ensure that we don't miss out. It's the combination of the two, both words and visuals, that is powerful.

Why is visual thinking so powerful?

We are hard-wired to think visually. Our brains have hundreds of millions of neurons devoted to visual processing, the equivalent to approximately 30 per cent of the brain's cortex. In comparison we have approximately 8 per cent for touch and 3 per cent for hearing. We interpret and make sense of the world around us using visual stimuli every day; we see colours; we gauge distance, speed and size; and we sense hazards, complexity, simplicity, depth and so much more in all aspects of our daily lives, often in a split second.

Our brains are designed to process information visually; in short, we process images much more quickly than we process words. Imagine drawing a circle on a piece of paper and asking someone what you have just drawn. It would take that person seconds to say 'a circle'. However, show the same person a written definition of a circle, for example 'a round plane figure whose boundary (the circumference) consists of points equidistant from a fixed point (the centre)', and ask the person what the words describe. To process this sequential text would take longer, perhaps not much longer, but it would definitely take more time. Looking at the picture of the circle is parallel processing; we take it all in at the same time. Reading the words is linear processing, which is more time-consuming, as it requires more effort to read each word and put them all together to make meaning. There may not be much in it in terms of time, but in the fast-paced world in which we live any time-saving device is useful!

It's part of our make-up as humans. We've been doing it for years, using cave paintings, hieroglyphics, murals, maps and diagrams to tell stories and make sense of the world; it works.

It's universal. Different cultures, peoples, organizations, businesses and groups have their own languages. It takes time and effort to learn these. Using visuals helps to cross these barriers, whether you're talking about social or business interactions. Brains love pictures!

Some business analysis examples

Visual thinking complements business analysis so well that there are many different ways for business analysts to use the power of visuals in combination with words. Here are a few examples that are used widely and some that are used much less often.

Process models

A simple process model shows how work gets done, using a series of tasks. It shows the flow between tasks and decisions taken along the way.

Have you ever tried to write up a process in prose without any visual input? One of the authors, Penny Pullan, did once, and a fairly straight-forward process ended up as three large pages covered in words. This lost the clarity of what happened when, the flow through the process, and the view of the whole. By drawing out the flow visually, carefully identifying each task and decision, and linking them together, she rendered the whole process clear. She was able to see the big picture as well as each individual task. She could see how everything fitted together and its place within the whole. Another advantage of mapping out processes visually is that it's easy to see missing pieces, as well as any parts that are messy or overly complex and need fixing.

It's possible to draw out processes in a group setting. Here, sticky notes are invaluable, rectangular ones for tasks and square ones turned to make diamonds to represent decisions. Building up a process this way is far more

FIGURE 10.1 A process model, showing the process for refuelling a car

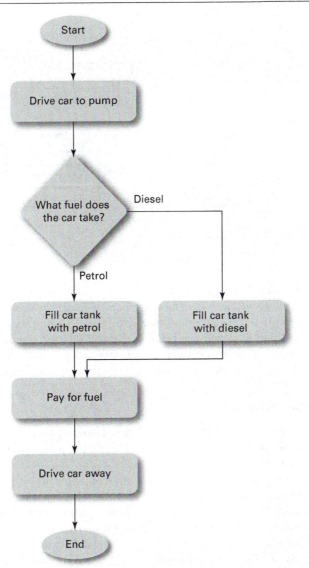

powerful for developing joint understanding among a group than a beautifully neat map drawn on a computer. People tend to assume that neat models drawn on a computer are right, so these can be intimidating and don't attract as many suggestions for improvement as sticky note models. Practice shows that people find it so much easier and less daunting to move a sticky note and suggest that it would be better elsewhere than to suggest a change to a finished-looking, computer-drawn model.

FIGURE 10.2 Ideas on sticky notes formed into clusters

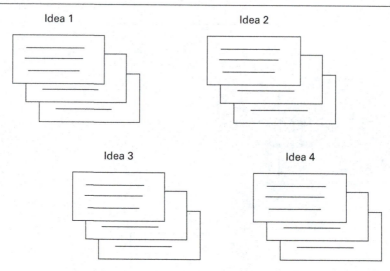

Process models support communication with stakeholders throughout the project, from those working in the current process to those who need to build a solution that will support future processes. These models are also invaluable for those who will need to test that the solution works.

Other diagrams used extensively in business analysis include organization charts, data models and fishbone diagrams among many others.

Clustering ideas

Idea generation is an important part of any change process. This means coming up with ideas, some of which will form the future state that will replace the current state.

One way to capture ideas as they come up from a group is to write them down on sticky notes, one note for each idea. Use thick marker pen so that people can read the writing from afar. These notes can be grouped into clusters of related ideas. It's then easy for the group to see how many related ideas there are and to evaluate each group in turn. Instead of sticky notes, it's possible to use pieces of card and to stick them on to a large piece of paper with repositionable adhesive instead.

Tables

Tables are really useful for comparisons and making decisions, as well as for showing where things fit. In Table 10.1, a RACI matrix or responsibility chart is used to make clear precisely what sort of responsibility each person has for each action. The options are R for 'responsible' (the person who will

TABLE 10.1 A RACI matrix for this chapter

	Penny: editor/ author	Vanessa: author	Malcolm: proof-reader	Julia: publisher
Write chapter	AR	R	I	
Draw pictures	A	R		
Proofread	C	C	AR	
Accept	C	I		AR

carry out the action), A for 'accountable' (the person with whom the buck stops), C for 'consulted' and I for 'informed'. The other option is nothing, which means that the person is not involved in this action in any way. For example, in Table 10.1, Penny and Vanessa shared the R for the responsibility of writing the words for this chapter, with Penny ultimately accountable (A) as editor, while Malcolm as proofreader wasn't consulted but was informed (I) when the task was complete.

Tables like this are useful when information is clear and fits neatly into one category or another. They are often used to evaluate criteria before making a decision.

Mind maps

Mind maps start with a central theme, then branch out into several sub-themes and then continue breaking down into as much detail as needed. Mind maps can be used for taking notes when interviewing stakeholders as well as for group meetings. Penny Pullan finds them useful for keeping track of all the business analysis tasks that need to be completed on a project and used one to plan the contents of this chapter.

Free drawings

Rarely used by business analysts, perhaps because of lack of confidence in their drawing skills, free drawings can be very powerful. For change projects, using a journey metaphor can work very well. Imagine a project viewed as an arrow travelling along a road to a distant goal. Along the road, there are twists and turns, bridges and possibly rock-falls. Groups will quickly grasp this metaphor and start thinking intuitively about what the bridges, rock-falls and other elements might represent.

FIGURE 10.3 A simple mind map for this book

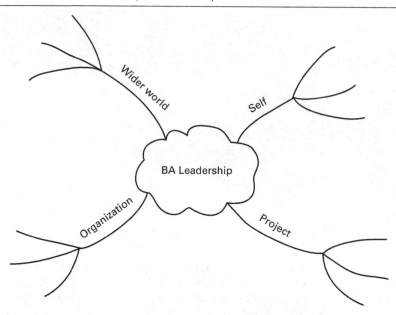

FIGURE 10.4 A free drawing representing a project

Simple pictures engage the brain. There is no need to draw in the details, as the brain will fill in the gaps. Simple pictures that are hand-drawn allow for changes and invite others to add to them.

FIGURE 10.5 A mandala showing the team of authors for Part I of this book

James Archer

Kate Stuart-Cox

Joseph da Silva

Authors of the Self section chapters

Corrine Thomas

John Niland

A form of free drawing, rich pictures are used to capture a holistic view of a business issue or problem. They are usually hand drawn by individuals to get an overview of a situation that would be very long and complex if written down in text alone. They show the main people and systems involved in the issue, along with their views. Also shown are the relationships between these and any other problems or questions. There is no strict format for rich pictures, which are part of the soft systems methodology by Peter Checkland, covered in Chapter 19.

Mandalas

Mandalas are circular in form, with a central theme and with other ideas spread around it. While not yet widely used in business analysis, a very useful example would be a team mandala, as shown in Figure 10.5. The team name is central, and the names of all the individuals involved are arranged around the team name. This is a very powerful way to convey the unity of the team and to show how everyone is working together. With virtual

FIGURE 10.6 A graphic recording: passionate people making a difference

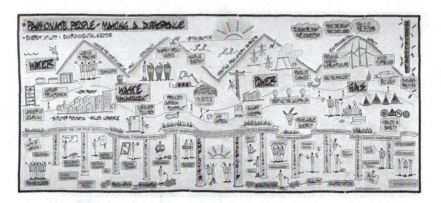

Drawn up by Vanessa Randle and used with permission.

teams, it's even more important to draw up these team mandalas, with a head-and-shoulders photograph of each team member, so that everyone can 'see' everyone else and how the team fits together. Mind maps are a form of mandala.

Graphic recordings

Graphic recording is done by a person, known as a graphic recorder, who listens to a group and draws up a visual in real time summarizing the key ideas, themes and connections from the session. It uses a combination of graphics and words to sum up the session. The graphic helps to focus the session, to show people that they've been heard, and connects different ideas together. After the event, the output becomes a very useful memory jogger to remind people of the session and the key themes that came up.

At the time of writing, only a handful of business analysts have trained as graphic recorders, but those who have report how very engaging it is for their groups and how memorable the outputs are.

To sum up

Visual thinking comes naturally to many business analysts. It brings in spatial, spontaneous and synthesizing thought patterns alongside the more linear and analytical thought patterns that tend to come when using only words.

Visual thinking helps business analysts to see the big picture of a situation, to clarify problems, to fill in missing pieces and to simplify complexity. With groups of people, it does all this and more. It engages people by making abstract things more tangible and therefore easier to grasp. Groups are able to see tacit assumptions made clear, as they develop joint understanding. With a good facilitator, they can explore possibilities, asking 'What happens if...?' With good visual support, the discussion in the group remains focused and they don't have to cover the same ground over and over again. Visuals help people to see relationships between issues, people and systems. This is the core of business analysis.

People who see a visual they've worked on as part of a group will remember much more than just the picture in front of them. It will jog their visual memory to bring back memories of how this shared artefact was built up and the discussions in which they took part.

The human brain will fill in any gaps, so simple pictures that communicate the essence of an idea are quite enough. These also allow for improvements and changes, so even if you feel artistically challenged why not take the next step in bringing visual thinking to your analysis?

About the authors

Penny Pullan is co-editor of this book and Vanessa Randle is a leading UK graphic recorder. Together they help business analysts and others to use visual thinking through **www.graphicsmadeeasy.co.uk**.

References and further reading

Cadle, J, Paul, D and Turner, P (2010) *Business Analysis Techniques: 72 essential tools for success*, BCS, London

Gray, D, Brown, S and Macanufo, J (2010) *Gamestorming: A playbook for innovators, rulebreakers and changemakers*, O'Reilly, Sebastopol, CA

Osterwalder, A and Pigneur, Y (2010) *Business Model Generation: A handbook for visionaries, game changers and challengers*, John Wiley & Sons, Hoboken, NJ

Roam, D (2008) *The Back of the Napkin: Solving problems and selling ideas with pictures*, Portfolio, New York

Roam, D (2011) *Blah, Blah, Blah: What to do when words don't work*, Portfolio/Penguin, New York

Sibbet, D (2010) *Visual Meetings: How graphics, sticky notes and idea mapping can transform group productivity*, John Wiley & Sons, Hoboken, NJ

Through the stage door: design thinking to refresh business analysis

TAMSIN FULTON

This chapter will take you through the wings and into the arena of my work back stage, enabling innovation in public services. I work behind the scenes with the people who deliver services, from firefighters to food safety officers, to develop new services and new ways of doing things. It's about creating change *with* people, using tools from design thinking to get to the next step in the innovation cycle: to create engagement and collaboration to try out new ideas, quickly and cheaply.

The design thinking principles I bring to refresh business analysis are:

1 spending time with people;
2 visualizing insights and ideas;
3 co-designing and collaborating;
4 prototyping ideas through to implementation.

Spending time with people

In my work back stage, I engage staff and other stakeholders to explore and develop new services and new ways of doing things. I want to reconnect staff with the users of their service to understand how the service works from the perspective of the people they serve and to better understand the experience of their service users, their needs and capabilities, and engage them along the innovation journey.

Senior leaders find the process a powerful way to reconnect and think differently about a service. Having found a way for the chief executive of a local authority to participate as a volunteer at a council-funded coffee morning for older people, it was difficult to get him to leave the community centre. The experience gave him important insights into volunteer services for older people but also into the wider context of local community provision, including public transport, library services and leisure facilities.

Spending time with people is a simple approach to quickly getting an idea of how things work and where the opportunities and challenges lie. A variety of techniques can be used individually or in combination when spending time with people at work – observing, interviewing, shadowing, intervening, participating – depending on the context in which you are working.

I use the participatory approach of action research when I want to observe and reflect on a specific role or context. An example of this approach was joining a Safer Neighbourhoods team of police community support officers on their eight-hour evening shift. This approach was useful too when I participated in a soup run at Westminster Abbey as part of an exploration of co-production in services for the homeless. This enabled me to walk in the shoes of a volunteer and engage with service users on how things worked from their perspective. For example, it turned out that five soup runs appear every Sunday evening and not one from Tuesday to Thursday. One service user went on to suggest coordinating volunteer groups round a weekly rota to solve this strikingly basic flaw. For my study it was another example of the missed opportunity to utilize the capacities of service users through an exclusive focus on a need.

For theatre productivity in a hospital, shadowing presented a more practical approach to understanding how staff worked in an operating theatre. Shadowing is not about asking people what they want but observing, reflecting and identifying needs through discovering how things work.

Working with front-line staff to shadow team members and those in supporting teams helps staff to take on a neutral role, suspend their perceptions about how they think the service works and look at the service with fresh eyes. The mismatch between what the service thinks it does and what occurs in practice and the knock-on effects to the way a service is delivered are revealed through the experience.

Take time to capture what you find. Ask yourself:

- How well are interactions working (between colleagues and with service users)?
- How do people feel (in providing the service and experiencing it)?
- What is the impact of roles and rules (on the service and the way people work together)?
- What challenges do you notice (along the service journey and its supporting processes)?

Capturing and sharing the experience of spending time with people are a vital part of the design process. Photos and video are great for bringing research to life. Visualizing insights and findings makes it easier to share and reach a common understanding of the service. The next section explores some of the techniques for visualizing these.

Visualizing

Every time you visualize an idea you cross a bridge. All along the innovation journey, visualization is used to move ideas on through the design phases, from insights to ideas, ideas to prototypes, and prototypes to implementation. Visualizing what you have found through spending time with people is the bridge to turning insights into the project scope and brief. Articulating what you have found in a visual way makes it easy to share your findings with others, generate a dialogue and debate and build on what you have found.

Ask yourself:

- How can you best share the new insights you have found (eg photos, a vox pop, a diagram or a customer journey map)?
- What do you want your visual to achieve (enlightenment, debate, consensus or action)?

Design for debate is a powerful way to provoke discussion through a visualization of an issue you have identified. For example, in a research project about anti-social behaviour, local residents displayed my postcards in their windows to mark out the invisible borderline of a local authority dispersal zone (UK Government, 2003) (the Anti-Social Behaviour Act 2003 gave police new powers to disperse groups in authorized areas). With local authority agreement, a police superintendent can designate a defined area as a 'dispersal zone' for a period of up to six months. The purpose was to generate discussion and debate among the local residents themselves and also to engage the wider community outside the dispersal zone.

Design for debate aims to provoke a strong response and focus attention, so it can be an extreme example of something you have found or think you will find in the future if things don't change. In an environmental project looking at local authority teams active in the street environment, I visualized my research findings to show not only the expected local authority teams but also the outbound teams working for Transport for London, the London Fire Brigade, the Metropolitan Police, the Probation Service, housing associations and various community and voluntary groups. Visualizing theses active teams helped to drive the project towards coordinating the activity of outbound teams from across the public, private and voluntary sectors, not just the 33 London boroughs.

Visualizing insights helps people to understand your research and findings quickly, and helps you to move on to the next stage. I made a visual diary of my shift with the Safer Neighbourhoods team to capture the kinds of behaviours encountered and considered anti-social by the team. For the operating theatre, I created a storyboard to capture day-surgery patients going from the ward to surgery and back to the ward. In this way I was able to succinctly share insights from several patient journeys within a single agenda item at a theatre productivity board meeting.

Once the challenges are agreed the brief is better defined and the team is ready to move on to generating lots of ideas. Visually capturing this process not only forms a record of the ideas, but helps identify gaps and synergies and find the big ideas.

Having selected some strong ideas to take forward, visualizing these quickly means you can easily share and talk about them. It also helps other people give feedback and build on them, allowing you to review and refine your ideas, returning for more feedback to continually evolve the ideas. In a housing project an idea was formed around letting clients know where they could expect to be housed before they reached the interview stage to reduce confrontation at interviews and 'no-shows' at property viewings.

As ideas develop the visualization needs to become more sophisticated. A quick sketch at the beginning is great for exploring the initial idea with others, but as you want to find out how your idea could work in practice people will need a more tangible concept to collaborate on and make it work for them.

The housing team next explored visualizing the actual information they wanted clients to have and produced a map showing where people had been housed in the last year. They took it to colleagues, and the map was refined based on what the team heard until it was ready to test out live in the service with clients. This became their first prototype version.

Co-designing and collaborating

Collaboration keeps people at the heart of what you do and goes beyond spending time with them to gain insights. It means involving others in generating ideas, testing, giving feedback and implementing solutions.

Ask yourself:

- Who should you involve in your idea (service users, their families, colleagues, managers, partners, commissioners)?
- How will you involve them (gathering insights, generating ideas, giving feedback, testing out and building on solutions)?

Ideally, a team collaborating on a project would be drawn from different professional backgrounds and roles to bring a mix of perspectives to explore the spaces within and between their work and to cross-pollinate ideas. In any phase of the project, the team can call in other people with specialist knowledge or experience to help shape and overcome challenges. Input might come for example from someone who represents a new type of service user, a colleague in another department or a contact in a partner organization. Collaboration is a tool that helps to lower boundaries around teams and organizations and bring together the best people you know to nurture innovation.

An idea can come from anywhere, anyone can contribute and everyone is listened to. Design thinking brings this 'equality' dynamic into the process, most noticeably with rules for brainstorming new ideas. Rules like 'Defer judgement', 'Build on the ideas of others', 'Go for quantity' and so on all help to create an equal environment in which ideas can flourish collaboratively.

The organizations we identify as being most innovative, like Google, Hewlett-Packard, Valve Corporation and IDEO, most often have flat organizational structures and an innovation process based on multidisciplinary collaboration. The Department for Business, Innovation and Skills lists 'flat structure' as its top tip for innovative organizations (UK Government, 2013).

However, most organizations in the private and public sectors have hierarchical structures in place, limiting the collaboration potential of all the professionals and groups they have working, reinforcing silo thinking, producing unequal ideas and missing rather than nurturing opportunities for innovation. Projects in this hierarchical context need to create 'free spaces' where colleagues can come together on an equal basis to collaborate and develop creative solutions to challenges that don't respect the organizational boundaries between functions, teams and management structures.

Creating and sustaining a shared belief in a 'free space' is tough, especially in the early stages when the team move on from asking 'How are things done?' to asking 'Why are things done?' The team are exploring new ways of doing things, unlearning how things are done and challenging the barriers they encounter. These can come in the form of team roles and functions, process rules that govern the nature and sequence of activities, fuzzy operational definitions and system rules that layer up over time, determining what and how things are done, even though they may no longer relate to the reality of the service. Management's role is to permit and encourage this questioning and exploration and where possible free up the space around the idea, so that the idea can be explored and the potential gauged, outside the limitations of the status quo.

The challenge is to steer focus towards achieving the desired outcomes while leaving the approach open and fluid to practically discover how best to achieve the desired outcome through prototyping. This means managers not halting an idea too early because it rubs against a defined way of doing things. It requires them instead to have faith in the design process and a willingness to let ideas play out to their natural conclusion in a simulated environment, the 'free space', and see the value in staff learning through the experience of exploring and tackling an idea.

Driving change can become a struggle at this point, but through identifying the barriers and pushing these up the management tiers – to see what can be facilitated further up the hierarchy – the wheels of your fledgling idea can stay on. Remember, during an innovation process, disruption to the way things are currently done is positive.

Another huge challenge that collaboration helps overcome is people's natural fear of change and resistance to being changed. Leadership is critical in ceding control to the team on how they reach an outcome, even if the outcome is set, and facilitating an open environment in which expected outcomes can be delivered in new ways. The point is for everyone to be involved in the change and feel ownership of it – to contribute and shape workable solutions.

The final principle from design thinking, prototyping ideas through to solutions, helps keep colleagues engaged and in the driving seat. As ideas are dropped or merged with other ideas because they don't work or aren't strong enough to create change, managers are reassured that only workable solutions get taken forward.

Prototyping ideas through to solutions

Prototyping is all about taking an idea quickly into a real environment or trying something out (in whatever way is practical to you) and learning from doing it. There are three ribbons of activity during prototyping:

- making your prototype;
- establishing metrics;
- creating an environment in which to test out your prototype.

Often it is practical to split the idea into individual mini-prototypes that set out to answer specific questions or components of your idea. As you find answers and challenges through asking people how it could work better for them, you respond to what you learn by creating successive prototype versions, until the desired outcomes are achieved.

Making your prototype

Once you have talked the idea through with colleagues from other teams, listened to their feedback and revised and reviewed your idea again with colleagues, you're ready to lift your idea off the paper and give it some form and function. The aim is to take your prototype to colleagues, service users, providers and anyone else touching on the delivery, as a more interactive and better-articulated version of your initial idea.

Early prototypes need to be rough and ready so that people feel inspired to build on the idea. You are not presenting solutions at this stage; you are inviting others to explore the concept, and the prototype itself should communicate your willingness to go back to the drawing board.

Custom-made cards are useful to represent information you might want to exchange between colleagues; a storyboard can illustrate a scenario of how you see your idea working; role play can help you test out how an interaction might work in practice.

Bring your idea to life just enough for people to understand what you are trying to do, but also leave space for them to contribute and reshape.

Establishing metrics for your prototype

Take time to plan and document your prototyping. Ask yourself:

- What are you going to prototype (the full idea or an element of it)?
- What do you want your prototype to achieve (the questions you are trying to answer, the outcomes you are looking for)?
- How will you prototype your idea (how will you present it, where and with whom)?

After each round of prototyping, gather your team to review and reflect on what you have heard and learnt, and stay alert to unintended consequences or unexpected use or reactions. You may go round this process two, three or more times, improving the measurable impact of the prototype with each successive round. All along the prototyping process, ideas will morph and merge with other ideas and some will get dropped, allowing only effective and efficient prototypes that meet the organization's objectives and the desired outcomes for service users to move to implementation.

Creating an environment in which to test out your prototype

Keeping the space open for people to contribute equally along the development path is critical in creating a solution that will work and get taken up in practice. It comes back to doing things *with* people rather than *to* them, allowing people who do the work to bring the change.

Decide who best to test out your idea with. Draw up a list of people with a mix of perspectives, roles and seniority, both internal and external. Try to present your idea in a neutral way, as one of a few ideas put out there to try to solve a problem you have identified. Share the challenge you are trying to overcome, the insights you visualized earlier and how your idea might work. Observe and capture their reactions and comments. Take notes, but also pictures or video, if you can, to help you later reflect on what you learnt.

Decide how and where you are going to test your idea. This will inform the design of your prototype and help you set up the test environment in physical and conceptual space. The approach is to assemble a microclimate that reflects a future state, so you might ask people to work together who wouldn't normally do so, change the sequence or remove steps in the current process. On a small scale and in a constructed environment, each idea must prove itself to work in practice before it can be moved into a live environment.

Conclusion

Seeing projects move to implementation as they meet their desired outcomes around organizational efficiency and service quality is a very rewarding process in itself. As better ways of working are developed and readily taken up by staff, tangential benefits like better timekeeping, reduced sickness levels, job satisfaction, better communication and team working surface too. These softer elements, together with the practical knowledge to create change, form an environment in which innovation can continue to thrive at a grass-roots level because of a new openness and willingness to change and adapt to new situations as they arise.

About the author

Tamsin Fulton MA (RCA) is a service design consultant.

References and further reading

Brown, T (2009) *Change by Design: How design thinking transforms organizations and inspires innovation*, HarperBusiness, New York

Design Council (2005) Double Diamond design process, www.designcouncil. uk/designprocess

Dunne & Raby (2007) Design for debate, http://www.dunneandraby.co.uk/content/bydandr/36/0

IDEO, Design thinking and innovation firm, www.ideo.com/uk/

UK Government (2003) Anti-Social Behaviour Act 2003, http://www.legislation. gov.uk/ukpga/2003/38/part/4

UK Government [accessed 21 January 2013] *The Innovative Organisation: Business processes and culture* [Online] http://www.bis.gov.uk/policies/public-sector-innovation/resources/creating-an-innovative-culture/the-innovative-organisation

12 Business analysis, leadership and agile

CHRIS MATTS AND KENT J McDONALD

When we considered the best way to address the topic of business analysts as leaders from an agile perspective, we thought of many different approaches we could take. We decided to discuss the topic in a fashion that embodied the way we view the very broad issues of leadership and agile.

'Agile' as used in agile software development is a label applied to multiple approaches for software development that share the values and principles as stated in the Manifesto for Agile Software Development (**www.agilemanifesto .org**). This label was first used to refer to software development approaches when the manifesto was written by 17 practitioners and consultants in Snowbird, Utah in February 2001. Since that label was first coined, the use of agile approaches, whether actual or proclaimed, has become increasingly popular. Unfortunately many teams are adopting agile in name only by following some of the practices and proclaiming that the team is doing agile. We think being agile is a more appropriate route to go where the goal is not agile itself, but rather to deliver value to customers in frequent increments with consistent reflection, adaptation and learning, with collaboration among stakeholders.

We view leadership as leading by example, and share our learning with others. In this case there are followers from the perspective that they weren't the first ones to figure out how to address specific problems. Leadership of this fashion does not rest in one person, but floats around the team based on who has a particular expertise. This type of leadership is very exciting because it actually improves the effectiveness of everyone involved. Those who learn something from the current 'thought leader' are getting the benefit of the new knowledge, but the thought leader gains also, because he or she may get a clearer understanding of a particular topic as a result of explaining it to someone else. Looking at problems from multiple different perspectives can often be very enlightening.

We view agile as collaboration among stakeholders to deliver value to customers in frequent increments with consistent reflection and adaptation. A key aspect of that concept is continuous learning, which is where we find that leadership and agile overlap.

With that in mind, we chose to answer a series of questions related to how we actually perform business analysis in an agile fashion and lead by example while doing it. As we discussed our answers, we found that we had arrived at the same approach to doing things through different experiences. As a result, we chose to answer these questions collectively with the occasional diversion where our experience or practices differed. We hope that you find this format helpful for identifying the bits of information most helpful to you in any given situation.

What do you do to prepare for a new project?

The last time one of us (Chris Matts) prepared for a new project was several years ago, and we'll describe the experience from his perspective:

> It was a year or two after I learnt about agile and I took on a role as head of business analysis and project management for a group. I had decided to train the group in agile so that they could be more effective and achieve more while at the same time work less hard. I hit the ground running, comfortable in the techniques I would teach the group so that they could be more effective with the tools they were using. As a result it was several weeks into the assignment when I realized that none of the group were trained as business analysts or project managers. My predecessor had been an accountant and had hired a department of qualified accountants. The group had pretty good knowledge of the domain but did not have any technical skills. As a result I had to pull back and reassess the situation. I focused on training in basic technical skills. I think I lost some credibility in the fact that we had been talking about agile techniques and then needed to pull back and focus on basic technical skills.

Since that experience and similar ones for Kent McDonald, we do not specifically prepare for a project. We continually keep a lookout for new skills and techniques that we can add to our toolkit. It is not enough to be aware of the techniques; we also need to study them and, if possible, try them out to understand their strengths and limitations.

What's the first thing you do when you start a new project?

There is no first thing we do on a project. There are a number of things that we do in an opportunistic manner to gather as much information about the project and its context as we possibly can:

1 Get to know the people involved.
2 Understand *why* we are doing the project.
3 Understand *what* we are trying to achieve.
4 Get something done.

Getting to know people involved in a project goes beyond simply creating a stakeholder map to show who can influence the outcome. It means meeting the people and getting to know what they are like and how they interact with others, and giving them a chance to learn about us. In particular we stress the importance of collaboration and focus on achieving results. Our favourite tool for getting to know someone is the humble cup of coffee. Ideally we go out of the office and meet in a coffee bar, but if we can't do that we will try to find an atrium, a café or as a last resort a meeting room.

Many project teams do not have a shared understanding of why their project exists, so when we start a project we ask 'Why?' We keep asking 'Why?' until someone gives an answer that aligns with increasing revenue, protecting revenue or reducing costs. Once we know, the most important thing is to ensure everyone else on the project knows why as well.

Alongside the 'why', we also worry about 'what' we are going to deliver. Sometimes it's necessary to work with the business investor to understand the 'what' (the problem the investor is trying to solve) before the 'why'. Once you can demonstrate that understanding, you can then lead the conversation to understand the 'why' and possibly suggest an alternative solution.

As soon as we can, we try to get something real done. Creating documentation does not count. Changing a process, implementing training or getting some software into production does. Whenever we try to do something, we quickly discover a number of impediments to getting anything done. Identifying these impediments early is vital to future success. Who are the people and process points that will get in your way? Which committees or departments act as gatekeepers to protect the way things currently work? Once we have identified them, we usually have to drink lots and lots of fine coffee to build relationships with the people who will be able to make things happen. Trying to get things done also helps to identify those 'organizational anti-bodies' that oppose the change.

What techniques do you use?

Think about getting your toilet fixed. Which plumber would you prefer? One turns up in a Mercedes in a smart suit. He has a shiny tool box containing a gold-plated hammer. When he arrives, he takes the hammer out and asks to be shown the problem. The other plumber has already visited to check what your problem was. She arrives in a van full of the tools most likely to solve the problem. On arrival she announces that she has more tools and can call on colleagues for even more if necessary. Which would you prefer to fix your toilet?

We try to learn as many techniques as we can when the opportunity presents itself, even if we rarely use them or if it's 'not our job'. You never know when a particular technique may be relevant.

As well as learning techniques we intend to use, we also learn about the ones we do not intend to use. This is so that we can have a robust discussion with someone who wants to use something that we consider is inappropriate in the context. 'Hold your friends close, and hold your enemies closer still' is a maxim that applies to tools and techniques as well as people.

How does learning fit with business analysis in agile?

We would argue that the value of business analysis is structured learning. There are three steps to business analysis:

1 Find the question.

2 Find the answer.

3 Transfer the knowledge to everyone in the project.

We'll describe these in reverse order.

Knowledge transfer is getting the knowledge out of your head and into the heads of the other project members. Traditionally this is something that was achieved using 'documentation', requirement documents and analysis artefacts such as entity-relationship models and use cases. Once you realize the goal is knowledge transfer rather than documentation, you have many more options for how you transfer that knowledge. At the start of a project, our preference is to use a whiteboard or flip chart to draw on and talk people through the ideas. What we normally find is that people will ask questions that lead to new insights. If we start with a PowerPoint presentation, it discourages people from asking 'dumb' questions, as they feel it is a more complete idea. The use of a whiteboard or flip chart encourages more interaction and makes the session more into a conversation than a monologue. People can sustain interest in a subject for longer if they can direct the learning. Use of PowerPoint commits you to an agenda and an order of delivery. When we've delivered the same material several times without it being modified by questions and clarifications, we will then create a PowerPoint deck. This is to complement the interactive sessions. Documentation was often pushed forward as the solution to the remote location problem where you could not use a flip chart to explain things to people. Skype video and similar services have blown this argument away. We now zoom a camera into focus on just the flip chart and have a session as if the people were in the room. For a negligible sum you can get group video and screen share on Skype. No longer do we need to force the agenda using PowerPoint.

Finding the answer is what we normally call 'issue resolution'. Once we have the question, anyone who understands it (and will understand the answer) can ask the question. Often, finding the answer is simply finding the right person and getting the answer. Sometimes the process is a bit more involved, especially if a number of people need to agree on an answer or if no one knows the answer.

Finding the question is arguably where business analysts add the most value. They approach the domain and learn about it in a structured manner using the traditional business analysis tools as structured learning tools. The tools allow them to structure the knowledge they discover so that they spot gaps and identify when something does not fit into their model of understanding. Feature Injection contains a process called 'Break the Model', which is a modified version of David A Kolb's experiential learning circle. 'Break the Model' can be used to structure the use of wire frames, entity relationship models, use cases and state models to discover examples that document the domain.

What documents do you produce?

We should dissect this question a bit. By 'documents' do we mean the actual artefacts that contain information teams produce and used to use to measure progress, or did we really mean models that the team uses to understand the problem better?

If the first definition of documents was meant, then we produce only those documents that our stakeholders request and, before producing anything, understand why those documents are needed. We also generally ask our stakeholders to prioritize those requested documents right alongside the features being considered. In effect we ask them to consider which is more valuable, a set of documents, or new capabilities.

If we really meant models that help the team understand the problem and possible solutions, then we use whichever models help us gain that understanding. We changed the term from 'documents' to 'models' because most of the things created while the team is trying to understand the problem really don't need to be kept around afterwards. Documents don't have any value other than as a historical record used for future reference and so tend by their very nature to hang around and become out of date.

What we don't do is 'always do a BRD' or 'always do a functional design spec' or whatever mind-numbing names have been created for things that attempt to persist in requirements information. This perspective serves to reinforce the 'requirements as an end in themselves' mindset that we are trying to leave behind.

Do you only do analysis when you work on projects?

We do analysis all the time. In fact, analysis is often much more valuable if it is done before a project is started. Setting up a business value model to figure out if a project is worth it can be a quick way to save an organization a lot of money.

How do you know when you are done with analysis?

We know we are done with analysis for a given project when the project is over and we have measured whether it was a success based on the objectives we identified at the beginning.

A better question may be: 'How do you know when you are done with analysis for a given iteration?' The answer is: when we have a sufficient number of examples so that the team can begin delivering the functionality committed to for that iteration. Some teams we have worked with have called this a set of consumable requirements.

Then again, we are always finding additional refinements we can make to our understanding of the problem and potential solutions, so perhaps the proper response to the question is 'What value is there in knowing when you are done with analysis?'

How do you hand off information to the developers and testers?

The quick answer is that examples are used to specify the system. They form the contract between the business analyst/tester pair and the development teams. See our discussion about knowledge transfer in the response to the 'How does learning fit with business analysis in agile?' question above.

How do you make people change?

The simple answer is you cannot make people change. You can only inspire them to want to change. You can force a way of working on them, but if they do not want to do it they will subvert it or drop the approach as soon as you turn your back on them.

You haven't mentioned user stories; where do they fit in?

User stories help us to defer commitments. They are good mechanisms for having meaningful planning and scope discussions, but are woefully inadequate for describing the problem and solution by themselves. Kent McDonald likes to call them atomic planning units because they are ambiguous enough to allow adult discussions about what is and is not included in a particular product.

So what can you do with this information?

Now it's our turn to ask a question to which you provide the answer. Think about the information we shared above and relate it to how you have thought about business analysis before. Are these ideas a great departure from how you are used to behaving on projects, or do they sound fairly familiar? Your answer to that question indicates how easily you can fit into a leadership position on an agile team through adopting continuous learning.

About the authors

Chris Matts is a consultant who is writing a graphic novel on project risk management using Real Options.

Kent J McDonald is an author and consultant who is active in the business analysis and agile software development communities.

Further reading

Adzic, G (2011) *Specification by Example*, Manning, New York
Matts, C and Adzic, G [accessed 19 January 2013] InfoQ [Online] http://www.infoq.com/articles/feature-injection-success
Pixton, P *et al* (2009) *Stand Back and Deliver*, Addison-Wesley, New York

The iterative business analyst – increasing insight, reducing waste, delivering value

13

MELANIE ROSE

Iterative delivery involves developing and releasing systems or products in small increments, giving developers and business owners a chance to learn from early releases and adapt the approach or requirements based on these learnings. It's a concept favoured by many agile methodologies and start-ups and, conceptually at least, it's a no-brainer. Why wouldn't you want to release something quickly in a small, low-cost, low-risk way in order to establish whether you are on the right track? You could save money and significantly reduce the risk of launching something that users don't need or don't like. But most companies are not start-ups and, for the vast majority, a move to iterative delivery represents a significant culture shift and is easier said than done.

I wanted to explore ways to drive iterative delivery thinking that could be applied in more established organizations. First, it was important to understand why it is hard for some companies to release iteratively.

Organizational impediments to iterative delivery

Organizations love a big-bang release

Most board members would freely admit that an all-singing, all-dancing launch is something they relish – when it goes well. The longer you wait, the longer the list of features and services you have to wow the market with and the more time you have to develop high-profile marketing campaigns and launch events. But a big release can be your enemy. The bigger the launch, the more egg on senior management's faces if the product does not work as expected or is not what customers want.

Gut feel or research is preferred to feedback

Every organization has its share of people who are meant to be experts on what the customer wants. From marketing managers to user experience analysts, some jobs are all about being right about what the product should *do*. This makes it harder to accept end-user feedback that contradicts these carefully honed ideas. But that's what often happens. As Eric Ries admitted in one of his lean start-up talks, in his early days developing a 3D social networking site, when test users gave him feedback he didn't like, he asked for different test users! Over time, he realized that, as long as he got it early enough, negative feedback was a hugely positive thing that enabled him to build a better product for his target audience. This lesson is one worth promoting. Today Ries's site – IMVU – typically has over 100,000 people online at any one time across 90 countries.

Quick means dirty

Unsurprisingly, there are a lot of quality fears around delivering small increments quickly. Some of this fear comes from the idea that a 'minimal' feature set – a term often used around agile and iterative delivery – means something rather lo-fi, spartan and full of bugs. There is no excuse for compromising on quality in the areas that your stakeholders demand, but there are negotiations to be had and tough decisions to be made. And that's exactly where the iterative business analyst comes in.

Big funding demands a big plan

Whether it's an executive board, parent company or venture capitalist, no one wants to provide 18 months' worth of funding only to be told 'We'll release feature *x* in two weeks, and then we'll see.' An extreme example, yes, but generally there'll be expectations of getting some bang for the bucks that will require careful management. The research/gut-feel issue also applies to the funding conversation. No one wants to fund a project that is going to fail, but most projects can't guarantee success until launch. In this catch-22 situation, you may need to make some high-level commitments – with caveats – but focus on the early win that can be delivered and try to stop short of a detailed release plan.

It will be hard to manage communication around small increments

It's true that managing communications (and expectations) in multiple small bites is more challenging. On the receiving end, there is the risk of 'communication fatigue' and stakeholders feeling underwhelmed by myriad drip-fed changes. Sponsors and product owners need support in trying to find new, inventive ways to communicate changes and engage the audience on an iterative basis. Instead of regular e-mails, do a showcase or demo periodically. Invite prospective users to test-drive the new service. Recruit ambassadors to spread the word.

Steering a course towards iterative delivery

These are not insignificant fears, yet much of the literature around agile topics does little to address them. So now that you understand some of the blockers, how you can lead change in this area?

Business analysts are better placed than most to see that research and rationale can be misguided or flawed, that assumptions can be hidden. They can add real value through understanding the broader strategy, clarifying the objective(s) and breaking down requirements in order to release early, get feedback and refine a plan. Most crucially of all, an experienced business analyst can apply pragmatism and a nuanced approach to understanding and influencing the right people in order to address the fears, uncertainties and challenges of business stakeholders in order to get there.

Bear in mind, though, that this is a journey. There will be no overnight successes. Most companies won't change the way they work unless there is an obvious benefit in doing so. And why should they? Promoting iterative delivery because it's the 'agile' thing to do (and, believe me, I have heard people talk this way) will not win much support. Neither will trying to force change without understanding key stakeholder doubts, fears and scepticism.

The biggest revelation for me was the fact that asking the right 'stupid questions' in an informal way over a sustained period was surprisingly effective in bringing about change. It was often those informal conversations, without any particular agenda, where we asked business owners about their experiences and lessons learnt, that seemed to trigger new thoughts and possibilities. Demonstrating your understanding of the work gives you credibility when making suggestions, but of course it's always better to question first, so that people can think through the issues and reach their own conclusions.

In general there were five guiding principles that seemed to help these conversations progress:

It's all about the greater good

You don't have an agenda. The only thing you care about is the company's bottom line and finding the most efficient way to deliver on the company's strategy and stated objectives. Those who have gone in to win an ideological fight or to pit one department against another are the ones who fail. It's not about you or them. That's why business analysts are perfect for this, because the best ones can be professionally agnostic.

Take a genuine interest in the anticipated benefits

This is where you can sniff out assumptions or uncertainty in business cases. Many projects or changes start out with a proposition along the lines of 'If we do this, this will happen' or 'If we build this, people will use it or buy it.' How do we know? Who can we ask, and how soon can we get something in front of them so that we know for sure?

Understand stakeholder fears

Fear is a natural emotion when change is afoot. Spending a long time getting something 'right' and releasing it when it's 'perfect' are so ingrained as a practice that deviating from it is an unnerving prospect. When trying to uncover ways to do things differently, it pays to explore these fears. If only one element of the product or service were to be launched, what would that feel like? What is the biggest challenge for the sponsor or stakeholder on this project? There are lots of different ways to ask this: 'What keeps you awake at night on this project?' 'What do you think will happen when we launch this?' 'Who will be most affected by the change?' 'If we could solve only one problem today, what would it be?' In the answers to these questions lie your clues to where there might be opportunities to alleviate these fears. Look for ways to learn early and remove uncertainty. An informal approach (with no agenda, remember) is required to build trust. You are all on the same side.

Focus on outcomes, not solutions

In so many organizations, the solution has already been described in great detail, yet the outcome for the user is lost. Outcomes are quite different from objectives. An outcome-focused approach asks: 'What will the customer be able to see or do as a result of the change?' 'What will be different about this process when we have made this change?' The outcome is the only thing you have to hand that will help you establish whether or not the change has been a success and as such should be championed. Reporting is a classic example. 'We need x report containing x information in x format.' To put it another way, 'Who needs to do what as a result of this information and what is their biggest problem at the moment?' Out of these kinds of questions may come not only what you expect in terms of outcome, but what might be delivered as a first cut (can you find a small way to solve the biggest problem, or start solving it, right now?).

Assess which tools you need, when and to what extent

As a business analyst, you have an impressive toolkit at your disposal, but this is the time to be pragmatic about its usage. It's worth applying an 'include to exclude' rule of thumb to your thinking when it comes to the classic headings in business requirements specifications. While a lengthy and detailed document is not required, the headings work well as a checklist that will ensure you consider the full scope and impact of the work. Ask relevant questions and flag your discoveries around impact analysis, non-functional (but so crucial) elements, stakeholder analysis and known risks. Employ use cases to promote focus on outcomes, and focus on non-functional areas to mitigate quality risks. Process flows are effective in supporting effective business implementation. The pragmatism required is around how much you do and when you do it. Most business analysts know that a high volume of documentation won't get read. Use cards, sticky notes and interactive sessions, little and often, to get consensus and communicate new requirements.

Starting small, testing the water

So now you've identified the pain points or areas of greatest uncertainty, how can you convince your stakeholders that they can test the water early without losing face? Here are some techniques that I've encountered over the past couple of years, all of which, with a few adaptations, can be used to get early feedback:

Pretotyping

This movement and manifesto have been developed by Alberto Savoia, director of engineering and 'innovation agitator' at Google, Jeremy Clark, founder and CEO of FXX, and Patrick Copeland, senior director of engineering at Google. The trio were inspired by Jeff Hawkins's early forays into the personal digital assistant (PDA) market in the mid-1990s. Hawkins, the founder of Palm Computing, mocked up a PalmPilot with wood and paper and then carried it with him for a few days pretending it was a working device. His objective was to learn if he would actually use such a device before he incurred the expense of building a working prototype. Pretotyping differs from prototyping in that the main objective of prototyping is to answer questions related to building the product: Can we build it? Will it work as expected? How much will it cost to build? The purpose of *pretotyping* is to answer questions about the product's appeal and usage: Would people want this product? Will they use it as expected? Will they continue to use it? Think about what your organization could do to gauge the appetite for your proposed product in real terms. Link to a product or function not yet developed; how often does it get clicked on or requested? Don't forget to ensure your placeholder or holding page manages expectations effectively. Create an online newsletter or blog before you write a book to gauge appetite for the content; mock something up like the PalmPilot. This is not market research; this is more tangible and requires you to present users with something with which they can engage so they can meaningfully comment on its viability.

Experimentation – employing a scientific method

Accepting that much of what we do is an experiment, or an attempt to prove a hypothesis, is at the core of iterative delivery. Inspiration for managing this 'scientific method' effectively can be found in Mary and Tom Poppendieck's (2003) book *Lean Software Development*. Any business analysts worth their salt know an assumption when they see one. The challenge is to express that assumption as a hypothesis, design an experiment to test that hypothesis, measure the impact or outcomes of the experiment and devise the next one. It's not easy to do this on major projects from a standing start, so perhaps think about opportunities to approach a smaller, more peripheral project or initiative from a scientific perspective. Focus on ensuring the hypothesis is specific, as endless tweaking without clear, discrete objectives will not deliver quality feedback.

Segmentation

This concept extends the experimentation idea in that you deploy your experiment only to a subset of the users defined by you. It provides the opportunity to test the hypothesis or change on a small segment of users before rolling it out more widely (or deciding to roll it back). Most businesses can identify an area of their operation that could be a segment for a new product or service. The trick is to build enough lead time in between iterations to incorporate feedback, typically planning two iterations to allow time to get feedback on the first while working on the second. In addition, you need to ensure your segment is well chosen. A group of sales managers selected to trial a new booking system may not have the same concerns as their staff who will use the system on a day-to-day basis. A/B testing is a form of segmentation in digital environments, but there are ways to manage this through other kinds of service provision or industries.

Early adopters

Early adopters are different to those in a segment in that they are self-selecting trial users. They are often heavy users or 'fans' of a product or service, meaning that they are often naturally enthusiastic about testing a new offering. Be aware that this can skew results where your early adopters may be such aficionados of your product that they may not accurately represent the majority of customers. A computer game that launched to some early adopters was deemed too easy, but on launch the wider market found it difficult. Adobe run pre-release programmes, engaging user groups to solicit early feedback on new features and bugs. Similarly, Microsoft presents 'community technology previews'. An early release of Vista, for example, enabled Microsoft to find out that it took users hours to copy files across and made amendments accordingly.

Beta versions

While beta versions often pertain more to web development companies, they can be useful when rebuilding or upgrading any existing feature, service or functionality. Users can opt to use the beta version and complete a short feedback form. People can be nervous about quality on beta products or versions. Exploring perceptions around this can tell you where the trade-offs are. Are your stakeholders happy to have fewer functions with a more finessed look and feel? Will they accept more features or more complex functionality but with a more white-label format? From the BBC to Dictionary.com, many popular sites have used beta versions to get a feel for what users think before rolling products out more widely. It should be stressed that the trade-offs should, along with the relevant engineering practices, inform your definitions of quality. How can you use your toolkit to ensure that, regardless of the scope, quality is maintained through the piece? There is also a risk that change-averse users will not opt to try the beta version and you will not get much feedback. If you are not getting much take-up for the beta version, you can make it the default (as the BBC did) to drive engagement, giving users the option to switch back to the 'old' version until it is decommissioned.

Delivering value, one step at a time

In our consistently uncertain economy, iterative delivery is a must if organizations want to reduce the risk of expensive projects failing to grasp and address customer needs. You have only to think about the column inches devoted to government IT overspend, failed dotcoms, and companies with customers wielding burning torches over unpopular features or changes to see why there is value in testing the water.

If you can apply your business analysis skills, behaviours and techniques with a generous dash of pragmatism and influence, you can lead change. You can start small. You can reduce the risk of high-cost failure, alleviate fear and add value. You are an iterative business analyst.

About the author

Melanie Rose is the business analyst team lead for Totaljobs Group and has delivered requirements and governance on Prince 2 and Scrum projects for over 10 years.

References and further reading

Brandenburg, L, http://www.bridging-the-gap.com/
Denning, S, http://www.stevedenning.com (on outcomes and delighting the customer)

Haynes, L *et al* (2012) *Test, Learn, Adapt: Developing public policy with randomised controlled trials*, Cabinet Office, London, http://www.cabinetoffice. gov.uk/resource-library/test-learn-adapt-developing-public-policy-randomised-controlled-trials (gives a great insight into how the government applied a scientific approach to developing public policy)

Modern Analyst, http://www.modernanalyst.com

Pichler, R, http://www.romanpichler.com/blog/

Poppendieck, M and Poppendieck, T (2003) *Lean Software Development: An agile toolkit*, Addison-Wesley, Boston, MA

Ries, E (2011) *The Lean Startup*, Portfolio Penguin, London

Ries, E, http://theleanstartup.com/

Ries, E, http://www.startuplessonslearned.com/

Savoia, A, Clark, J and Copeland, P, www.pretotyping.org

Knowledge sharing and analysis with patterns

14

ALLAN KELLY

> According to leading management thinkers, the manufacturing, service, and information sectors will be based on knowledge in the coming age, and business organisations will evolve into knowledge creators in many ways.
>
> According to [Peter Drucker] we are entering 'the knowledge society', in which 'the basic resource' is no longer capital, or natural resources, or labour, but 'is and will be knowledge'.
>
> (Nonaka and Takeuchi, 1995)

Patterns are all around us; it is simply a question of whether we see them and whether anyone has documented them. Patterns are recurring events, situations, constructions and ideas. They occur over and over again. Things that happen once are not patterns, but we label them as patterns when they recur several times.

Business analysts will recognize the same business problem occurring again and again, often in different situations. Sometimes identical business requirements are identified and there is an opportunity to reuse requirements that had been previously gathered. These are two obvious reasons why business analysts should be interested in patterns.

A pattern exists for a reason. A pretty design on a tie, a sheet of wallpaper or a dress is just that, a pretty design. These patterns exist to decorate people and places; attractiveness is no small matter. When these designs are used again and again, they take on meaning: they are used again and again for a reason.

The pattern on a tie may simply be there to make a businessman look good, but it may also serve to identify him as a member of an association, a clan or his old school. Similarly, a pattern on a dress may make the woman wearing it look good, but it may also help to identify her or convey authority and legitimacy (think of a nurse or airline steward). Wallpaper may look nice, but we would choose different wallpaper for a gentleman's club to that for decorating a baby's nursery.

Things recur for reasons; things repeat for a reason.

In the 1970s the architect Christopher Alexander devised the 'pattern form' to codify his thinking about architecture. Using patterns, he documented the ways in which buildings are located, laid out and constructed in recurring ways for reasons he came to call 'forces'. Traditionally, the logic behind these designs was handed down by word of mouth and through participation. Today, those who study these things would call this 'tacit' knowledge and would say it was communicated through stories and legitimate peripheral participation, ie being allowed to observe and assist one who has this knowledge.

Alexander also believed that this knowledge was being lost. Modern architecture and modern society separate architects and builders from those who use the buildings, so he set about codifying the patterns that made buildings the way they are.

By the early 1990s the software engineering community faced a knowledge transfer problem. Knowledge of how to build computer systems effectively existed, but was confined to a few experts. Even when the knowledge was widely known it was difficult to share. The rapid growth of the discipline needed a new way of communicating this knowledge.

In the late 1980s a few engineers in the software development community began to look at Alexander's pattern ideas. Bruce Anderson, Kent Beck, Grady Booch, Jim Coplien, Ward Cunningham, Erich Gamma, Ralph Johnson and others set about applying Alexander's ideas to software. One result of this was the formation of the Hillside Group (www.hillside.net) to promote these patterns. Like Alexander, they used this approach to codify tacit knowledge so that it could be communicated and shared in a wider community.

The patterns identified by Alexander and the software community were not created by them. Patterns can, and do, exist independently of documentation.

The world is full of undocumented patterns. Only a few of all possible patterns are documented. To those that are documented, the title 'pattern' is awarded. These patterns codify events and constructions that happen again and again.

Building on Alexander's ideas, each formally documented pattern contains:

- the problem the pattern is addressing;
- the context in which the pattern is found;
- the forces that make it hard to solve;
- the solution;

- how the solution is constructed;
- the consequences of implementing the solution.

There are different formats and styles in which patterns adopting this approach might be written, but in general, as long as they consider these elements, we may term them 'Alexandrian patterns', or just 'patterns' for short.

Ever since software professionals started writing patterns there have been some patterns that concern themselves more with the business than the technical side of the profession. For example, the patterns in *Organizational Patterns of Agile Software Development* (Coplien and Harrison, 2004) are more about organizational form than software development. The ideas put forward in *Fearless Change* (Manns and Rising, 2005) originated in the software community, although many of these can be applied in any environment. More recently I published 38 business patterns in *Business Patterns for Software Developers* (Kelly, 2012).

Worked example: segmented customers

Patterns are often described as 'a solution to a problem in a context', but this description is a little too brief. The best way to explain patterns is to look at one. Let's dissect the segmented customer pattern, one many business analysts may recognize. This pattern and the related patterns mentioned are taken from *Business Patterns for Software Developers* (Kelly, 2012).

The first thing to note about a pattern is the name. All patterns have a name that should be evocative of the solution and usually describe the end state rather than the process of creating that state. A good name will draw the reader in from the very beginning. The name is important, because it creates a vocabulary, a language, which serves as a short cut to the ideas. When people share a knowledge of patterns they can use the names alone to communicate large, quite detailed ideas and understanding.

All patterns start with a problem statement. In the case of segmented customers this is: 'Your customers all seem to want different things. How do you know what features to provide, what documentation to write and what services to offer?'

Problems do not exist in isolation, so patterns commonly give a context, a setting in which the pattern applies. In the case of segmented customers the context is: 'A company, team or other organization that is creating technically complex products used by a variety of customers, perhaps with different objectives.'

While a pattern will do its best to state an explicit context, it is always worth remembering that there is also an implicit context. In the case of segmented customers this is a series of patterns dealing with the software industry, or rather the software industry as it exists in the early 21st century.

Christopher Alexander's patterns in *A Pattern Language* (Alexander *et al*, 1977) includes patterns such as Nine Per Cent Parking and Ring Roads. Now, 30 years on, these patterns look quite rooted in the 1970s US urban context.

Problem and context are the first two sections of the pattern and frame the issue to be addressed. A third section, forces, examines what makes the problem hard – after all, if it were easy to solve it wouldn't be worth writing about. Usually there are multiple forces, which often contradict one another and interact to make a solution difficult – or at least non-obvious. Forces for segmented customers are: 'One product may be used in different organizations and by different people, but the needs and usage pattern will vary between groups. Trying to satisfy everyone is worthy, but is likely to mean that nobody is completely satisfied. Potential customers are not equal: they differ in needs, scale and budgets.'

Within a single organization there are multiple people with multiple roles placing different demands on the product. Users will have different requirements because they fulfil different roles and because they will have individual preferences.

Developing new products and enhancing existing ones involve making judgements and guesses about how your product will be used. Many scenarios can be imagined, which can sound reasonable, but may be unnecessary. Some scenarios will contradict each other. Analysing all cases would be expensive and time-consuming.

In writing forces it is common to juxtapose two conflicting forces by the use of the word 'but', eg 'Trying to satisfy everyone is worthy, but is likely to mean that nobody is completely satisfied.'

Once the problem space has been thoroughly explored the author presents a solution: 'Segment your customers into different groups and address the needs of each group separately. Groups are defined by discernible attributes and characteristics that allow you to differentiate one group from another. Working with definable groups avoids generalizations that do not describe any one group accurately.'

Solutions usually start with an opening statement describing the general solution: the thing you have to build or do to resolve the problem. The best patterns then delve into the details of how you go about building this solution. Segmented customers' full solution is about half a page long. For some patterns the solution can be the bulk of the pattern. Particularly with technical patterns, authors may separate the solution statement section into 'solution' and 'implementation' to make this divide clearer.

Importantly, a pattern solution needs to describe a recognized approach that has been applied more than once. Informally, a 'rule of three known uses' exists here. My personal preference is to start writing my patterns from the known uses and solution and work back to the problem and forces through the examples.

After the solution a section follows examining consequences. This describes how the forces are resolved after the solution is applied and highlights any downsides such as negative consequences or liabilities.

Finally, bringing up the rear of the pattern are a number of sections that, while sometimes omitted for brevity, lend weight to the pattern. These deal with the known uses or examples that validate the reoccurrence of the pattern, related patterns or other related work and sometimes common variations of the pattern.

However, a pattern is not just a set of modular sections – problem and solution, forces and consequences, etc – that happen to fit together. The pattern must also work as a whole thing and stand as a thing of beauty. A pattern needs to possess, as Alexander said, 'the quality without a name'. We don't write patterns about Enron-style accounting or Lehman Brothers trading, because such practices do not make the world a better place. When writing a pattern it is imperative that authors strive for beauty and wholeness, with the aim of creating something that improves the world, or at least their little bit of it.

Story

Another way of thinking about a pattern is as a piece of literature that tells a story. A problem, a difficult situation, is described to the reader, who is then led through the analysis of the problem before being shown the solution. Comparison has been made to the 'Aha!' moment in fiction when the solution surprises the reader and relieves the tension.

While decidedly more analytical than an average novel, patterns share many of the characteristics that Denning (2001) suggests are seen in stories that communicate knowledge and promote action. The trick with a good pattern is to make it as readable as a short story while communicating understanding.

Patterns and sequences

While an individual pattern can, and should, be useful on its own, usefulness multiplies when patterns are considered together. Patterns cluster together in languages because they address related problems. Indeed, the end point for one pattern may well be the starting point for another. The consequences at the end of one pattern are the starting point for the forces of the next.

Pattern sequences exist where several patterns run together. Figure 14.1 shows how segmented customers may result from using customer understanding. Once the customer base has been segmented, core product only or whole product might be used to serve particular segments. Potentially both patterns could be used for different segments. Additionally, or alternatively, the company may use expeditionary marketing to probe the market segment to see what customers want. This might be through the use of simple product variations (which keep costs low). A company may also choose to deepen its understanding of a segment by hiring in a representative customer, as described in poacher turned gamekeeper.

FIGURE 14.1 Pattern sequence from business patterns

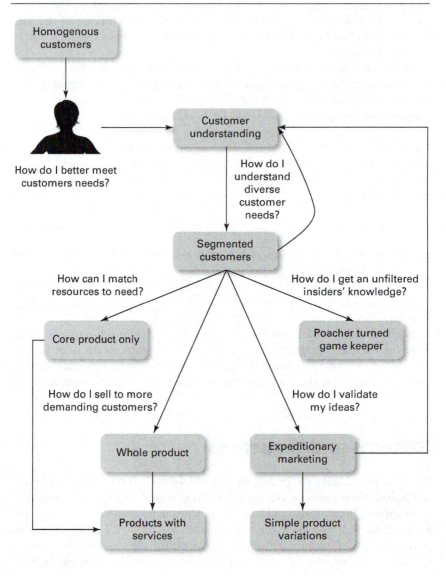

Using patterns

Probably the most common way to use patterns is for sharing knowledge. They solve specific problems in context. The extensive collaborative review process that most of the patterns mentioned so far have gone through helps to identify and document the tacit knowledge that can be lost using other approaches.

Of course, one could mechanically read all of any of the books mentioned and more, and remember the patterns. While I have read some pattern books from cover to cover, I tend to browse new books and read the patterns that interest me. Reading one pattern frequently leads you to read another related pattern, and then to the building of your own sequences from the solutions that interest you.

Knowing that these patterns exist and that they can be called on is useful in itself. They become more useful when a team share the vocabulary and can talk patterns. Dialogue progresses more actively when teams share language and understanding.

So far we have described patterns as a means of sharing captured knowledge, but there is another way to view them: as a knowledge capture tool. Before knowledge can be shared it must be captured. The same qualities that make patterns powerful communicators make them powerful capture tools.

While capturing and sharing are in one sense different sides of the same coin – in order to be shared it must be captured first – they differ in one critical way: in the person who benefits. When sharing, the audience is the reader who benefits from the knowledge of others. When writing, the audience is the writer, benefiting from a deeper understanding of the problem and solution.

The discipline and thought process necessary to define the elements of a pattern and to assemble them in a readable form mean that the person who learns most from a pattern may well be the writer. Certainly in writing my own patterns I have learnt more about the patterns and subjects they concern.

Indeed, the analysis required to write a pattern constitutes a useful analysis technique in its own right and is sometimes referred to as 'pattern thinking'. Even when three known uses are unknown or when no solution is known, there can be great value in asking and understanding 'What is the problem?' and 'What are the forces that make this problem difficult?'

Finally, in the case of the business patterns language and perhaps other pattern languages, there may be value in actively breaking the pattern or sequence and doing something differently, in other words doing something different to the norm, innovating.

Conclusion

How you use patterns is up to you. You can use them as short cuts to a solution: match a problem you see to an existing pattern and apply the solution. You can scale this up by moving from individual patterns to whole sequences.

The next step up is sharing these patterns with others, creating a common vocabulary to allow a team to communicate more effectively and build shared understanding. Sharing language is an important step to sharing vision.

Whether your patterns are general patterns (with three known uses) or specific to the context the team is in, it should not stand in the way of knowledge capture and sharing.

First of all, get to know some patterns. In addition to the many published books (a few of which I have mentioned above), there are many patterns freely available on the internet. One word of advice: start with patterns that have been reviewed through one of the PLoP (Pattern Languages of Programming, a legacy name) conferences. These patterns have benefited from review cycles.

Second, pattern conferences are open to all. They are a great place to learn about patterns and even better places to take your own patterns. The conferences exist to help authors improve their work. I don't believe I would have written two books, and much more, had I not started attending EuroPLoP.

About the author

Allan Kelly is the author of *Business Patterns for Software Developers* and works for Software Strategy.

References

Alexander, C *et al* (1977), *A Pattern Language*, Oxford University Press, Oxford

Coplien, J and Harrison, N (2004) *Organizational Patterns of Agile Software Development*, Pearson Prentice Hall, Upper Saddle River, NJ

Denning, S (2001) *The Springboard: How story telling ignites action in knowledge-era organizations*, Butterworth-Heinemann, Oxford

Kelly, A (2012) *Business Patterns for Software Developers*, John Wiley & Sons, Chichester

Nonaka, I and Takeuchi, H (1995) *Knowledge Creating Company*, Oxford University Press, New York

Manns, M and Rising, L (2005) *Fearless Change: Patterns for introducing new ideas*, Addison-Wesley, Boston, MA

Dealing with uncertainty

15

RUTH MURRAY-WEBSTER AND PENNY PULLAN

What do we mean by uncertainty, and what is risk? Shouldn't a business analyst leave risk management to the project manager? What is the risk management process, and what do we need to consider at each stage? How do we deal with the fact that individuals perceive risk so differently? What is risk facilitation, why is it necessary and why does this role fit many business analysts so well? This chapter addresses these and other questions about how business analysts can best deal with the inevitable uncertainty that comes with change.

What do we mean by uncertainty?

People who want to provide leadership for change need to be able to deal with uncertainty.

While almost everything to do with change is uncertain, not all of this matters. For example, it is unlikely to make a difference to most projects if the sun is shining or there will be grey, cloudy skies tomorrow. Only some aspects of uncertainty matter, those that might affect our objectives, and we call these risks. From now on, we will focus on these using the definition that 'Risks are uncertainties that matter' (Hillson and Murray-Webster, 2007).

People often confuse issues with risks. Issues are problems that are happening now, with no uncertainty about them at all. These need to be managed, of course, but they need to be dealt with separately from risks; otherwise the current issues are likely to overshadow future risks.

While risk in the English language has rather negative connotations, uncertainty that matters could work both ways, positively as well as negatively. It's important that we are aware of positive opportunities as well as negative threats. The process for risk management applies to both, and it's important to make the most of positive risks. By adding this side into the way you deal with uncertainty, you will be ahead of many organizations.

FIGURE 15.1   Risk can be positive, as well as negative

While many business analysts work within the world of *financial* risk management, this chapter is about risk management *in general*. It is designed for people leading change and to help them engage others in this work.

But isn't risk management for the project manager?

When Penny Pullan first started encouraging business analysts to consider risk management as part of their role, many came back to her stating that it was a project management task. Her answer was that those engaged in business analysis work closely with stakeholders in the change, usually much more closely than project managers do. Business analysts build up strong relationships with people involved and learn to see the world from their perspective. Surely, as part of this, risks will emerge that otherwise would remain hidden from the project manager. A business analyst who is a leader for change will want to work closely with the project manager, sharing the risks that they find and working together to deal with them. To be able to do this, it's important that business analysts have a good understanding of risk, the risk process and the human aspects of risk, which is what the rest of this chapter will cover.

The risk management process

There are steps in the risk management process which can be expressed as a series of questions. We will run through each in turn, with a few pointers for each. For more details, see Pullan and Murray-Webster (2011).

How much risk can we tolerate?

Before taking on a change and the risks involved, it's important that there is an understanding of how much risk the organization can tolerate. How much capacity is there for dealing with risk? How much appetite does the organization have for taking on risks in return for possible rewards?

This step includes knowing who the stakeholders are and their objectives, as well as how these objectives will be measured. How important is each objective compared to the others? How much risk can be tolerated for each objective?

What's risky and why?

This step is where many project managers and business analysts start their process, but doesn't mean much unless there is a clear understanding of how much risk the organization can tolerate. So, if you are tempted to start here, go back a step.

We suggest that you start by exploring the positive opportunities, the risks that could make your project go even better and have a positive impact on your objectives. It's much easier to come up with opportunities before thinking about all the threats! Once this is complete, then move on to the negative threats, the risks that could harm the achievement of your objectives. For each risk, make sure that you have a clearly identified owner who will be responsible for managing that risk and keeping an eye on it over time.

It's very easy to provide woolly risk statements that are so vague that different people interpret them in very different ways. To avoid this, use the structure of cause–risk event–effect to make sure that the following are crystal clear:

- the underlying *cause* of the risk;
- the uncertain *event* itself;
- the *effect* that the risk event would cause if it happened.

Here's an example of cause–risk event–effect: because heavy rain has caused local flooding, my car may get stuck when I am visiting my friend, resulting in delay and repair costs.

How much does each risk matter?

This step explores how much each risk matters, in terms of how likely it is to happen and the impact if it does happen. These are subjective judgements, and human biases and difference in attitude play a huge role here. The purpose of this step is to prioritize the most significant risks so we can target action in the right place.

As part of the first step – 'How much risk can we tolerate?' – we should have come up with clear scales for both probability and impact, making clear precisely what is meant by 'low', 'medium' and 'high'. When evaluating risks we have identified using these scales, it is best practice to analyse probability and impact separately. There is one probability that a risk event may occur, but many potential impacts. Disassociating the evaluation of probability and impact reduces the chance of bias influencing the prioritization.

How risky is this situation as a whole?

Many organizations leave out this step of looking at the situation as a whole, with all the risks viewed together. They miss out on a clear idea of the combined impact of all the risks on their objectives. If this step is missed, it is also difficult to include normal variability (such as productivity rates or currency fluctuations), as well as specific risk events, in the overall assessment of risk to objectives. To assess how risky the situation is as a whole you need a way of modelling the effect of uncertainty on your objectives. To get a good outcome you will need to identify any mutually exclusive risks, as well as looking at which risks are likely to occur together, and the cumulative effect of these.

What action shall we take?

In this step, the risk owner for each risk explores what actions should be taken to keep exposure to risk within the defined tolerances for each objective. There's a range of options available for both opportunities and threats:

- *Accept the risk*. Keep monitoring, but don't spend any time or money now.
- *Prepare a Plan B*. Accept the risk for now, but also prepare a Plan B just in case the risk occurs.
- *Treat the risk*. Can you reduce the uncertainty in some way? For threats, this is called mitigating the risk by reducing the probability and/or impact. For opportunities, this is called enhancing the risk by increasing the probability and/or impact.
- *Share the risk*. This is where you share the risk with others, perhaps other organizations, that can help you out. This is often called transfer, but it can be problematic (Pullan and Murray-Webster, 2011). An example is taking out life insurance to 'transfer' the risk to the life insurance company. Unfortunately, although your family would receive some money in the event of your death, this doesn't actually remove the fact that you still have to die for them to receive

FIGURE 15.2 All too often, risk registers are created only
for compliance

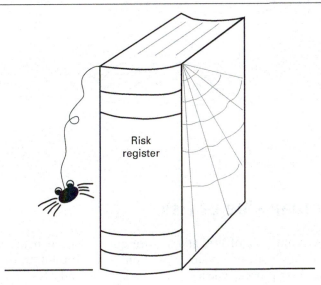

Risk
register

it. There are still impacts, even if the financial ones have been transferred!

- *Make it certain.* This is where you make sure that threats can't happen and opportunities do happen, usually by managing the cause of the risk event.

Be aware that, with all but the last of these actions, there will still be some residual risk. You also need to make sure that your chosen response doesn't create secondary risk that is greater than the original situation. The whole point is that you contain exposure within tolerance, without paying more money for the response than the risk would cost if it happened in the first place.

What's the current situation?

The risk assessment work above is only a snapshot in time. However, situations are dynamic, and risk management needs to keep pace. The best way for this to happen is that the whole change team make the risk process part of their everyday project life, using their risk register as a living, changing document and seeing the value that their work adds.

Unfortunately, this ongoing work is often not done properly, if at all. Risk registers are often created to tick boxes for compliance and then forgotten. This can lead to cynicism about risk management, as well as delivering little, if any, value.

FIGURE 15.3 Three strands of risk

Have I seen
this before?

What is my
automatic
reaction?

How I
perceive
the risk

How do I
feel about it?

The human side of risk

Risk is a natural part of life, and we are quite adept at managing risks on a day-to-day basis. For example, we don't need to think through a full risk management process whenever we cross a busy road. However, without thinking consciously about it, we check that it is safe to cross before walking across the road. If the road is too busy to cross safely, we walk along the road to a pedestrian crossing. It's common sense and a natural part of being a human.

Risk management in change projects is on the whole common sense. However, it is more complex, as there are several people involved in assessing risks and deciding what to do about them. Risks are, by their very nature, subjective, so in a group you're likely to find as many different views as the number of people present as to what the risks are, how much they matter and what to do about them!

There are very many different factors that can influence people's perception of risk (Hillson and Murray-Webster, 2007; Murray-Webster and Hillson, 2008). These can be seen as three strands of a rope:

- *Situational factors ('Have I seen this before?')*. These are the conscious, rational considerations that we use to think about a risk situation. They take into account things such as whether we have done anything similar before, how much we have control of the situation or how soon the situation might affect us. How close the risk is to us personally will affect this too, as well as the dynamics of the group we're in.

- *Subconscious factors ('What is my automatic reaction?')*. These include heuristics (mental short cuts based on our previous experiences) and many different types of cognitive bias. Heuristics can help us to reach an appropriate position quickly or can lead us astray. The trouble is that, as these are subconscious factors, we tend not to know which! Heuristics include intuition, availability (for example, recent data are most memorable), and anchoring and adjustment (we become irrationally attached to the first value suggested to us). The cognitive biases that silently influence human perception are too numerous to mention here, but include repetition bias (repeated data must be true!), optimism bias, the illusion of being in control (erroneous perception of manageability) and groupthink (the tendency of members of a group to value social harmony rather than exposing conflicting information).

● *Affective factors ('How do I feel about it?')*. This strand contains the factors based on emotions and feelings. These arise automatically or instinctively in a situation. Without us being aware, they have a bigger influence on how we perceive risk and react than the situational and subconscious factors. Fear, worry, excitement and attraction change the way we react in risky situations.

Taken together, these three sets of factors combine to influence each individual's perception of risk in any particular situation and therefore the choices he or she makes as a result (the person's risk attitude). Risk attitudes range from risk seeking, through risk tolerant to risk averse. As you can imagine, if it is difficult to understand the influence of each strand within individuals, it becomes even more complicated with a group! To manage risk well, however, we must try to be aware and to appreciate the influences. If we don't, we run the risk of believing that the process we have described is rational and objective. Human beings are 'predictably irrational' (Ariely, 2008), and the successful risk manager understands this and has ways of dealing with it through effective facilitation.

Risk facilitation

This is an area where business analysts with well-developed facilitation skills can make a huge contribution to change, even more so if they are aware of the factors that we've described above.

Business analysis focuses on requirements, which need to have an owner. This owner cares about them throughout and will test that his or her requirements have been met at the end of a project. In the same way, risks need to have risk owners who will care about them throughout the process. In both cases, it is very important that the owners and not the facilitators look after the risks. The facilitators need to facilitate and make the process as easy as possible, but never take over the requirements or risks. This can be quite a challenge, but nevertheless one that business analysts are used to.

As well as making risk management work as easily as possible, a risk facilitator can bring energy and life to what can be a dull and pedantic process. This is important in order to engage people, not just at the early stages, but throughout the ongoing monitoring and readjusting that takes place later on. Again, a good business analyst will have the skills to keep people engaged throughout a change, from the very start through to delivering the benefits at the end.

With many of the skills already in place, business analysts can be ideal risk facilitators, if they are willing to develop skills in risk and in understanding how to deal with all the complexity of factors that make human risk behaviour so interesting.

Conclusion

Dealing with uncertainty is a key part of working with change. Risk management processes involve asking questions and developing answers. Business analysts have many of the skills to be able to work as risk facilitators on their projects, working in partnership with their project managers and other stakeholders. Business analysts who are determined to be leaders for change can make very positive impacts on their projects in the area of dealing with uncertainty.

About the authors

Ruth Murray-Webster is a leading organizational change consultant, managing partner of Lucidus Consulting Ltd and is a visiting fellow at Cranfield School of Management.

Penny Pullan is the co-editor of this book and, together with Ruth, set up www.facilitatingrisk.com

References

Ariely, D (2008) *Predictably Irrational: The hidden forces that shape our decisions*, HarperCollins, New York

Hillson, DA and Murray-Webster, R (2007) *Understanding and Managing Risk Attitude*, 2nd edn, Gower, Aldershot

Murray-Webster, R and Hillson, D (2008) *Managing Group Risk Attitude*, Gower, Aldershot

Pullan, P and Murray-Webster, R (2011) *A Short Guide to Facilitating Risk Management: Engaging people to identify, own and manage risk*, Gower, Aldershot

Opinion piece
The first shoots of creativity

DAVID BASKERVILLE

All too often a business analyst is assigned to a project to identify requirements and write operational designs when, without fully understanding the problem, 'the business' has already chosen a solution. On these occasions, it's the responsibility of a business analyst to tactfully place the 'solution' to one side and to work to understand the real problem, gathering unique and robust requirements, and in turn deliver a more innovative design.

In today's environment, it is important for businesses to stand out from their competitors, so, when introducing new or enhanced products or services, business requirements should be as creative and innovative as possible. How can we, as business analysts, encourage others to think creatively as we help elicit requirements for new solutions?

Four years ago, I became interested in creativity. I had always been very logical in my approach to business analysis, with a methodical way of working. Despite this background, I could see potential in new, creative ways of thinking.

Further reading showed me how many of today's great designs originate from businesses using a range of creativity techniques. One such technique is SCAMPER (Eberle, 1996), which builds on the notion that most new ideas are modifications of something that already exists. This makes it a useful technique to use for process or product enhancement. Each letter in the word SCAMPER stands for a different approach you can adopt to modify the product or process:

S = Substitute;

C = Combine;

A = Adapt;

M = Multiply, Magnify, Minimize;

P = Put to other uses;

E = Eliminate;

R = Rearrange or Reverse.

An example of SCAMPER technique in action is Mars ice cream. Mars realized their sales of heavy chocolate bars declined during the summer months, so, in 1988, they decided to *substitute* the nougat filling with ice cream to create a new, unique product, the Mars ice cream bar. The ongoing success of this product allowed Mars to take advantage of its breakthrough to produce a wide variety of other chocolate, ice cream products (*The Times* 100 Business Case Studies, 2013).

I've used many such examples to help others grasp how powerful these techniques are and how they can deliver benefits for business. The stories certainly help to overcome initial scepticism.

Another creativity technique is Situation/Solution Reversal (also known as reverse brainstorming) (Hicks, 1991). This helps people to overcome their normal tendencies and thought patterns, by thinking about the opposite of what they are trying to do. We've found that analysts generate 20–30 per cent more requirements using this technique and, as it's proven so useful within our organization, we now include it in our business analysis induction training. Here's how it works:

1 Clearly identify the problem to be explored and write it down.

2 Reverse the problem. For example, an original problem of 'How can we decrease spending in this department?' when reversed becomes 'How can we increase spending in this department?'

3 Capture all the business requirements for the new, reversed problem. Once you have captured the reverse requirements, put them to one side.

4 Use your normal approach to capture requirements for the original problem.

5 Finally, compare these normal requirements to those generated by the reversed problem and ensure that each of the reverse requirements has an opposing requirement. (This is the step where we find 20 to 30 per cent more requirements.)

Above are two creativity techniques that we've found very useful in business analysis. If these techniques are researched and practised, within a short space of time creativity becomes natural and more qualitative, and creative and innovative solutions follow.

How has our business analysis practice incorporated creativity since then? We've created a website that is a repository of creative tools and techniques, with information as to how to use the tools to their full potential. We provide support to colleagues and other projects as they apply creative tools, leading to better, more innovative solutions. Why not do the same for your organization?

Creativity is contagious. Pass it on.

(Albert Einstein)

About the author

David Baskerville is a lead business analyst for a multinational financial services organization.

References

Eberle, B (1996) *Scamper: Creative games and activities for imagination development*, Prufrock Press, Waco, TX

Hicks, MJ (1991) *Problem Solving and Decision Making*, Chapman & Hall, London

The Times 100 Business Case Studies [accessed 20 January 2013] How Mars transformed the ice cream market [Online] http://businesscasestudies.co.uk/masterfoods/how-mars-transformed-the-ice-cream-market/introduction.html

PART III
Leadership within your organization

Introduction to Part III

Part II covered leadership within a project context. Part III provides a wider view, taking into account all the ways that business analysis needs leadership across organizations.

What do we mean by leadership within your organization?

Most business analysis takes place within a project. Some strategic business analysis, known as enterprise analysis, takes places before projects start, looking across an organization as a whole as well as the context in which the organization operates. All business analysis, even at a project level, benefits from leadership that takes into account this organizational context. The problems, processes, organizational structure, systems and infrastructure need to be understood, whether they fit neatly within a project scope or not.

What does Part III cover?

Part III starts off in Chapter 16 by exploring how to operate effectively as a business analyst inside an organization. It focuses on value: where value comes from, as well as how business analysis can focus on value and help the project to deliver it.

Changing culture is a daunting task in any organization. Chapter 17 argues that paying attention to the climate in projects, created by observable behaviours, will improve the results of projects. Chapter 18 focuses on global working and virtual teams, a way of working that has become commonplace in the 21st century. The chapter looks at why this is so and how business analysts can operate more effectively when working virtually and on global projects.

Chapter 19 looks at understanding what's happening within a business. It uses various flavours of systems thinking to understand a system and its purpose. It introduces systems dynamics and the viable systems model, and finishes by looking at how to reduce variation in processes.

Anyone working on change within organizations will come across power and politics. Chapter 20 explores why business analysts can't just ignore these, and goes on to suggest ways to improve business analysts' individual power and their management of politics. Many changes involve more than one organization, and Chapter 21 explores this. Starting with a single organization, it expands to cover how to manage relationships with stakeholders across several. Chapter 22 explores strategic thinking for business analysis, starting with an overview of strategy and moving on to practical suggestions for application.

Part III is rounded off by an opinion piece written by a senior business analyst in television on how to lead from the middle, which will echo with many.

There are further resources at **www.baleadership.com** for leadership within your organization. These include an article that looks at a variety of ways of modelling the business, introducing a range of different models and their uses, along with tips for success and pitfalls to avoid.

How does Part III relate to leadership in the wider world?

While business analysis is carried out within organizations, it's now a worldwide profession. These chapters will help business analysts to understand their organization's context, and analysts can look to the wider world to provide further opportunities to contribute, lead and make a difference beyond their company.

Operating effectively as a business analyst inside an organization

16

SIMON EDWARDS

Twenty years ago, my first meeting with my new project team didn't go as expected. As a new graduate, I'd been looking forward to the day's break from the graduate training programme to learn more about the project to which I'd been assigned. However, when I pitched up I was greeted by two analysts playing chess. They told me that the project was inevitably going to be cancelled, after a year spent on analysis, because it had lost the support of its sponsors. A few weeks later I got the call to confirm that the organizationally aware analysts had been right.

As this book's Introduction sets out, the role of business analysis is to turn strategic goals and visions into reality while adding value. The role should end only when the identified benefits and value to the organization have been realized, preferably not when the project has been stopped after a year's analysis.

So how does the organizationally aware analyst help ensure the project has value and then ensure the project realizes its value? This chapter explains that the organizationally aware analyst must focus relentlessly on the value the project aims to deliver, and provides a number of suggestions on how to do this. With this approach, the analyst can help lead the project to realize that value, irrespective of his or her level within the hierarchy.

Where does the value come from?

The first step is to look wider than the immediate project area and consider the organization as a whole. How does the organization itself add value? Many of the most successful firms follow one of three main approaches:

- operational excellence;
- product leadership;
- customer intimacy.

These approaches lead to very different cultures, and affect the way the project needs to operate. An operationally excellent organization is likely to focus on consistency, and have clear rules and little discretion to operate outside the rules. The organization focusing on customer intimacy will allow a great deal of flexibility for staff members to meet customer demands, and hence will have very different processes. The organization focusing on product leadership will emphasize the speed of being able to introduce new products and services. Effective business analysts will understand this, and build this into their approach. What works for the operationally excellent organization is unlikely to work for the organization that focuses on customer intimacy.

What is the problem we are trying to solve or the opportunity we are trying to realize?

Business analysts must seek to understand the underlying opportunity the organization is trying to achieve through the project, or the problem the organization is trying to solve. This is key, however late in the project the business analyst starts. And it is surprisingly easily lost as the project moves into the detail of analysis, design and execution.

The business analyst should speak up if the value the project set out to deliver can no longer be achieved: better that than wait for the post-implementation review of an unsuccessful project. McKinsey's surveys gave unclear objectives and lack of business focus as the most frequent cause of cost overruns (Bloch, Blumberg and Laartz, 2012).

What is the business case?

It is important to understand how the potential benefit coming from the project stacks up against the costs of the project. Not everything can be reduced to a financial benefit, but it helps to identify as much of this as you can. Failing to be clear about this is a great danger to the project, however much there may be support for the project at the start. For example, if the project is regulation-driven, consider the impact of not complying with the regulation. This could include the fines that a regulator might apply and, for a public company, the loss of market value through share price reductions, though the impact on reputation could be greater still.

This benefit can then be compared to the likely costs of the project. If you think the potential benefit is 10 times the cost, then the fact you have made some rough guesses of the cost doesn't matter too much: this should be enough to gain confidence, and the support, to proceed. But if the benefit and cost are much closer, then it is worth looking to see if there are more valuable alternatives. You need to be sure that there is an opportunity in whose exploration it is worth investing a certain amount of time and money.

How important is time?

Timing matters. Any organization would put more value on having $1 now rather than in three years' time. We could take the $1 and earn interest over the next three years, so there is a time value to money.

The world also changes. If you are in an uncertain world, then going away for three years to do something that will then deliver a benefit runs the risk that when you come back at the end of your three years the world will have moved on.

The field of real options helps to assess the value that flexibility in an investment decision can give in the future. For example, infrastructure could be designed with the option to expand, so that it can produce more if needed. This may cost more to establish, but the option gives more value (Dixit and Pindyck, 1995).

What is critical for the organization?

The more the project is addressing an issue or opportunity that is significant to the organization as a whole, as well as to a department, the more likely the project is to succeed. In addition, you're more likely to be able to attract the time of people, and the resources you'll need. So an effective business analyst will look at how to link the project benefits to these wider objectives.

The wider context in which the organization is operating also informs the level of detail required within the business case. Suppose a benefit of the project is to improve efficiency, such that an activity that takes a person five days now will take four days in the future. That's equivalent to saving 0.2 of a person. In an environment where there are many opportunities, but constrained by the availability of people, this would give a significant benefit, as it means an extra day each week that a person can spend doing something else. But, if the overall environment is one of cutting costs, the project works only if this translates into a cost saving. Perhaps individuals' contracts mean they would be compelled to work only the four days for four days' pay. In other cases, you can't save 0.2 of a person, so how does the saving come? The cost reduction would come only if there were five of these benefits so that a whole person could be saved, and only if the saving offset the redundancy costs or natural turnover meant that the saving would occur by not replacing a leaver.

What does this mean for project trade-offs?

The business case should establish the priority attached to the inevitable project trade-offs between cost, time and quality.

Does the market opportunity disappear if the project takes too long to deliver? Generally, the best returns come from being an early provider of a product or service; in this case it will be better to deliver quickly even if it costs more, because the benefits from early delivery will outweigh the incremental costs. Or, in a cost-saving project, it may be worth incurring additional costs earlier so that a big cost gain can be realized more quickly. But in other cases cost may be the overwhelming constraint. If there's a risk that an aeroplane will fall out of the sky if you don't get it right, then quality trumps everything.

The trade-off against time is an important one for the business analyst to bear in mind. Many business analysts will know the consequence of poor requirements leading to much greater cost if errors are fixed later in the project. But that doesn't mean it is always right to push back for more time: it may be that the risk of an error, and the potential cost of fixing it later in the project, is outweighed by the benefit of the earlier delivery. So if the business analyst does wish to push back for more time it is important to consider the impact on the value the project aims to deliver.

What does it mean for the business analyst to focus relentlessly on value?

Value and the requirements phase

The business analyst always needs to keep in mind the view of what the project is trying to achieve. Once you've got to the stage of 'We have decided how we're going to do it', it is easy to become focused on the 'how' and to lose sight of why we're doing it in the first place. This is particularly important for business analysts, because once the project is under way they are going to start talking to people about the detail of what is wanted. Very often that's not going to be the person who's sponsoring the project, because you'll need to be operating at a more detailed level. You'll need to deal with a range of different people, not all of whom may have bought into the whole idea of the project in the first place, and who may not be aware of the broader objective you're trying to achieve. Instead they may be looking for the opportunity to implement their pet projects.

Effective business analysts are more than simply order takers who are writing down whatever they're being told by the person they're speaking to. Don't operate like the person at the McDonald's counter taking an order for a Diet Coke to go with a burger and chips. Instead, the effective business analyst operates more like the sommelier in a restaurant. Just as the sommelier seeks to understand what the customer is looking for in a wine, and brings his or her own knowledge to help customers decide given their food choices, the business analyst needs to be prepared to challenge what's being said and bring his or her knowledge of the project's aims into the conversation.

This makes the business analyst's task both hard and interesting. You need to build and maintain a working relationship with the people that you are asking for requirements, but you need to be able to challenge them. You need to get to the point of understanding how the requirement relates to the goals of the project. Sometimes the people you're speaking to may not be sure themselves and will resent being challenged on this.

Business analysts who have taken the time to really understand what the project is trying to achieve, and are able to explain it, will be in a better position, because they will be credible in the eyes of the people with whom they interact.

What are the considerations for global projects?

The imperative to 'seek to understand' is particularly important on global projects, which aim to implement in a consistent way globally. The particular challenge this brings for a business analyst is to understand whether a request for local variation should be accepted as a genuine requirement. The business analyst needs to question whether a requested difference arises because 'that's the way we like to do things here' or because there absolutely is a regulation or feature of the environment that means it does have to be done differently. If you're thousands of miles away it's harder to tell.

The business analyst needs to invest in gaining an understanding of the local environment and building the trust of the people he or she needs to deal with. Building trust is going to be harder when you can't walk up to people's desks and see them face to face. This will require substantially more effort than it would to build that trust locally, but this investment is needed to get an equivalent level of input and support.

How does the organizationally aware business analyst help the project?

The business analyst can show leadership by helping support communication activity around the project. McKinsey state that one of the four dimensions of 'value assurance' for a project is focusing on managing strategy and stakeholders instead of exclusively concentrating on budgets and scheduling (Bloch, Blumberg and Laartz, 2012).

At their most effective, business analysts articulate the vision for the project throughout their conversations. For example, the conversation 'We have decided to do a project to implement this computer system and your bosses have said you must give time to me to outline the requirements' is a very different start from 'We're trying to move into a new market, and to do that we need to implement this computer system.' This is backed up by Gary Yukl's research that shows that the most effective way of achieving change is through articulating a vision ('inspirational appeal'), and this is more effective than techniques of citing someone in authority (such as a project sponsor) in order to get people to cooperate (Yukl and Tracey, 1992).

The organizationally aware business analyst has a big part to play in stakeholder management. At their best, business analysts are regarded by the business as part of the business and by the project team as part of the project, so they are an effective bridge between the two. This comes from being able to talk the language of business and show that business concerns are understood, but also through delivering what the project needs.

Business analysts are likely to have met with a number of people across the organization in defining and determining requirements, and in getting requirements agreed. This helps them to understand the different focus that different people and different roles bring. This becomes critical to the project succeeding in the end, because the project succeeds when people change their behaviour.

Preparations for change

What at first may seem a lull in work for the business analyst, once requirements have been signed off and before something needs to be tested, is a great opportunity to work through questions such as 'How do we get this accepted?', 'How do we make this change happen?' and 'Who needs to be more convinced than they are?'

A lot of my experience has been on implementing IT-dominated projects, and there is a danger of becoming too focused on delivering the system and too little on preparing the individuals who are going to be using the system so they will get the full value out of the system. At the extreme this neglect has resulted in the old system being kept on as well as the new system being implemented.

We know from our success, or otherwise, in following New Year's resolutions how hard it is to change what we do, and it is no different for organizations.

Developing training is part of this preparation, but as important is truly empathizing with the individuals who need to change. For example, suppose a system eliminates the need for spreadsheet manipulation and gives more time to analyse. At first glance, this may seem attractive, but maybe the individuals get a sense of achievement through using the spreadsheet to produce some output. They might be less clear what is required when they have more time to analyse, and feel less certain about what they are delivering. The effective business analyst can deliver real value by ensuring that the expectations for the individuals affected are clear prior to systems implementation, and that guidance is provided to help them meet those expectations.

Implementation process and testing

One of my most successful projects was helped in the testing phase because we had established a clear understanding of the expected value. The aim of the project was to improve capacity so that we could increase trading volumes without sacrificing control. Each day we reviewed defects identified in testing, and followed a simpler decision process: could we achieve the desired capacity despite the defect? If we could, it could wait. If not, we needed to fix it. Appropriately enough the computer system was called FOCUS, and it succeeded because that's exactly what the project team did: focus on the intended value.

How does the business analyst help the project deliver the value?

The strongest indicator of an outstanding business analyst is leadership. This provides a strong and committed mindset, the willingness to step up and take a leading role, the courage to challenge appropriately and respectfully at all levels of the organization, and the drive to make a difference.

This chapter has set out how the organizationally aware business analyst can help lead the project to realize the full value available. This knowledge of and focus on value enables the business analyst to make a real difference to the project and the organization, even when working with people who are more senior, more knowledgeable or more experienced.

Working in this way, business analysts have credibility through their organizational knowledge and will demonstrate their strategic value to the organization. As well as ensuring that the project succeeds through delivering value, this will increase the range of career opportunities that become available to the business analyst.

So what became of the chess-playing, but organizationally aware, business analysts? They learnt the lessons of the unsuccessful project, although it did reduce their opportunity to play chess in office hours. Within five years the more senior of the pair was the head of the department, and within 10 years the more junior had become CIO of the organization.

About the author

Simon Edwards has 20 years' experience as a business analyst, project and programme manager in international banks in London, UK.

References and further reading

Bloch, M, Blumberg, S and Laartz, J (2012) Delivering large-scale IT projects on time, on budget, and on value, *McKinsey Quarterly*, October, http://www.mckinseyquarterly.com/Delivering_large-scale_IT_projects_on_time_on_budget_and_on_value_3026 (accessed 1 December 2012) (this outlines the findings of research conducted by McKinsey and the BT Centre for Major Programme Management at the University of Oxford as well as the McKinsey surveys mentioned in the chapter)

Brooks, FP (1995) *The Mythical Man-Month*, anniversary edn, Addison-Wesley, Boston, MA (an influential and still relevant study on large-scale programming projects, which provides good insight into the requirements process)

Dixit, AK and Pindyck, RS (1995) The options approach to capital investment, *Harvard Business Review*, May–June, pp 105–15, http://hbr.org/1995/05/the-options-approach-to-capital-investment/ar/1, also available at http://web.mit.edu/rpindyck/www/Papers/Options_Approach.pdf (this sets out the 'real options' approach to factoring real-world uncertainties into assessing projects, distinguishing this from the typical approach of using net present value to determine cost–benefit)

Hammer, M and Champy, J (1993) *Reengineering the Corporation: A manifesto for business revolution*, HarperBusiness, New York (this provides a good guide to challenging the processes that businesses follow, and what it takes to succeed with change)

Reimus, B (1997) The information system technology system that couldn't deliver, Harvard Business Review Case Study, *Harvard Business Review*, May–June, pp 22–35, http://hbr.org/1997/05/the-it-system-that-couldnt-deliver/ar/1 (in the guise of providing advice to a CIO, this helps to show the importance of focusing on business value)

Treacy, M and Wiersema, F (1993) Customer intimacy and other disciplines, *Harvard Business Review*, January–February, pp 84–93, http://hbr.org/1993/01/customer-intimacy-and-other-value-disciplines/ar/1 (provides more information on the implications of a company's choice of source of value)

Ullah, P (2011) *Collaborative Leadership in Financial Services*, Gower, Aldershot (the book's focus is on technologists within capital markets, but it is of wider interest as a source of tools on working collaboratively to succeed; informed by research into what makes a project successful, it emphasizes the difference real clarity on the desired outcome makes for a project's chance of success: only 3 per cent of projects that succeeded reported unclear goals and outcomes, compared to 41 per cent of projects that failed (p 171))

Yukl, G (2012) *Leadership in Organizations*, 8th edn, Prentice Hall, Upper Saddle River, NJ (this contains a number of case studies as well as theory around managerial effectiveness)

Yukl, G and Tracey, JB (1992) Consequences of influence tactics used with subordinates, peers, and the boss, *Journal of Applied Psychology*, 77 (4), pp 525–35 (the research cited in this chapter that shows that 'inspirational appeal' is most effective at gaining commitment laterally or down the organization is set out here)

Context, climate and culture

17

ANDY WILKINS AND KATE STUART-COX

Introduction

One of the key reasons for projects not realizing their full potential is that context, culture and climate are often all but ignored. This chapter starts with trying to unravel some of the muddle between the concepts and so provide business analysts with a productive way forward.

Many technically trained people tend to think that the only important stuff is the 'hard' stuff, and they tend to dismiss the 'soft' stuff as unimportant, unnecessary and at best elusive. The other 'get out of jail free card' to deflect from having to do anything is that context, climate and culture are the remit of senior management, human resources (HR) or organizational development (OD) and are not their business. However, it is the 'hard stuff' that is easy and the 'soft stuff' that is hard. Both are clearly needed, but we find that more attention needs to be paid to the 'soft stuff' once a minimal level of 'hard' resources is available.

Business analysts need to be thinking and conceptualizing themselves on a different basis if they or the profession want to credibly help in the leadership for change space. We have used the International Council of Management Consulting Institutes (ICMCI) Common Body of Knowledge as a reference point and lens for business analysis work in the field of consulting. Specifically, business analysis is seen as towards low in consulting competence, breadth of managerial/organizational competence, and depth of specialist technical/professional competence (ICMCI, 2013).

The aim of this chapter is to help you grow in consulting and managerial/organization competence. It will begin to help you be more ready, willing and able to pay attention to the 'soft stuff' of context, climate and culture, which often by the way only requires no appreciable resources except awareness, attention and thoughtfulness. 'The bulk of what we do to cultivate this creative, passionate workforce costs nothing' (Think with Google, 2012).

FIGURE 17.1 Two key aspects to context

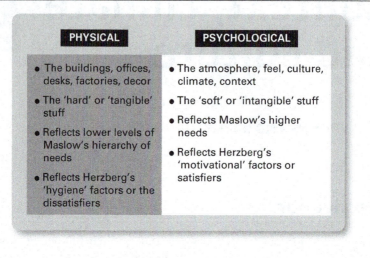

PHYSICAL

- The buildings, offices, desks, factories, decor
- The 'hard' or 'tangible' stuff
- Reflects lower levels of Maslow's hierarchy of needs
- Reflects Herzberg's 'hygiene' factors or the dissatisfiers

PSYCHOLOGICAL

- The atmosphere, feel, culture, climate, context
- The 'soft' or 'intangible' stuff
- Reflects Maslow's higher needs
- Reflects Herzberg's 'motivational' factors or satisfiers

Context, culture and climate

When we refer to the terms 'context', 'culture' and 'climate', there are many conceptions that come to mind, and in this chapter we propose a productive way of viewing these terms. Any context can be seen to include both physical and psychological aspects.

From the work of Frederick Herzberg (1987), we know that the physical context (buildings, offices, decor) is a hygiene factor. This means that the physical spaces in which we work need to be good enough, and if they aren't it can lead to dissatisfaction. However, a fabulous physical environment does not do much to stimulate us.

Research also suggests that people cost 8 to 10 times more than the physical accommodation and that people are infinitely more valuable. This means that, once the physical conditions are acceptable, there is much more to be gained by addressing the psychological aspects of the context that affect people at work – the culture and climate.

However, quite often in everyday organization jargon, the concepts of 'climate' and 'culture' are used synonymously. 'Climate', like 'culture', is often used as a fluffy catch-all word to cover anything and everything that is elusive and/or 'soft'. However, climate is different to culture; and, whether you believe in gravity or not, if you step out of a second-floor window you will hit the ground. Similarly, whether you believe in climate or not, it is either helping or hindering social ('soft') and economic ('hard') results in your organization.

FIGURE 17.2 Climate and culture

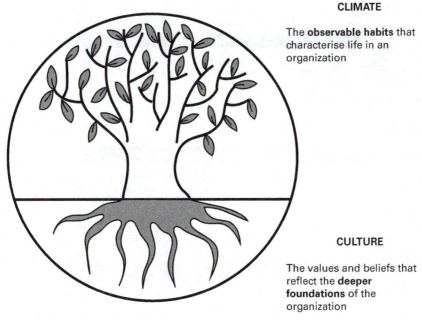

CLIMATE

The **observable habits** that characterise life in an organization

CULTURE

The values and beliefs that reflect the **deeper foundations** of the organization

Adapted from Ekvall (1996).

There are three distinctions between climate and culture that it is really useful to understand:

1 Culture is a broader concept, which, if you need to understand it, means you will need to look at the entire organization. If you focus on climate it is much more situational and so you can use individuals and their perceptions of a group or division or other units of analysis. Climate is scalable.

2 Culture tends to be relatively descriptive, meaning that one culture and its attendant assumptions and values are no better or worse than others, whereas climate is more normative, meaning that we are looking for environments that are better for certain things. Climate is measurable.

3 Climate is distinct from culture in that it is more easily observable and more amenable to improvement efforts. Climate is changeable.

As a result, we believe it is far more useful to work on climate than culture. Indeed, it has been suggested that, even when successful, cultural interventions can take nine years or more to implement and embed, while climate improvements can be implemented and measured within seconds. It is often easier to kill a company and start afresh rather than try to change the culture!

FIGURE 17.3 Climate as an intervening variable

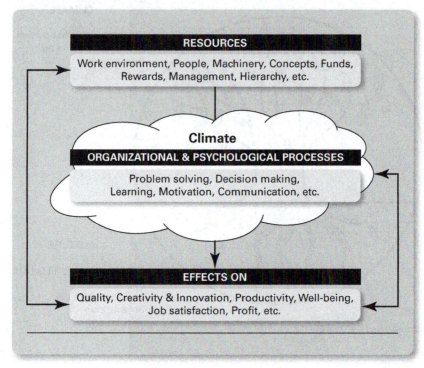

Adapted from Ekvall, Swedish council for management and work life issues, 1991.

Thus a climate is observed behaviours or habits, and the term 'climate' is borrowed from the world of weather to help demonstrate that climate is situational in the sense that, as with the weather, it can be different in different locations. For example, we can walk into one meeting with a dark, unproductive climate and walk out of that meeting into another where there is a sunny, productive climate.

The good news is that, because it is situational, we can, if we choose to attend to it, do a lot to influence our workplace climate.

Climate and its impact on your work

The outputs of an organization are dependent on its climate, and the outputs of a business analyst are dependent on the climates you encounter as well as the climate you create around yourself. Intuitively you already know this to be true – of course there will be a correlation between the climate and business success!

Think back over your career to the work situation that provided the most satisfying working environment for you. Now, contrast that one to the opposite – the one that provided the least satisfying working environment. You are probably instantly able to see that your personal enthusiasm and the level of your creativity paralleled the work environment. But what dimensions of the environment do you think were most important? And if you wanted to improve the working climate what specifically would you do?

Climate is an intervening variable, which has the power to influence processes such as communications, problem solving, decision making, learning and motivation. Organizations use resources such as people, money, buildings and equipment in their processes and operations. These operations have different effects at different levels of abstraction, such as:

- high or low job satisfaction among employees;
- high-quality or low-quality products and services;
- radically new products or incremental improvements in the existing ones;
- commercial profit or loss.

Climate has an important influence on organizational outcomes, but the effects in turn influence both resources and the climate itself. Therefore organizational climate has much to offer business analysts in terms of its ability to help explain the behaviour of people in the workplace.

FIGURE 17.4 Nine dimensions of climate that influence people

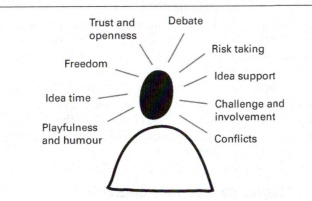

The nine dimensions of climate

So, while climate is important, it is also often poorly understood, so let's look at the dimensions of climate. Each of the following questions assesses one of the nine dimensions of the climate. Although the full questionnaire, called the Situational Outlook Questionnaire (SOQ), is far more complete and accurate, thinking about these questions could be helpful. As you read each question, consider how your team, project or organization might answer it on a scale of 1 (a little) to 5 (a lot):

1 *Challenge*. How challenged, how emotionally involved and how committed are we to the work?

2 *Freedom*. How free are we to decide how to do my job?

3 *Idea time*. Do we have time to think things through before having to act?

4 *Idea support*. Do we have a few resources to give new ideas a try?

5 *Trust and openness*. Do people feel safe in speaking their minds and openly offering different points of view?

6 *Playfulness and humour*. How relaxed is our workplace – is it OK to have fun?

7 *Conflicts*. To what degree do people engage in interpersonal conflict or 'warfare'?

8 *Debates*. To what degree do people engage in lively debates about the issues?

9 *Risk taking*. Is it OK to fail when trying new things?

How to influence climate

One of the risks of context, climate and culture being in the 'organization' part of this book is that you might be thinking that you have a 'get out of jail free card' not to have to think about climate because it is an organizational issue and not something you can do anything about. However, since climate is local and situational, it is not just the remit of your corporate HR or OD department or CEO; it is something you need to put on your agenda if you are really serious about wanting to be seen to be 'leading change' or 'turning strategic goals and visions into reality while adding value'.

So what can you do personally to help create a healthy climate? The following outlines five general strategies that can be taken to help establish and improve each of the climate dimensions.

General strategies to promote challenge and involvement

1 Take time to collaboratively establish goals.

2 Celebrate the accomplishment of key milestones.

3 Develop and maintain a shared set of values or norms.

4 Create ways for people to participate.

5 Ensure the use of fair process.

General strategies to promote freedom

1 Ensure that outcomes (projects, deliverables or delegated tasks) are well defined, but let individuals develop their own means for obtaining them.

2 Provide clear structures that enable people to work within boundaries in an autonomous and creative way.

3 Reward people who take initiatives.

4 Make resources readily available (eg people, time, equipment, finances).

5 Share power and decision making where possible.

General strategies for promoting trust and openness

1 Establish and reinforce 'norms' (or agreed guidelines and practices) for operating together.

2 Involve the group in some activities that help the people to get to know each other better.

3 Be clear about expectations from colleagues.

4 Bring to the surface the often hidden aspects such as assumptions, beliefs, values and personality type that influence working together.

5 Do what you say you will do (DWYSYWD).

General strategies for promoting idea time

1 Convene special-topic working sessions.

2 Devote some time during each team meeting to exploring one new idea.

3 Get really clear on the top priorities – the wildly important goals.

4 Get skilled in facilitative leadership and creative problem solving or use someone in meetings who is (using creative problem solving doubles outputs and halves the time).

5 Build some slack into projects.

General strategies for promoting playfulness and humour

1 Have designated places for sharing jokes, funny stories, etc and display significant personal artefacts: personalize your workplace.

2 Encourage some wild and silly thinking.

3 Reinforce the guidelines for divergent thinking; particularly defer judgement and allow freewheeling.

4 Use cartoons and visuals to convey data humorously.

5 Get skilled in facilitative leadership and creative problem solving or use someone in meetings who is (people who use creative problem solving smile and laugh more than twice as often).

General strategies for reducing conflict

1 Identify common goals and expectations among people who are experiencing tension.

2 Take some time to do some role playing, socio-drama, exaggeration and caricature to help people see the effects of conflict.

3 Bring to the surface the source of tensions.

4 Have clear policies and strategies to deal with personal complaints, difficulties and conflicts, especially ways of signalling tensions.

5 Be crystal clear about roles, who makes key decisions and how they are made.

General strategies for promoting idea support

1 Develop a deliberate and professional way for hearing and responding to ideas using a tool like Advantages, Limitations, Uniques, Overcoming (ALUO).

2 Keep the criticism of ideas focused on the idea, not the person.

3 Get skilled in facilitative leadership and creative problem solving or use someone in meetings who is (people who use creative problem solving provide over twice as much verbal support and 10 times less verbal criticism) (Firestien and McCowan, 1988).

4 Establish peer-based seed programmes, funds or resources for special projects and ideas.

5 Find ways to collaborate and share ideas and information.

General strategies for promoting debate

1 Actively encourage people to take and share different viewpoints and perspectives.

2 Separate generating from focusing and follow the guidelines whenever possible.

3 Model active listening; generously seek the whole thought being sent before responding.

4 Be open to different points of view and willing to exchange your opinion and ideas on them.

5 Value diversity; use cross-functional and cross-cultural teams, and hold frequent organizational conferences on key thematic issues.

General strategies for promoting risk taking

1 Reinforce the importance of learning from mistakes.
2 Avoid judging your ideas before they are put forward.
3 Develop a productive working relationship with a sponsor for change to help provide 'air cover'.
4 Provide 'stretch' goals of projects and tasks.
5 Provide simulations or opportunities to enable the floating of new and riskier ideas.

To conclude

In our work with clients we consistently find that the view of the workplace climate is related to the level in the organization of the rater. The higher up the organization, the better the climate appears to be. It is a little like flying over London at 30,000 feet. From that height it looks just fine, but at street level you begin to notice the challenges, and it is at the street level that work gets done.

As you think about how to improve your climate, be sure to improve the foundation, beginning at the street level. One of the most powerful aspects of attending to your work climate is obtaining deliberate insights about something that has a profound effect on those you work with as well as business results.

About the authors

Andy Wilkins and Kate Stuart-Cox are founding partners of Perspectiv. Andy is also an honorary senior visiting fellow at Cass Business School.

References and further reading

Akkermans, HJL, Isaksen, SG and Isaksen, EJ (2008) *Leadership for Innovation: A global climate survey – a CRU technical report*, Creativity Research Unit, Creative Problem Solving Group, Buffalo, NY

Davis, T *et al* (2001) *Innovation and Growth Survey*, PricewaterhouseCoopers, London

Ekvall, G (1987) The climate metaphor in organizational theory, in *Advances in Organizational Psychology: An international review*, ed BM Bass and PJD Drenth, pp 177–90, Sage, Beverly Hills, CA

Ekvall, G (1996) Organizational climate for creativity and innovation, *European Journal of Work and Organizational Psychology*, 5 (1), 105–23

Firestien, RL and McCowan, RJ (1988) Creative problem solving and communication behaviors in small groups, *Creativity Research Journal*, 1, pp 106–14

Herzberg, FI (1987) One more time: how do you motivate employees?, *Harvard Business Review*, 65 (5), September–October, pp 109–20

International Council of Management Consulting Institutes (ICMCI) [accessed 20 January 2013] Common Body of Knowledge [Online] http://www.icmci.org/download/?id=6972570

Isaksen, SG (2007) The climate for transformation: lessons for leaders, *Creativity and Innovation Management*, 16, pp 3–15

Isaksen, SG (2007) The Situational Outlook Questionnaire: assessing the context for change, *Psychological Reports*, 100, pp 455–66

Isaksen, SG and Akkermans, HJ (2007) *An Introduction to Climate*, Creative Problem Solving Group, New York

Isaksen, SG and Akkermans, HJ (2011) The creative climate: a leadership lever for innovation, *Journal of Creative Behavior*, 45 (3), September, pp 161–87

Isaksen, SG, Dorval, KB and Treffinger, DJ (2011) *Creative Approaches to Problem Solving*, Sage, Thousand Oaks, CA

Isaksen, SG and Tidd, J (2006) *Meeting the Innovation Challenge: Leadership for transformation and growth*, Wiley, Chichester

Schneider, B, Brief, AP and Guzzo, RA (1996) Creating a climate and culture for sustainable organizational change, *Organizational Dynamics*, 24, pp 7–19

Think with Google (2012) [accessed 25 January 2013] Passion not perks, http://www.thinkwithgoogle.com/quarterly/people/laszlo-bock-people-ops.html

Global working and virtual teams

PENNY PULLAN

What do we mean by global working and virtual teams? Why are virtual teams becoming ubiquitous? What are the specific challenges of global working and virtual teams and what opportunities do they present us with? This chapter addresses these and other questions about how business analysts can best deal with global working and virtual teams, and covers some practical techniques to make the most of this new way of working.

What do we mean by global working and virtual teams?

In this chapter, we define virtual teams as any team where at least one team member is working apart from the others (Settle-Murphy, 2013). Global working involves virtual teams whose members span different countries, cultures and time zones. Global business analysis work usually involves global projects.

Why global projects and virtual teams?

> While businesses and companies are increasingly multinational we are more frequently facing projects with participants representing various cultures, having different native languages, working in different time zones and locations. In other words, this is the world of global projects. Global projects are practically creeping into the life of companies of all sizes from small enterprises to the biggest leading players.
>
> (Kähkönen, 2010)

People who want to provide leadership for change in the 21st century are likely to need skills in working as part of virtual teams and as part of global projects. Strong global trends are driving the growth of virtual working, including:

- outsourcing and offshoring;
- globalization;
- home working and telecommuting;
- spending cuts;
- higher fuel prices.

Many workers who wouldn't consider themselves telecommuters work from home at least one day a week, if not more. Even volcanic ash clouds and threats of epidemics have played their part! Organizations are focusing on the need to reduce the costs of travel, as well as the time taken travelling, carbon emissions produced and the inconvenience involved. Technological advances have made it easier and cheaper than ever before to collaborate virtually, with voice, screen and video sharing now available at little or no cost.

Challenges and opportunities

Virtual working requires specific ways of working to engage stakeholders, especially on global projects. People engaged in such projects need to understand and work with differences in culture, language, location and time zones. These bring challenges, from straightforward ones, such as finding times when everyone is able to meet, to complex ones, such as building trust remotely. They can also bring opportunities, ranging from gaining access to the best people in the world regardless of location, working around the clock on projects by 'following the sun', to reduced pollution, travel and, sometimes, labour costs.

Success does not come from just applying whatever works in the face-to-face world to virtual teams. In particular, it can be very difficult to create a culture of openness, trust and mutual support in a virtual team. While face-to-face meetings have the benefit of body language to support communication, this is usually missing or, at best, diluted in virtual teams. It's very easy for team members to become disengaged and frustrated, often silently tuning out without others noticing.

Many other factors come into play when change happens through global projects and programmes. These include:

- diverse locations in which stakeholders and the project team are based;
- diverse country cultures;
- diverse mother tongues;
- diverse time zones;
- diverse technologies, especially when working across more than one organization;

- diverse organizations involved, which can themselves have very different cultures and ways of working.

Good virtual collaboration technology alone isn't the answer to all these factors. You need specialized skills and competencies to make global working and virtual teams work well. We'll touch on these throughout the rest of this chapter.

Cross-cultural skills

We need a certain amount of humility and a sense of humour to discover cultures other than our own; a readiness to enter a room in the dark and stumble over unfamiliar furniture until the pain in our shins reminds us where things are.

(Trompenaars, 1993)

Trompenaars's advice applies to business analysts working across different organizational and country cultures. They need to understand how attitudes, beliefs, behavioural norms, basic assumptions and values can influence project stakeholders. Then they can learn how to adapt their own style to the different cultures involved.

A typical example of this is a UK-based business analyst working in a virtual team with an IT development team based in Bangalore, India. Here, it's important for the UK-based business analyst to be aware of the culture of face saving that is strong across much of Asia and the Middle East. I know of many such UK analysts who have asked the direct question 'Did you understand that?' and received the answer 'Yes.' However, as the work progressed, it became clear that this wasn't the case. The UK analyst would have done better to check understanding by asking open questions about how the developer would proceed, preferably in a one-to-one situation. Of course, this is assuming the cultural stereotype applies to everyone, as each person is an individual. Nevertheless, I find that the stereotypes can be useful until I get to know individuals and their own preferences.

Use of appropriate technology

There has been such a proliferation of new technologies that many think that technology alone will enable virtual teams and global working. However, technology is just one of many factors. What is more important is choosing and using the appropriate technology to support the work people are trying to do together as well as their communication preferences. Think of the choice between travelling to the office to use your company's top-of-the-range video suite for a 6 am meeting and taking the meeting from your home as a conference call. Which would you prefer? I know what my preference would be!

FIGURE 18.1 The time and place grid, populated with some of the technologies that support each quadrant

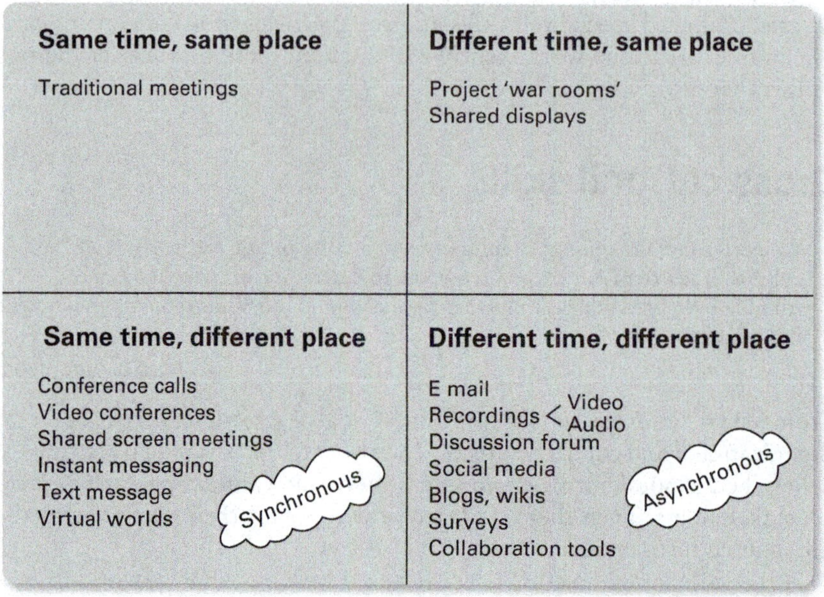

<table>
<tr>
<td>

Same time, same place

Traditional meetings

</td>
<td>

Different time, same place

Project 'war rooms'
Shared displays

</td>
</tr>
<tr>
<td>

Same time, different place

Conference calls
Video conferences
Shared screen meetings
Instant messaging
Text message
Virtual worlds

Synchronous

</td>
<td>

Different time, different place

E mail
Recordings < Video / Audio
Discussion forum
Social media
Blogs, wikis
Surveys
Collaboration tools

Asynchronous

</td>
</tr>
</table>

Figure 18.1 shows the huge range of technologies available to support virtual working, and the list is growing all the time. Virtual technologies fall into both of the lower two quadrants – same time, different place (synchronous) and different time, different place (asynchronous). While people often think of audio- or videoconferencing or shared screens for virtual working, not all interactions in virtual teams need to be synchronous, especially when the team is spread across the world in a variety of time zones. There is a whole range of technologies that support asynchronous interaction, and business analysts will find these complement same-time interactions very well. Social media, for example, have been used to build relationships across virtual teams as well as share information outside project meetings (Harrin, 2010). Surveys can be useful for gathering initial requirements, and there are other asynchronous collaboration tools to support idea generation and modelling.

Effective virtual teams

Setting up

The initial kick-off meeting of a project is a good time to set up a virtual team for success. During this kick-off, it is important to set a clear vision for the work to be done and agree the goals that need to be achieved. The role of each team member needs to be articulated clearly and agreed, so everyone knows who is doing what.

At this early stage, it's important for the team to agree how they will work together, covering both the processes that they will follow and the ground rules that will govern how they interact and behave with each other. Such ground rules might include simple things, such as working hours in each country and whether it is acceptable to call people after office hours, as well as more complex issues, such as decision-making processes and how problems will be dealt with.

If it is at all possible, I recommend bringing a virtual team together face to face for this initial kick-off meeting. This gives people the chance to get to know each other and build up trust. When tough times come and challenges emerge later in the project, this trust will be invaluable.

Keeping people participating

In a virtual team, it's all too easy for team members to get caught up with local work or whatever is happening locally, losing focus on their virtual work. After all, by being remote, a virtual project is 'out of sight' and can too easily become 'out of mind'. A facilitative leadership style that takes into account each team member's situation, as promoted throughout this book, works much better than telling people what to do.

To sustain participation, ensure that there is a 'level playing field' as far as possible in your virtual team. An example of this is varying the times of meetings so that everyone has some meetings that are convenient for them, even if others need to work outside office hours. This is a way of sharing the pain so that everyone in the team is 'in it together'.

Consider relationships across the team. Business analysis works at its best when business analysts have good relationships with their stakeholders. In virtual teams, it's best, in addition to meetings, to arrange one-to-one calls with people where you need to build up and retain trust. Think too about asynchronous ways of keeping in touch. Would a team wiki or collaboration tool help to keep people participating?

Running effective virtual meetings

Before

Virtual meetings need more preparation than face-to-face meetings, in order to command the team's full attention. In addition to the crucial meeting start-up steps described fully in Chapter 7 and shown in Figure 7.1, there are additional steps in preparation for effective virtual meetings:

- *Choose which technology you will use* to support the purpose of the meeting. Will everyone have access? If not, consider reverting to simpler technology that everyone can use.

- *Test the technology before the meeting* and have a back-up plan to which you can revert in case it does not work for everyone. An example is having a pack of slides to send to participants by e-mail in case the shared screen application doesn't work for everyone.

- *Share the jobs around the team.* It's vitally important to keep meeting participants engaged. A good way of doing this is to share the jobs around the team. This could mean that different people run different parts of the meeting or take roles such as timekeeper or action-scribe.

- *Consider how to include a visual element* in your meeting. It's so tempting for participants to divert to reading e-mail or doing other work, especially if there is nothing for them to look at. To overcome this, make your meeting as visually interesting as you can. Share business models or even hand-drawn graphics, just as you would use a whiteboard in a face-to-face meeting.

- *Prepare a team photo map*, with photos of each team member imposed on a map, showing everyone's location and time zone. This can really help participants relate the disembodied voices of the virtual team to real people and remember the time differences involved.

- *Plan to use narrative* to keep people interested. Thorpe (2008) has shown that remote participants are more likely to stay engaged and retain information afterwards when storytelling styles are used rather than sharing lists.

During

Start up your meeting with the meeting start-up steps shown in Figure 7.1 and discussed in Chapter 7. The 'how we work together' ground rules are particularly important for successful virtual meetings, and you can build on those you developed when setting up the team. Some typical ground rules might include:

- *Say your name before making any contribution.* This feels very strange at first, but is really important to ensure that everyone knows who is speaking. After a few minutes, people will get used to it and say their name naturally. Without it, only those familiar with people's voices will know who is speaking.

- *Mute your audio if you are not speaking.* This works well if the audio quality is poor or compromised by background noise. While it reduces noise and interruptions, it also cuts down on the speed with which people can contribute, so only use it if you need to.

Throughout your meeting, focus on facilitating collaboration, engaging people and working together to meet the objectives you have agreed.

In addition to using visuals and a narrative style described earlier, polling is an effective technique to keep people engaged. Let people know in advance that you will be asking them for their input and views throughout the meeting. This makes it much more likely that they will keep focused, as they never know when they could be asked for their input.

I usually plan for virtual meetings to last no more than an hour, or at most 90 minutes. Beyond this, it becomes difficult to keep people engaged.

Before the end of the meeting, recap the actions that have been agreed and explain how these will be followed up. Also review the session. What went well? What would make it even better next time? If you use the results of these reviews for the future, meetings will improve over time.

After

It does seem to be more difficult to get people to take action after virtual meetings compared to face-to-face meetings. Perhaps participants feel less commitment to their virtual colleagues, or perhaps trust is missing. As lack of action can destroy what fragile trust already exists, this can become a vicious circle.

To make actions more likely to stick, ensure that they are documented clearly in the meeting and then followed up carefully afterwards. Ensure that everyone is clear on what they need to do and that they feel committed to carrying out their actions. It might be that some actions need amending. After all, an imperfect action that gets done is far better than a perfect action that never happens!

Conclusion

Global projects and virtual teams are becoming commonplace in business analysis work. With a little preparation and a lot of understanding, business analysts can work effectively when they can't be face to face. A facilitative leadership style is effective, taking into account the needs of each person in the virtual team.

About the author

Penny Pullan is the co-editor of this book and hosts the annual Virtual Working Summit: www.virtualworkingsummit.com

Further reading and references

Binder, J (2007) *Global Project Management: Communication, collaboration and management across borders*, Gower, Aldershot

Harrin, E (2010) *Social Media for Project Managers*, Project Management Institute, Newtown Square, PA

Kähkönen, K (2010) The world of global projects, *Project Perspectives* (International Project Management Association), **XXXII**, p 3

Lipnack, J and Stamps, J (2010) *Leading Virtual Teams*, Harvard Business School Publishing, Boston, MA

Pullan, P (2013) Managing people in virtual project organizations, in *The Gower Handbook of People in Project Management*, ed D Lock and L Scott, Gower, Aldershot

Settle-Murphy, N (2013) *Leading Effective Virtual Teams*, CRC Press, Boca Raton, FL

Thorpe, S (2008) Enhancing the effectiveness of online groups: an investigation of storytelling in the facilitation of online groups, PhD thesis, Auckland University of Technology, Auckland

Trompenaars, F (1993) *Riding the Waves of Culture: Understanding cultural diversity in business*, Nicholas Brealey, London

Systems thinking for business analysts leading change

EMMA LANGMAN

Systems thinking is a vast topic. While many proclaim to be experts, I concur with CW Churchman (1969), who said 'There are no experts in the systems approach.'

As a business analyst, you already think in systems. You just may not know that this is what you do. In fact, you could do this when you were just five years old; you just didn't know the jargon. What questions did you ask? Things like 'How does water come out of this tap?' and 'Why is the sky blue?' If you have noticed that today's problems are often caused by yesterday's solutions (Ackoff and Addison, 2006) then you can think in systems. And if you've ever exclaimed in frustration that this project is facing the same issues that your organization has faced before then you are ready to learn how systems thinking can help.

My aim in this chapter is to provide a broad overview of systems thinking and explain its importance to the business analyst who is serious about leading change. After looking at some key concepts, I will share some systems thinking approaches. There are many more and much to learn, but I hope that this chapter will at least provide a launchpad for further explorations.

Writing a chapter about systems thinking is a bit like writing about how to surf. It's actually something you really learn with practice. I hope to give you enough confidence to pull on your metaphorical wetsuit, grab a metaphorical surfboard and dive in! Good luck, and enjoy the journey.

What is systems thinking?

I said that systems thinking is a vast topic. I lied. It is virtually infinite in the areas that it touches and the thinking that it enables. Those people involved in systems thinking quite quickly find themselves pondering deeply philosophical and even spiritual dimensions of our existence as human beings on this planet. We will not be exploring this in detail in this chapter, but you might find Ackoff's discussion about the difference between the deterministic Machine Age (with its Machine Age God) and the emergence of the Systems Age of interest as additional reading. Certainly, *Creating the Corporate Future* (Ackoff, 1981) is an extremely relevant read for business analysts leading change.

Are there different types of systems thinking?

Systems thinking tells us that everything is connected to everything else. However, many people first come to the subject through practical work like process modelling, process improvement, lean or Six Sigma. These are increasingly referred to as 'linear systems thinking' methods. What people mean by 'linear systems thinking' is that there is a clear goal and that systems thinking can help us to improve iteratively, to get towards that goal. For example, if I want to reduce the cycle time to deliver a particular piece of work (report, component, etc), then one of these techniques might be appropriate. If business analysts can help their organization to overcome 'silo thinking' and evaluating 'value' and 'non-value' work using these methods, this can lead to significant improvements at an operational and project level. However, these techniques are not generally appropriate for looking at large-scale organizational or societal change.

The second type of systems thinking methodologies tries to understand, manage and 'lead' very large and complex systems. These work where defining the problem is part of the problem. Some of these models help create clarity, transparency and control, such as Beer's viable systems model (Beer, 1979, 1981). Others focus on the ideas of emergence and the difficulty that arises with 'soft systems' and the multiple perspectives held by human beings (Checkland, 1981). These approaches are particularly useful when looking at large-scale change or 'wicked and messy' problems where there is no known or knowable answer (such as alcohol misuse, crime, or how to get people to look after their health). You may remember *Nudge* (Sunstein and Thaler, 2008) being a major hit some years ago with government policy makers. Systems thinking is older, richer and deeper than the concept of 'nudge', but you may already be getting a clear understanding of why there isn't an easy-to-read 'airport book' about it!

For business analysts, these ideas are very important. We are no longer in the world of slow-changing economic and societal trends. Companies, public sector organizations and charities can no longer get by if they stagnate or 'continuously improve'. The challenges thrown at today's business analyst are now rarely 'Analyse this specific problem and recommend a

FIGURE 19.1 Business analysts need to work with different stakeholder views

solution', but something bigger and less defined like 'Work out how we cut costs by at least 10 per cent in a year, while still improving customer service.' The key tools of the soft systems approach (root definitions and rich pictures) are an essential prerequisite, getting much more clarity on 'what needs to be done' before attempting to work out 'how to do it'. The 'soft' part of the system is the fact that we are talking about 'mental models'. The systems in question are not the prison itself (which we can build and touch) (see Figure 19.1), but our opinions, views and 'paradigm' about what that system is about.

Understand a little about your system before you start

It is really important to be clear, as a business analyst, whether you are planning an intervention in a 'closed' or 'open' system. According to Ludwig von Bertalanffy (revered in systems thinking circles as the father of open systems theory), organizations are 'open' systems. Essentially, what this means is that they do not operate like machines, based on routine, repetitive and predetermined tasks. Rather, they are constantly interacting with the environment in which they find themselves. In other words, the metaphors of biology and self-organization are more relevant to you, as a change agent, than the ideas of physics and well-oiled, predictable interactions. You can read more about von Bertalanffy in Robert Flood's accessible book *Rethinking the Fifth Discipline* (1999).

It is essential to know if you are working with a 'closed' or 'open' system in order to avoid costly and potentially dangerous mistakes. For example, if we imagine that the work of social services is a 'closed' system, we could apply lean or other 'linear systems thinking' approaches to speed up the processes. We could easily (for example) speed up the process for taking children into care. That's simple. What is much more difficult is working out which children are at sufficient risk of abuse or neglect to require them to be taken into care. For that kind of issue we need to understand multiple perspectives, risk and complexity. The higher the risk, the more important it is to look at a situation from all angles.

Whenever we are working in systems thinking, it is essential to define the boundaries of the system of interest. There are actually *no* systems in the world. Or, to put it another way, there are *infinite* systems. They only exist when we choose to place a boundary around a real (hard) system, or our model of our thinking about a system (soft).

Recognize that most systems thinking occurs in people's heads

When using soft systems we are *never* drawing a model of a system. Rather, we are attempting to represent people's mental models (or thinking) about the system. This is a clear distinction between 'soft' and 'hard' systems thinking. It's a bit like saying 'There is no such thing as reality, only people's perceptions of reality.' Another way of putting it is that 'The map is not the territory.' No matter how good the map is, it is only our understanding of the territory it covers; it is not the territory itself. However, if the business analyst is to deal successfully with complex and challenging organizational change, this type of mental agility is essential in this day and age.

Define the boundary of your system of interest

Whether dealing with hard (real) or soft systems (models of thinking about systems) it is important to draw some kind of 'boundary' around that system. Systems are effectively defined by their boundaries and their purpose (whether this is designed or emergent). For business analysts, this is a key issue.

Failure to be clear about the whole system leads to all kinds of wasted investment – like building a school building in the Third World, but not thinking through the long-term details (like providing a teacher,

FIGURE 19.2 Even with a clear intended purpose in mind, a system may still create something else

books, curriculum, etc). One of the most extreme examples I have seen of too narrow a boundary on a system was an engineering company that built a large signal-controlled roundabout without an electricity supply to the lights. It can be a big mistake to draw the boundaries of a system too narrowly. Of course, care must also be taken not to make the system boundaries so wide that you are paralysed by the size of the task ahead of you. However, since a system can be understood only by its role in the system within which it belongs (the suprasystem) (Ackoff, 1981), we must always go 'out' before coming back 'in' again with our thinking.

Understand the purpose of the system

There are two key schools of thought about purpose. For those working in a 'hard systems' and 'closed system' frame of mind, life is simple. Define the purpose (call it a vision, mission, etc) and then align everyone through perfect processes, to ensure that it is delivered. When it comes to delivering predetermined projects, this is obviously a key step. Methodologies like Prince 2 are predicated on a clear purpose, requirements, timescale, milestones and so on.

Unfortunately, most organizational challenges now are less clear cut. The business analyst must first analyse what the system (the organization) already does. This builds on Beer's (1979, 1981) concept of POSIWID (the purpose of a system is what it does). Now that the business analyst is expected to lead change, he or she must act more like an internal consultant. Rather than relying on mission statements and board-level PowerPoint presentations, you must be able to 'sniff out' the reality of what is going on within a team, department or organization.

Start to draw a model of how people think about the system

In order to be able to model people's thinking (or your own thinking) about the system, you can use some useful, scalable models. Two that are particularly helpful are: 1) systems dynamics archetypes; and 2) the viable systems model.

Systems dynamics

Similar to rich pictures, systems dynamics archetypes are simple diagrams that help us to diagnose and communicate what is happening in our project, team, organization or society. The 'archetypes' are blueprints of patterns of feedback that you are likely to see in the world. You can read more about this in Senge's classic *The Fifth Discipline* (1990).

In systems thinking, the terms 'positive feedback' and 'negative feedback' have very specific meanings and do not mean 'good' or 'bad'. Positive feedback means that the more I do something, the more I get of something else. Figure 19.3 gives a good example.

The way out of this unhealthy 'positive feedback' loop is simple (in theory!). One could decide not to worry about one's weight, or eat something healthier – or eat the chocolate but burn off the calories in the gym. This 'negative' feedback loop would then link to my 'positive' feedback loop. Indeed, one action (such as walking the dog) might have an impact in more than one area. If I were to walk more, I might feel less depressed *and* eat less chocolate *and* burn off more calories *and* thus reduce my weight. By drawing a simple archetype, it is easier to start to see where it is possible to intervene.

The 'shifting the burden' archetype is another wonderful pattern – about stopping cutting down trees long enough to 'sharpen the saw' (Covey, 1989). A typical work example is the use of agency staff as a result of rapid turnover in a call centre. This places additional demand on the learning and development department (to train up the temps), who pull help from their friends in recruitment, who then don't have time to recruit appropriate full-term staff. Meanwhile, the business analyst would like to do some work to solve the fundamental problem causing the high staff turnover (perhaps an

FIGURE 19.3 A classic 'positive feedback' loop with negative results

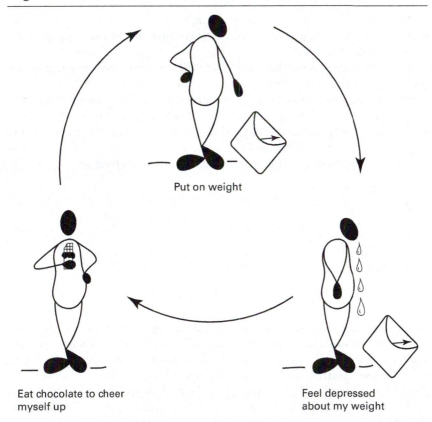

Put on weight

Eat chocolate to cheer
myself up

Feel depressed
about my weight

IT or other process issue), but can't, because none of the staff working in the call centre know the processes well enough to be able to help with the analysis that could drive the improvement. And, of course, the staff costs are also going through the roof!

An accessible primer for the business analyst looking to explore this part of systems thinking is *Thinking in Systems: A primer*, by Diana Wright and Donella Meadows (2009).

The viable systems model (VSM)

This model is a particularly powerful piece of the systems thinking toolkit (Beer 1979, 1981; Hoverstadt, 2008). Owing to its fractal nature, it can be applied to an individual, project, team, department, organization or even entire nation (as Stafford Beer did in Chile).

The VSM is a key element of the area of systems thinking that is known as cybernetics. Norbert Wiener defined cybernetics as 'The science of communication and control in the animal and the machine' (Wiener, 1948). This has more recently been interpreted as 'the science of effective organization'.

While the use of the word 'control' might seem to suggest a 'closed system' view of the world, cybernetics is very clear that it exists in an open system – indeed an infinite open system.

Upon first sight, the VSM is a horrifically complicated and offputting model. However, with a little practice, it is can become an extremely useful item of the business analyst's armoury. I have chosen the unusual step of *not* reproducing a picture of this famous image here, for the very reason that it can be offputting. Instead, I'd like you to imagine five mini-systems that work together at a human level and can 'grow' to be useful even when imagining them acting on the world stage. These are known as:

1 operations;
2 coordination;
3 control;
4 intelligence;
5 policy.

Operations

When business analysts are designing teams, you might think of each person as an operational unit within System 1. Nowadays, business analysts are often asked to be involved in organizational redesign or organizational effectiveness. Restructuring without an appropriate theoretical model like the VSM is little more than rearranging the deckchairs on the *Titanic*.

Whenever you are asked to be part of these conversations, bear in mind the UK train system. If your train is late, you complain to the train operating company, which gives you a refund and then seeks to blame the rolling stock company or Network Rail. This 'horizontal' model of railways is likely to be changed to a 'vertical' model with track, stock and operations in one area being under one franchise. Of course, this will lead to a different set of interactions and different arguments.

The way that you organize your operational units affects everything else. When you design an operational system, think at length about how 'cutting the operations' in different ways (by technology or geography, for example) could have unintended consequences.

Coordination

Just as with a railway network, every project and organization needs some type of clear coordination. To see why this is so important, simply imagine a railway without a timetable. It wouldn't be very effective, would it? While coordination isn't the most exciting concept, it is nevertheless absolutely key to a smoothly running system.

Control

The local control of the operational system (and its coordination) is the job of System 3. This is all about making sure that everyone is clear about what they are supposed to be doing, and has the resources to do it. This is where day-to-day HR and finance processes fit. It is important that these are clear and well designed, but not so rigid that, when something comes along in the wider system, the organization cannot respond.

Cybernetics enables work and resources to be shared out appropriately. This area of control is a key part of good supervision and management. Scholtes (1997) gives some fantastic advice about how this can be done much better than the traditional 'appraisal'.

Intelligence

The fourth 'system' is the 'eyes and ears' of a country, organization, department or team. This is about seeing what might be coming over the horizon. Just as with our surfer at the start of this chapter, it really is only possible for the business analyst to be fully effective when he or she is looking at what the future challenges to the project or organization might be – not just what is visible now.

This area can often be overlooked, particularly during tough financial times. Being a business analyst who is working hard on helping your organization to come up with a more efficient carburettor is all very well, until your competitor produces a fuel injection system without you knowing about it (after Deming, 1994: 9–10). Successful projects, teams and organizations are always looking towards the future.

Policy

A large part of the job of System 5 is about the long-term ethics, values and policies of an organization. Rather like a modern-day monarch, when things are going well System 5 doesn't have to do much. Its main role is to make sure that there is a good balance between System 3 (day-to-day management) and System 4 (forward-looking activity, research, etc). If too much time and money go into System 4, then the organization may fold before the new ideas can get to market. On the other hand, if all the effort and focus are going to System 1 (through System 3) then we're back to being an excellent provider of defunct products or services. That can be the beginning of the death spiral.

Monitoring

In Patrick Hoverstadt's easily digestible book (2008) he describes 21 different 'pathologies' that organizations can get if they don't look at themselves through a systems thinking lens like the viable systems model. While most organizations have several of these 'pathologies' the top three

FIGURE 19.4 System 5 is essential to the long-term viability of the overall system

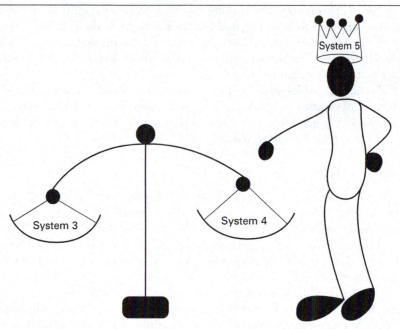

are: separation of resource from workload (bricks without straw); inadequate coordination; and 'the control dilemma'.

The control dilemma is where management are out of touch with what is happening 'on the ground'. They are also not looking over the horizon with System 4. When an external shock hits, something goes wrong in System 1. Then 'Management, fearing a loss of control of the situation, press the sub-systems for information and reports… operations [are] undermined by micro-management… prompting ever more micro-management' (Hoverstadt, 2008). This issue is also explained well by Joiner (1994) as the 'big cog and little cog' model. One of the key roles of business analysts today is surely that of helping senior management to understand and carry out the role of monitoring effectively, so that this situation can be avoided.

Designing your solution to absorb variety

Now that we are on the subject of monitoring, it is well worth taking a short meander into the wonderful world of variety, variation and data.

Even with 'linear' methodologies, such as lean, the new systems design will fail if it cannot manage the variety that is placed upon it. A great example of systems that don't help when there is high variety is that of

'Press 1 for *x*' telephone systems. Everything works fine as long as you have a standard enquiry or problem. The same is true in healthcare; hospitals sometimes have difficulty treating unusual illnesses outside standard 'patient pathways'. For more on this area of thinking (which is based on Ashby's law) you might like to read Weinberg (2001).

The practical implication of variety for the business analyst leading change is to consider how much variety you can afford to attenuate (absorb). Compare shopping in Lidl and Waitrose to see how the more variety you demand (eg different products), the better the overall customer service experience is likely to be, but the more costly it is to provide that service. It is important to design systems so that they can absorb appropriate levels of variety.

Reducing the variation in your processes

Variation is often confused with variety, but is a separate concept within systems thinking. Think about 'flow' of work through a team, water through a pipe, or customer calls into a contact centre. Traditional management approaches work on averages. Thus call centre metrics of target call durations are used to try to drive up productivity. This is not a good planning method, since there will be variety in the content of the calls, and variation in the number of calls coming in. Rather, the use of statistical process capability charts can revolutionize the effectiveness and efficiency of your team or department's work.

To read more about the problems with standard metrics, a good starting point is John Seddon's books (1992, 2003). You may also find the works of Dave Gaster (2006, 2010) of interest. His approach, known as Visualising Transformation™, is somewhat similar to the stables of lean and Seddon's Vanguard method, but also draws on soft systems methodology and other parts of systems thinking. The diagrams and pictures are particularly interesting if you are involved with data mining or business intelligence as part of your role.

For a fantastic, accessible introduction into the world of statistical process capability (SPC), I recommend Wheeler's *Understanding Variation: The key to managing chaos* (1994) and Scholtes's *The Leader's Handbook* (1997). The key point to notice about accessing systems thinking through the 'window' of variation is that the way that organizations look at data affects everything else too. By being clear about what data are telling them, business analysts can help their organizations avoid overreacting to 'common cause' variation (day-to-day wobbliness in data) and respond promptly to real signals that something is happening. This is worlds apart from the traditional approach to performance data of comparing 'this week' with 'last week' or 'the same week last year'!

If this chapter has inspired you to look at the 'non-linear' aspects of systems thinking, you may like to explore chaos theory, complexity and emergence. A good place to start is Dave Snowden's Cynefin model (2000, 2002) or his many YouTube videos. Another, brain-widening author that I highly recommend is Fritjof Capra, particularly *The Web of Life* (1996).

Final thoughts

Since everything is connected to everything else, it is quite difficult to suggest a 'right' place to start your journey with systems thinking. It also depends a good deal on your experience to date. However, if you follow this chapter's suggestions, it should help you to think through the system and the various issues, such as closed/open, soft/hard, variety/variation, purpose and boundaries.

This is a huge topic, and there really are no 'experts'. Jump in and give it a go with iteration, creativity, curiosity – and a joyful noticing of emergence. Wherever you are now, draw a 'systems boundary' around something that interests you and start trying out some of these methodologies and approaches as you continue in your quest to become ever more successful in leading change.

About the author

Emma Langman specializes in using systems thinking approaches for helping her clients to lead change through her company Progression Partnership Ltd: **www.progressionpartnership.com**

References and further reading

Ackoff, RL (1981) *Creating the Corporate Future: Plan or be planned for*, John Wiley & Sons, New York

Ackoff, RL and Addison, HJ (2006) *A Little Book of f-Laws: 13 common sins of management*, Triarchy Press, Axminster

Beer, S (1979) *The Heart of Enterprise*, John Wiley, London

Beer, S (1981) *Brain of the Firm*, 2nd edn, John Wiley, London

Capra, F (1996) *The Web of Life: A new synthesis of mind and matter*, HarperCollins, New York

Checkland, P (1981) *Systems Thinking, Systems Practice*, John Wiley, London

Churchman, CW (1969) *The Systems Approach*, Dell Publishing, New York

Covey, S (1989) *The Seven Habits of Highly Effective People*, Simon & Schuster, New York

Deming, WE (1994) *The New Economics for Industry, Government, Education*, 2nd edn, Massachusetts Institute of Technology, Boston, MA

Flood, RL (1999) *Rethinking the Fifth Discipline: Learning within the unknowable*, Routledge, London

Gaster, D (2006) *Quality or Politics? Achieving excellence in public service delivery*, Nisbet Media, Broadstone

Gaster, D (2010) *Visualising Transformation*, Word4Word, Evesham

Hoverstadt, P (2008) *The Fractal Organization: Creating sustainable organizations with the viable system model*, John Wiley, London

Joiner, BL (1994) *Fourth Generation Management: The new business consciousness*, McGraw-Hill Professional, New York

Scholtes, PR (1997) *The Leader's Handbook: Making things happen, getting things done*, McGraw-Hill, New York

Seddon, J (1992) *I Want You to Cheat! The unreasonable guide to service and quality in organisations*, Vanguard Consulting, Buckingham

Seddon, J (2003) *Freedom from Command and Control: A better way to make the work work*, Vanguard Consulting, Buckingham

Senge, P (1990) *The Fifth Discipline: The art and practice of the learning organization*, Doubleday, New York

Snowden, D (2000) Cynefin: a sense of time and space, the social ecology of knowledge management, in *Knowledge Horizons: The present and the promise of knowledge management*, ed C Despres and D Chauvel, Butterworth-Heinemann, Waltham, MA

Snowden, D (2002) Complex acts of knowing: paradox and descriptive self-awareness, *Journal of Knowledge Management*, 6 (2), May, pp 1–14

Sunstein, C and Thaler, R (2008) *Nudge: Improving decisions about health, wealth, and happiness*, Yale University Press, New Haven, CT

Weinberg, GM (2001) *An Introduction to General Systems Thinking*, Dorset House, New York

Wheeler, DJ (1994) *Understanding Variation: The key to managing chaos*, Longman Higher Education, Harlow

Wiener, N (1948) *Cybernetics: Or control and communication in the animal and the machine*, Hermann & Cie, Paris and MIT Press, Cambridge, MA

Wright, D and Meadows, DH (2009) *Thinking in Systems: A primer*, Routledge, London

20 Dealing with power and politics

SARAH COLEMAN

Power and politics are subjects that are often considered predatory, unsavoury and focused on self-interest. There is a certain irony that at work we recognize the value of a politically adept manager, but at the same time many of us prefer to be left alone to get on with the job and we try to rise above 'dirty' politics.

We are often uncomfortable with these topics and we can show the battle scars to prove it. As a consequence, they are rarely talked about openly and objectively in organizations, and are rarely challenged; instead, they simmer beneath the surface as the 'elephant in the room'. And yet power and politics pervade most organizations and have a strong impact on the way they operate to take decisions about the allocation of resources, how conflict is resolved, how cooperation and collaboration are supported and where the organization should head.

These are all excellent reasons why, as a business analyst who is a real asset to your organization, you need to become that 'politically adept manager' who is aware of the politics of the situation and the organization and of the power bases of the groups you will need to influence and carry with you.

Why should I be interested? I just want to get on with my work

As a business analyst, you spend a lot of time trying to make things happen and get things done either for yourself, in order to meet expectations and deadlines, or on behalf of others. Often, you will be faced with making decisions and solving problems that exceed your formal authority within the organization.

Many of the important decisions in organizations and projects involve the allocation of scarce resources (typically personnel, expertise, budget, technology, capital equipment, etc). With competing requirements for these resources, organizations have to decide how they allocate them, for better or for worse. As a result, decision processes often involve bargaining, negotiating, influencing, trade-offs, alliances, collaborations and jockeying for position by many different self-interested groups even within a single organization.

A deteriorating business climate, redundancy programmes, cost cutting and the drive to improve productivity have resulted in leaner and flatter organizations. This means that the range of formal authority and power has decreased and, instead, more emphasis is being placed on collaboration and matrix working across functions and divisions. Things no longer get done in today's complex work setting simply because someone issues an order and someone else follows it, so how can we successfully operate without the traditional authority of hierarchy to support us? This puts a premium on using our own ability to build relationships, recognize and use our bases of power, use influence, and collaborate and build alliances with others to achieve results.

The traditional organizational model may no longer exist, with its multiple layers of authority, but power bases still exist. How can you identify, establish and use these to achieve what you need to and fulfil your responsibilities to your team, project or organization?

On a personal level, if you want to get ahead in your career then understanding the power bases and becoming politically 'savvy' are important skills. When challenges arise, the ability to read the politics involved and understand how to use power and influence can help you move your agenda forward. It can also help you become aware of, and actively cultivate relationships with, those people who can help you move your agenda forward. Equally, they can help you to understand which individuals or groups you shouldn't upset or exclude.

Power and politics – a cautionary note

The typical organizational chart illustrates the legitimate authority and delegated power: the more senior the position, the more formal the authority and power held by the individual and recognized by the organization. However, it won't reveal much about which other individuals or groups hold particular power or influence, who are thought leaders or who help shape attitudes and beliefs within the organization. Identifying informal networks and remapping the organization will help you to understand the complex network of relationships that exist across functions and divisions. When I first moved into a global ICT business as a programme director leading very large, complex, high-profile projects I was advised on day one to build my own informal network fast in order to make things happen. The organization had plenty of formal processes and procedures, but making those relationships, creating mutual dependence and identifying the informal power

TABLE 20.1 Types of personal and positional power

Sources of power			
Personal (based on relationships with others in the organization)		**Positional (based on the formal channels of authority in the organization)**	
Expert	Having knowledge, experience, judgement	Legitimate	Based on one's position in the organization: the 'right' to command
Referent	Wanting to be like or associated with someone else, valuing that person's networks and contacts	Reward	Having the ability to reward desirable behaviour in others
Information	Possessing or having access to particular and necessary information needed by others	Coercive	Having the ability to punish, sanction or prevent
Connection	Based on who one knows – vertically and horizontally, inside or outside the organization ('networking' and building alliances)	Process	Subset of legitimate power; having control over the methods of production and analysis

Adapted from French and Raven (1959); Hersey and Blanchard (1982).

bases made the difference when favours needed to be asked and called in for the benefit of the client and the organization.

What is power?

When spider webs unite, they can tie up a lion.

(Ethiopian proverb)

In crude terms, 'power' may be defined as the ability to get someone to do something you want done, or the ability to make things happen in the way you want. It is a topic that often gets ignored in development and training, and many of us feel that power is something someone else possesses in the organization, rather than ourselves.

French and Raven (1959) and Hersey and Blanchard (1982) identified a range of sources of power, positioning them as personal (based upon an individual's relationship with others in the organization) or positional (based upon the formal channels of authority within the organization).

Kotter (1985) regards power as a driving force for bringing about change in organizations, and Moss Kanter (1983: 216) identified three sources of power: information (for example data, technical knowledge, political intelligence, expertise), resources (for example funds, materials, space, staff, time) or support (for example endorsement, backing, approval, legitimacy). Both view power as a positive force and recognize its role in bringing about change; moreover, they recognize that individuals can have power and influence in organizations regardless of their specific role or authority.

How can I improve my power?

What are some practical ways in which you, as a business analyst, can improve your power base?

Take the time to *cultivate good working relationships* based on respect, perceived need, obligation and friendship. These take time to develop and are often based on mutual trust. Scholtes (1998) suggests that trust consists of two basic dynamics: 1) I trust you if I believe in your competence and your benevolence so that, if I know you are good at what you do but that you don't care for my welfare, I won't trust you; and 2) if I know you will look out for me but can't do what I need you to, I still won't trust you. Covey (2008) looks at 13 key behaviours common to leaders who engender high levels of trust.

Develop your expertise and extend your understanding of the organization, the project, professional tools and techniques. Keeping abreast of current thought and good practice in business analysis enables you to build your personal credibility and profile within the organization.

If your work is recognized as being important to the organization's success, *promote it*! Shout loud and clear about how and why you, your project or your team are aligned with (and working to further) the organization's ambitions and targets. Not only are you in a good position to bargain and negotiate for resources and support, but this is also an opportunity to enable you to promote yourself by establishing a credible reputation and track record. Set expectations and make sure they are met or exceeded. Many of us are modest and self-effacing, believing that a job well done will be enough to bring us the recognition and reward we seek. Well, that modesty also brings with it a certain amount of invisibility, and if you choose to be invisible it is much more difficult to gain the resources you will need to succeed. Most organizations are meritocracies, but you still need to bring yourself to the attention of those who matter: get some coverage for your team or project in the in-house magazine or other in-house channels.

Establish some positional authority. If, as a business analyst, you work with matrix management and virtual teams in virtual locations you will typically lack formal, positional power. You may have the responsibility and accountability to produce results, but you don't often have the formal authority to go with it. This means that in some instances you have to bargain, negotiate and persuade other managers for their resources, which leads back to the idea of building good working relationships, especially if there is the opportunity to create some reciprocity or obligation on their part.

Actively manage your power relationships and power bases. Power relationships and power bases are dynamic, not static; they are fluid and can be redefined. As such, they need review, reappraisal and renegotiation.

Don't give your power away. Sometimes we fear the consequences of our power; sometimes we fear the responsibility and commitment that come with power. If you choose to give away your power, someone else will benefit. It may also be that you do not recognize your own strength in any power relationship and so unconsciously make a gift of it to someone else. In this case, start looking at what you bring to the relationship.

Look at power as the capacity to mobilize people and resources to get things done, and you will start to recognize it as a useful and legitimate tool for managing effectively; furthermore your team or project will benefit from having a politically capable manager.

What is politics?

> One of the penalties for refusing to participate in politics is that you end up being governed by your inferiors.
>
> (Plato)

Pfeffer (1993) described politics as the art of using influence, authority and power to achieve goals. In *Leading with Political Awareness*, the Chartered Management Institute (2007) reports that 'the most common understanding of "politics" – agreed on by 59 per cent of managers [from the views expressed by the 1,495 senior managers responding to the national survey in 2007] – is of alliance-building to achieve organizational objectives'. This is political behaviour, then, that is distinguished by a sense of personal integrity and is a means to achieve collaboration, build alliances and resolve differences, all of which can help deliver individual, team, project and organizational objectives. Compare this with the traditional view of politics as self-interested and self-focused.

Pinto (1996) concludes from interviews with successful project managers that it is almost impossible to be successful in organizations without a basic understanding of, and willingness to employ, organizational politics. He describes three positions that people typically take when faced with organizational politics: the Naïve, the Political Sensible and the Shark. The three positions lie on a scale as shown in Figure 20.1. Each has their own view, intent, techniques and favourite tactics.

FIGURE 20.1 Three political positions: the Naïve, the Political Sensible and the Shark

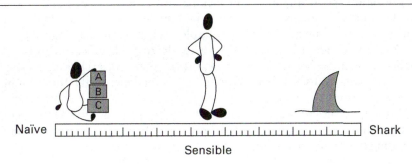

Naïve — Sensible — Shark

The Naïve thinks that politics is unpleasant and avoids it at all costs, relying instead on their belief that the truth will come out. The Sensible realizes that politics is necessary and uses it to further the goals of the project team, by networking, building contacts and giving and receiving favours. Negotiating, influencing and bargaining are favourite tactics. The Shark sees politics as an opportunity for selfish gain, using manipulation, deceit and possibly fraud to achieve their ends. This can include misusing information and bullying people.

FIGURE 20.2 Baddeley and James model

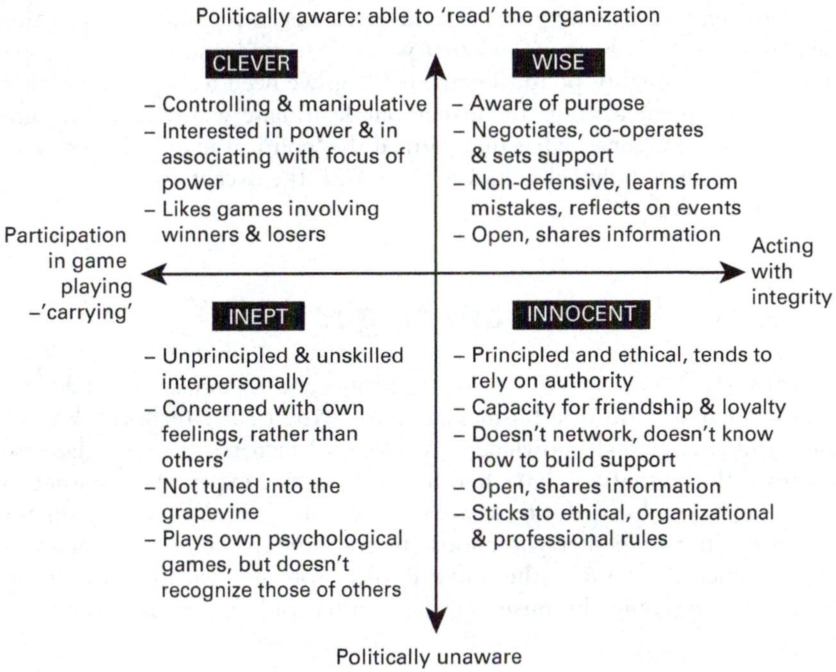

Politically aware: able to 'read' the organization

CLEVER
- Controlling & manipulative
- Interested in power & in associating with focus of power
- Likes games involving winners & losers

WISE
- Aware of purpose
- Negotiates, co-operates & sets support
- Non-defensive, learns from mistakes, reflects on events
- Open, shares information

Participation in game playing – 'carrying' ←——————→ Acting with integrity

INEPT
- Unprincipled & unskilled interpersonally
- Concerned with own feelings, rather than others'
- Not tuned into the grapevine
- Plays own psychological games, but doesn't recognize those of others

INNOCENT
- Principled and ethical, tends to rely on authority
- Capacity for friendship & loyalty
- Doesn't network, doesn't know how to build support
- Open, shares information
- Sticks to ethical, organizational & professional rules

Politically unaware

Baddeley and James (1987) developed a model of political behaviour using two dimensions, relating first to the skills of 'reading' the politics of an organization (politically aware or lacking political awareness) and second to the skills individuals are 'carrying' into situations that may predispose them to act with integrity or play psychological games (psychological game playing or acting with integrity). As a result, they identified four distinct political behaviours (clever, wise, inept and innocent), each with its own characteristics and set of behaviours that an individual might adopt in different situations.

It is important to note that these are behaviours and not fixed traits. This is the good news, since it is possible to develop 'wise' behaviour by understanding the situation and adapting your reaction to it.

Managing the politics

There are many ways in which politics is used in organizations: some are sensible, benign and open and work towards a win at the individual, team, project and organization levels; others are coercive and negative and carry the threat of punishment or sanction. And, as an added complication, the political game-playing tactics will not be the same in every part of an organization and are typically influenced by the culture of that part of the organization. As business analysts, we don't always enjoy having to negotiate, persuade, influence and barter for resources that are needed for our team or project: we resent the time used in 'playing the political game' and that could otherwise be used for more constructive purposes.

However, on the assumption that this will happen regardless of what we personally want to happen, and that we need to understand when we are ourselves the target of political game playing, we need to find and develop appropriate political tools to further our legitimate goals. Harrison and Lock (2004) developed what they termed the 'political manager's tool kit', outlining various political tactics for use 'with the exception (we hope) of deceit and deception' (Table 20.2).

How far do you want to go?

A word about how far you want to go in your organization, and your personal career path in a business analysis expert role. Technical knowledge and commercial knowledge are 'hygiene' factors: these are the professional things that you have had to do, learn and experience in order to get as far as you have. But these are only the 'entry-level' requirements for senior positions whether you choose to continue in the business analysis expert function or make the move into a more general executive position. Understanding the business, the market and the product portfolio

TABLE 20.2   Political tactics

Gaining support from a higher power source or sources
Alliance or coalition building (gaining support from near peers)
Controlling critical resources
Controlling the decision-making process
Controlling the committee process and meetings
Use of positional authority
Use of the scientific element
Deceit and deception
Withholding, censoring or distorting information
Games

Adapted from Harrison and Lock (2004).

are certainly important, but the next step up to senior and board level is a little different.

It is about building strong relationships at all levels, becoming politically 'savvy', identifying your personal power base, and creating your personal brand, trust and credibility. How politically aware individuals are and how good they are at reading the situation and making it work to their, their team's or their project's advantage are often regarded as signs of professional maturity. This is where sitting down to take a long, hard look at your own personal and positional power, level of influence within the organization and attitude to office politics comes into play.

And finally

Power and politics are neutral tools but, like anything else, it is how both are used that makes the difference between being self-serving and coercive, and promoting your work as a business analyst in alignment with organizational success. They are often uncomfortable subjects but can also be seen legitimately as opportunities rather than threats. Moreover, power and politics are increasingly recognized as valid and effective elements of management and leadership in organizations.

About the author

Sarah Coleman specializes in business transformation and organizational change at Business Evolution (**www.businessevolution.co**) and is a visiting senior fellow at Lincoln University.

References and further reading

Baddeley, S and James, K (1987) Political skills model: reading and carrying, Office for Public Management and Ashridge

Baddeley, S and James, K (1987) Owl, fox, donkey or sheep: political skills for managers, *Management Education and Development*, **18** (1), pp 3–19

Chartered Management Institute (2007) *Leading with Political Awareness: Developing leaders' skills to manage the political dimension across all sectors*, Chartered Management Institute, London

Covey, SMR (2008) *The Speed of Trust*, Free Press, New York

Frame, J Davidson (2003) *Managing Projects in Organizations: How to make the best use of time, techniques and people*, Jossey-Bass, San Francisco

French, JRP and Raven, B (1959) The bases of social power, in *Group Dynamics*, ed D Cartwright and A Zander, Harper & Row, New York

French, R *et al* (2008) *Organizational Behaviour*, John Wiley & Sons, Chichester

Harrison, F and Lock, D (2004) *Advanced Project Management: A structured approach*, Gower, Aldershot

Hersey, P and Blanchard, KH (1982) *Management of Organizational Behavior*, 4th edn, Prentice Hall, Upper Saddle River, NJ

Kotter, JP (1985) *Power and Influence: Beyond formal power*, Free Press, New York

Moss Kanter, R (1983) *The Change Masters*, Simon & Schuster, New York

Pfeffer, J (1993) *Managing with Power: Politics and influence in organizations*, Harvard Business School Press, Boston, MA

Pinto, JK (1996) *Power and Politics in Project Management*, Project Management Institute, Newtown Square, PA

Scholtes, PR (1998) *The Leader's Handbook*, McGraw-Hill, New York

Stimson, T [accessed 1 September 2012] Sources of power [Online] www.consultcli.com/Sourcespower.htm

Partnering across organizations

ADRIAN REED

Introduction

There's no denying that projects can be complex endeavours, with multiple stakeholders both *inside* and *outside* the organization. Unfortunately, where there are stakeholders there can be conflict, competing agendas or disagreement. There may even be stakeholders who don't yet appreciate the value that good-quality business analysis can bring to a project or there might be pressure to deliver in a completely unrealistic timescale. Does this resonate with you? If so, you might feel that in order to work in these environments you need *very* broad shoulders!

It's possible to avoid or mitigate these issues by creating trust-based partnerships. Partnering with key stakeholders and functions both inside and outside your organization can help smooth over issues and create an environment where the focus is on 'getting the job done' rather than 'finding someone to blame'. Partnering involves consciously acting as an ambassador for change, being a consistent point of contact and creating long-term relationships. Rather than seeing business analysts as outsiders in an ivory tower, business stakeholders will start to see the value of structured change and the quality of business engagement on projects will increase. Rather than having adversarial relationships with suppliers, an environment is created where issues and problems can be discussed openly.

This chapter focuses on how to initiate lasting partnerships with functions and stakeholders outside your immediate team.

Partnering within an organization: becoming the business's first port of call

As someone who works in the field of business change, you are likely to find yourself regularly working across multiple functions, teams or business units within the same organization, whether that's within the company where you work or a client organization. While you'll hopefully find some supportive stakeholders, others might resent having an 'outsider' on their project at all. Partnering *within* an organization provides you with the opportunity to demonstrate the value of the business analyst role on your own terms. It helps to avoid 'body shopping', where stakeholders request analysts for specific tasks without giving them full visibility of the project objectives. Even when stakeholders are aligned and supportive, building long-term partnerships will ensure that they *stay* supportive and will ensure that they engage business analysts early in the project life cycle.

Partnerships will persist beyond individual projects, but will start on a single project. A significant milestone is getting a 'foot in the door' and getting the opportunity to demonstrate the breadth of benefit that business analysis can bring, initially on a single project. The ideal way of getting this engagement is to start top down, by engaging the sponsors or senior leaders within the business area that you're targeting. The question is: how can a business analysis practitioner or team get this top-level engagement?

Creating a compelling case

A key step towards gaining this top-level engagement will involve creating the opportunity to present your case to the relevant top-level stakeholders. In order to make the most of this opportunity, it's important to prepare your argument carefully and ensure you consider the worldview of the stakeholders. In doing so, it is useful to take the following themes into consideration.

Clarity: be clear on what a business analyst is (and isn't) in your particular organizational context

Stakeholders don't always understand the business analyst role, and subtleties of the role can vary between organizations depending on the level of organizational maturity and the structure. An important precursor to partnering with any stakeholder group is to have a clear definition of what the business analyst role entails in your particular organizational context.

One way of conceptualizing the business analyst role is in terms of breadth of engagement and depth of engagement. One of the reasons the business analyst role can be difficult to describe is that we operate in very different spaces depending on the individual project and project stage. For example, anyone who has worked on a data migration project will agree that you normally end up knowing the business data and the data model as well as (if not better than) the business and technical subject matter experts who actually use or process the data. However, the same business analyst may work on a project to define the organization's strategy, in which case he or she will be working at a much broader and higher level of abstraction.

We can represent these two continuums – depth and breadth – on a graph (Figure 21.1). People used to describe the business analyst as being the 'bridge' between the business and IT. This analogy is far too narrow

FIGURE 21.1 The business analyst zone

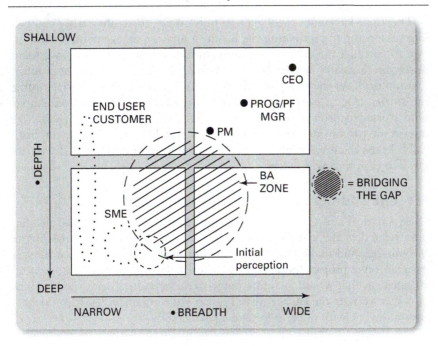

for today's business analyst role, a more apt description being the 'bridge' between the business and one or many solution providers (which may or may not involve IT). The business analyst role acts as the bridge between the stakeholders across the graph, and it's important that there's an understanding of where these lines are drawn in your organization. As you will notice from Figure 21.1, there is often an initial perception that the business analyst role is much narrower. It can be extremely beneficial to draw the graph from the perspective of your organization, to understand where the boundaries of the business analyst role lie (and where stakeholders think it lies). This helps inform your initial understanding of the stakeholders' worldview, which in turn can inform how you engage them. In order to engage them, it's important to form an emotional and logical argument, as described below.

Hearts and minds: create a logical and emotional argument for strengthening the engagement

As mentioned previously, a solid partnership spans beyond projects, but starts with a single project. In order to get deeper engagement on that initial project, it is useful to create a logical argument including facts, figures and examples. It is often useful to include quantifiable achievements from *within* the organization to show where business analysts have added value.

This argument can be used to start to plug the gap in perception over the boundaries of the business analyst role.

The logical argument will get you only so far; to create a truly compelling reason for strengthening the business analyst engagement, it's important to consider the emotional argument too. Often, as analysts, we focus purely on facts and figures. Some stakeholders will find this type of information 'dry'. As the old proverb says, 'Facts *tell*; stories *sell*.' It is often the *stories* from a presentation or meeting that the attendees remember. Find stories of project successes – and failings – to boost your case. It's important to consider your stakeholders' worldview. What (metaphorically) keeps them up at night? What are their major concerns? If you can tap into this, they will listen.

Present and persuade: present your case

Once a logical and emotional argument has been formulated and this has been related to the stakeholders' worldviews, it's time to get a meeting in their diaries and make your case. You can make your case whilst already engaged on a project (perhaps to call for a deeper or more autonomous engagement that would facilitate longer-term partnering with the business) or *before* you get the engagement. Present your argument, explain the benefits and work with them to initiate a partnership.

Delivering value, and shouting about it

Once you have your 'foot in the door', you have the opportunity to demonstrate the value that good-quality business analysis adds. Partnerships grow through establishing and reinforcing credibility; this is achieved through delivery. This can be delivery of valuable artefacts as well as valuable change. Sometimes creating a simple process map to help a stakeholder group solve a problem, while only representing a couple of days' effort, will be perceived as an extremely valuable win for the stakeholders themselves. It's important to shout about both the small and the big successes, so that stakeholders appreciate the value that's being added. This strengthens the partnership further and will enable it to grow over time.

Partnering outside an organization

Projects often rely on several organizations working together towards a successful delivery. The sponsoring organization may have engaged one or many solution providers, and perhaps there's also an IT integration partner or a third-party administrator (TPA) involved. Business analysts often act as the informal conduit between these parties.

This position can be made much more difficult as a result of the competing objectives of the organizations involved. Naturally, all organizations will have the same stated objectives (namely, to ensure the success of the project). However, there will be some implicit or unstated objectives too. For example, the sponsoring organization may want to deliver the project at the lowest possible price, while the solution provider may want to achieve the best possible profit from the job.

There are a number of different attitudes and approaches to managing relationships. At one end of the spectrum, there is managing a relationship as if it was purely transactional. Imagine buying a chocolate bar at a train station in a city you are visiting. You probably wouldn't care about the shop you bought it from, and you wouldn't think twice about going to the shop next door if it was cheaper. You're interested in the single transaction only, and aren't interested in building an ongoing relationship. You probably wouldn't care how much profit the shop was making – and if they sold something to you below cost price because they were struggling to attract customers, so much the better!

At the other end of the spectrum there's the longer-term relationship model. In this model, there's more of a focus on creating a sustainable situation where everyone wins. This is more like a relationship with a hairdresser; over time, the hairdresser gets to know you. He or she knows that what you ask for isn't always what you need or want, and feels able to give you advice. You make allowances when the hairdresser is away on holiday – perhaps you even schedule your appointments around this. You certainly wouldn't want the hairdresser to make a loss, as this would mean he or she wouldn't be able to service your future needs. Most importantly, the hairdresser will be a critical friend. If you ask for a 1980s mullet and it *really* wouldn't suit you, the hairdresser will diplomatically tell you (but the ultimate decision will, of course, remain with you).

A similar continuum exists for nearly all supplier–client relationships. Partnering across organizations helps minimize conflict by building and growing a trust-based relationship, towards the relationship-centric end of the spectrum. So what considerations need to be kept in mind when forming these types of partnership?

Roles and responsibilities

For any kind of partnering to work, there needs to be a clear understanding of who is doing what and when. In some circumstances, you may find that roles are duplicated across the organizations. This creates a situation that is ripe for misunderstanding, duplication and conflict.

It is therefore extremely important that roles and responsibilities are agreed as early as possible. It's as important to discuss what each stakeholder *won't* do as well as what he or she *will* do. A real challenge can occur when there are several business analysts, from different organizations, engaged on the same project. Take the scenario shown in Figure 21.2. The challenge, of course, is that each business analyst on the supplier side is

FIGURE 21.2 A web of relationships across organizations

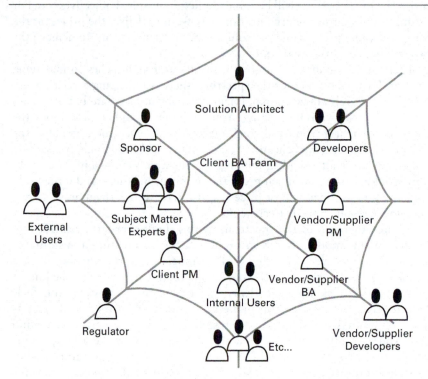

likely to be focusing *only* on the solution component that he or she is delivering. In a situation like this it's important to discuss and agree:

- *A single source of truth*. Which requirement catalogue or store will be considered the 'master'?
- *Avoiding duplication*. How will duplication be avoided, so that each requirement is only captured once?
- *Standards*. What standards, notations and software tools or repositories will be used?
- *User or business contact*. Who will speak to the users or business directly?
- *Change control*. What is the change control process and who owns it (particularly important when something that seems small for one solution component might have a huge downstream impact for another)?
- *Communication*. How, when and where will the team communicate?
- *Escalation*. How and when can issues be escalated, and to whom? What are the authority levels and who are the decision makers?

It is well worth taking the time to have these conversations up front.

Contracts and service level agreements

When third parties are mentioned, it's likely that the issue of contracts and service level agreements (SLAs) will come into the conversation. While these are undoubtedly important – and it's important that you know what each party is contractually obliged to deliver – the old adage applies that 'Rules are made to be broken.' This isn't intended to sound cavalier – it's just that partnering with an organization is about give and take. Sometimes suppliers might need an extra day above their SLA to deliver something complex. If it isn't business critical, why would you penalize them for this? It's much better to be pragmatic. In the same way, the SLA might say, for example, that four weeks' notice should be given prior to a new project starting, but since the organization has been working with you so long it routinely manages to achieve this in two weeks.

It's said that, when the contract comes out of the filing cabinet, the relationship is already dead. If you need to coerce using a contract then you may as well start looking for a new supplier (or forever accept that you are working on a transactional and potentially adversarial basis). That's not to say that conflict won't occur when deadlines are tight – and there may well still be disagreements over what is a change to scope, what constitutes a change request, and so on. However, by taking the view that the relationship is valuable and worth sustaining, it's much more likely that a win–win solution will be achieved.

Business tension

Ironically, one of the most difficult situations to manage relates not to the suppliers but to the business itself. Have you ever found yourself in a situation where things get tough and the business continually pushes and pushes the blame on to the supplier? This is an easy option; few suppliers will turn round and say 'Actually, this is entirely your own fault.' They certainly won't be this blunt if they value repeat business!

Working in a business analysis role gives a unique insight. As a completely objective insider you can act as a critical friend to the business. You can challenge their beliefs – with rapport – while also being prepared to receive a challenge back from them. This healthy discussion will often enable a business analyst to defuse a potentially ugly situation, simply by pointing out how the situation looks to an objective practitioner.

Conclusion

Partnering across organizations – whether internally or externally – will help avoid or reduce adversarial relationships. Partnerships are built through empathy, trust and developing an understanding of the way stakeholders view the world. These persist beyond project engagements, but start with a single engagement and shift the relationship from transactional to relationship based. When they work well they make life on projects more pleasant for all involved.

About the author

Adrian Reed is the principal consultant of Blackmetric Business Solutions and holds the position of marketing director of the UK chapter of the IIBA.

References and further reading

Brown, R (2007) *How to Build Your Reputation*, Ecademy Press, Penryn

Cadle, J, Paul, D and Turner, P (2010) The stakeholder wheel, stakeholder analysis and CATWOE, in *Business Analysis Techniques: 72 essential tools for success*, BCS, Swindon, pp 64–74

Gutsche, J (2009) *Exploiting Chaos: 150 ways to spark innovation during times of change*, Penguin Group (USA), New York

Heath, C and Heath, D (2008) *Made to Stick*, Arrow Books, London

Reed, A [accessed 2 December 2012] *Adrian Reed's Blog* [Online] http://www.adrianreed.co.uk

Thaler, R and Sunstein, C (2009) *Nudge*, Penguin Books, London

Strategic thinking for business analysis

22

DAV BISESSAR

This chapter is about strategic thinking for business analysis. Strategic thinking applies creative insight to generate ideas that a company can use, as well as scientific analysis to determine the best choice in a particular situation. Most of those in business analysis need to understand the strategy of their organization to be able to work with others to implement that strategy through projects and programmes of change. Some of those in business analysis will need to be able to formulate strategy as well, particularly those working in business and enterprise architecture.

Overview of strategy

What is strategy?

Strategy is the pattern or plan that integrates an organization's major goals, policies and action sequences into a cohesive whole (Quinn, 1980). Another definition expands this by saying that strategy is the overall plan for deploying resources to establish a favourable position (Grant, 2010).

There is a problem though. Very often the direction that should be taken is known, but the issue is following this direction through by taking all the actions and cultural shifts needed to make it a reality. David Maister comments that 'strategy is the diet, not the goal' (2008); the choice of a strategy that can be executed by the organization is difficult but vital if goals are to be realized.

Strategy, like business analysis, is both an art and a science. It needs both creativity and innovation, while being rigorous in analysis and fact finding.

Different perspectives

There are many different perspectives on strategy. Some authors see strategic management as linear, rational and planned, involving a top-down, step-by-step search for an optimal solution (Peters and Waterman, 1982; Kotler, 1994). In the case of a relatively stable problem space they suggest starting with requirements analysis and ending up with implementation. Other authors see strategy as emergent and incremental (Quinn, 1982; Mintzberg, 1987). This view takes into account that the reality of management is often quite different from textbook models. Strategy evolves over time through incremental 'muddling' steps (Lindblom, 1959) and adapts according to each situation. Here, strategists can react effectively to unexpected threats and opportunities. The interpretive view adds the importance of taking into account how the cognitive maps of managers can influence their perceptions of the environment and strategic responses (Johnson, 1988).

Strategy can be seen through the lens of systems thinking, described further in Chapter 19. Organizations are constrained by, but can influence, their external environment. The organization and its environment are considered as an interrelated system. Performance is determined by the integration and coordination of collections of different organizational activities. The behaviour of suppliers, customers, competitors and so on will determine the overall individual performance of the firm.

What differentiates business strategy from other kinds of business planning is competitive advantage (Ohmae, 1982). Thus the main purpose of strategic thinking is to enable a company to gain a sustainable edge over its competitors in as efficient a manner as possible. Examples of sustainable edge and competitive advantage are in terms of market share, cost of production, speed, and quality of service (Porter, 1985).

Why perspective matters

Over the years, approaches to strategy planning and thinking have changed. A hundred years ago, in stable and predictable business environments, command-and-control was the pattern of management, including strategy. Ideas and direction were set at the top and then driven down through every aspect of the business. Workers had little if any empowerment to give feedback, let alone to change things.

Since then, there have been huge changes, ranging from external forces such as globalization and economic uncertainty and the rise of social media, to internal forces including employee engagement and flatter hierarchies. Specific industries warrant different approaches to strategy. For example, in a high-tech industry providing cloud-based software solutions, the environment is very competitive, rapidly changing and difficult to predict. Here, it is important to be nimble and have flexible strategies that can adapt quickly to a fickle market. Another example is financial services. In the past, high barriers to entry prevented too much disruption in this sector. However, advances in technology, the worrying spectre of reputational damage resulting from the widespread use of social media, and the sheer dedication of people who want to do things differently are forcing a rethink, as new businesses emerge with new strategies.

Patterns of strategy

As described in Chapter 14, patterns can be really useful within business analysis and also within strategy development. Ohmae's (1982) 'four routes to strategic advantage' and Porter's (1985) 'generic strategies to competitive advantage' are good examples used by organizations in various combinations.

Four routes to strategic advantage

- *Key success factors (KSF):* resources are allocated to differentiate the organization relative to its competitors, towards improving a key success factor (for example economies of scale, or customer satisfaction). The key is to be different from other organizations by focusing on a critical element of success.
- *Relative superiority:* where your competitor's weaknesses are exploited using new technology or other strengths. If your services are more accessible compared with other organizations, then focus on this either by increasing relative prices or exploiting the value of your product in your marketing initiatives.
- *Aggressive initiatives:* these include challenging the premise of existing products and services to come up with industry-changing ideas, for example using a digital card in a camera instead of film, or the move from media ownership to the 'gym subscription' model where music or video is accessed from a remote storage system.
- *Strategic degrees of freedom:* embrace innovations in competitive products or markets by altering aspects of a product or service that contribute towards satisfying customers' objectives. For example, banks are moving towards providing money management tools that allow customers to monitor their spending by category.

Generic strategies

- *Cost leadership* is where the organization competes by aiming to be lower in price relative to the industry, most commonly driving this efficiency through economies of scale.
- *Differentiation* is where the organization creates products or services that are different in some way that is valued by its customers, for example a 'finest' food range compared with a 'value' label.
- *Focus (or niche) strategy* is where the organization focuses on a particular market segment or demographic.

Practical strategic thinking

Strategy must be actionable

Successful strategies need to be realizable – it's just not enough to create great strategy that cannot be implemented. The execution needs to be part of the thinking process.

It can be useful to think of strategy in two parts, separating what's possible from the effort of how to make it happen. Remember though that the two are interrelated and the 'how' must be tackled as part of testing the 'what'. Many transformative strategies have died because the organizations that created them couldn't implement them.

Understanding the what and how

There is no single correct way of thinking strategically. However, the author has found the following activities useful over the years.

A good first step is to get absorbed in the data, to develop a sense of the fundamentals of what is happening. What are the economic conditions in which your organization operates and what are the industry drivers and your differentiating internal capabilities? What are the key performance indicators that measure effective performance in your industry? Go beyond the standard measures of business performance, such as profit, revenue and earnings per share and include ones that reflect your industry. For example, in retail, you might choose metrics around stock, such as units sold per store, and sales records. In a non-profit charitable organization, you might choose number of children vaccinated per dollar donated.

The next step is to clarify the problem statement and generate hypotheses that solve that problem. Not focusing immediately on the problem is deliberate, as developing and testing your solutions are where you want to focus most of your thinking at this stage.

To get a sense of the business, some classic models of strategic analysis are useful here, so below are some tools that can help you to do this.

Step 1: frameworks used in strategic analysis

Whatever tools or models you pick, remember that they are abstractions of reality. These models allow you to see aspects of a business rather than the complex whole, in ways that allow you to make inferences. Remember that what's key is your own interpretation of the analytical facts, and your inferences of what the trends, numbers and issues tell you about the situation an organization is in.

Whatever models you use, try not to get paralysed by the analysis. It is very rare that the class of problems you are addressing in your strategic endeavour can be solved by complete analysis of the situation. Realistically, you are unlikely to have all the time or access to all the data you need.

Remember too that in reality most strategic tools are not used as prescriptively as they are in textbooks. The following frameworks are classic models used to analyse the external and internal environment of an organization.

External analysis – PESTLE

PESTLE breaks the external environment into several themes: political, economic, sociological, technological, legal and environmental. Considering the situation of each theme helps guide strategic decision making. Another variant is STEEPLE, where an ethical theme is added.

It's useful to think in terms of future trends as well as the current situation. This gives a view of the dynamics involved, rather than just a snapshot at the time of the analysis. This model can also be used to explore the impact on a competitor. An example here is a product manufacturer with a higher-than-average safety record. The manufacturer might welcome and even encourage increased regulation. Why? To 'shake out' competitors that are less able to keep up with any resulting required changes in design and manufacturing.

Industry analysis – Porter's five forces

Porter's (1985) five forces look at the bargaining power of suppliers and buyers, and the threat of potential entrants and substitute products or services. An example is how the introduction of music as MP3 files affected the CD market. Organizations find opportunities attractive in industries where there are few rivals, no close substitutes or alternatives, high barriers to entry and where suppliers and buyers have little bargaining power.

Internal analyses – SWOT and VMOST

SWOT analysis considers the internal strengths and weakness of an organization, together with its external opportunities and threats. The objective is to use strengths to take advantage of opportunities, while protecting against threats and shoring up weaknesses that are critical to success.

VMOST defines the vision of the organization together with its mission. Flowing from this will be the objectives, strategies and tactics.

Russell Ackoff (1987) describes the features of a good mission statement as:

- having some objective that can be measured;
- differentiating the firm;
- defining the business you want to be in;
- having relevance and being exciting and inspiring.

However, despite these good intentions, critics of such statements lament the lack of translation of such visionary statements into the reality of how the business is run.

These days, most firms reject the competitive posturing statements of the past in favour of more values-based slogans. Pepsi's famous historical mission statement of 'Beat Coke' has changed to 'The Power of One: By operating as one company, we unleash the Power of One, which gives us critical competitive advantages.' At the time of writing, the most prominent statement in the mission and values section of the firm's website is: 'At PepsiCo, we believe being a responsible corporate citizen is not only the right thing to do, but the right thing to do for our business' (PepsiCo, 2013).

Whatever the statement, in many cases the words are a reminder of a much wider belief about the firm and the reason for its existence and its values.

Stakeholder analysis – CATWOE

CATWOE (Checkland, 1993) is a soft system methodology framework that considers different stakeholder perspectives of the business system. Its relevance in strategic thinking is to capture the perspectives of people or entities affecting and influencing the organization's long-term performance. It considers:

- C = customers of the organization or people affected by the outputs of the organization;

- A = actors, entities or people who carry out the operations of the organization;

- T = transformation, ie activities of the organization that 'transform' the inputs into the products and services of the firm;

- W = *Weltanschauung* (worldview) or 'outlook', which lists beliefs about the organization's objective – a collective view;

- O = owners, the people who have responsibility for the business system(s);

- E = environment constraints on the organization or business system (for example the external analysis factors).

There are many other models of analysis (see Harding and Long, 1998; and Rasiel, 1999) that can help in strategy development or can help structure your thoughts (Minto, 2009).

Step 2: framing the problem and forming a hypothesis

One way to solve a problem effectively, building on the models and tools in Step 1, is:

1 *Form a problem definition.* Commit to paper your own rigorous definition of the problem, even if you have already been given a suggested solution. Make your problem statement action-oriented and SMART (specific, measurable, achievable, relevant, and

time-bound). Next, frame the problem in terms of the situation and complications facing the organization. Then use key findings from the analysis tools and models. Once you've nailed down the scope and known constraints (eg financial), this definition will affect outcome.

2 *Develop your hypothesis.* Instead of analysing everything and working through each possible solution, see if there are a few that immediately jump out at you. There are many ways to solve most problems; you only need one that works. So, rather than evaluate them all, try using your insights from the internal and external analysis tools to come up with a plausible answer. Have the courage to be brave and to challenge traditional thinking – a good technique is simply to ask thought-provoking questions. For example, what would happen if you made a mass market version of a high-end brand? Try to make sure that your top hypotheses are mutually exclusive and completely exhaustive (MECE).

3 *Determine the minimum amount of analysis you need to do to test your hypothesis.* For example, if there's one piece of key data that would determine whether a hypothesis is true or not, use that first rather than evaluate all its elements. If you wanted to increase the number of blood donors, your hypothesis might say you need to increase awareness. You could test this hypothesis by surveying people in the catchment area to determine if this is a factor. Also, beware of strategic bias (Kahneman, 2011); use appropriate fact-based analysis, not just data that supports your position.

4 *Does the solution pass the 'So what?' test?* Having come up with a strategy, make sure it's not just another obvious answer such as 'Increase profits by lowering prices and conducting advertising.' Your solution needs to be compelling and have an air of ingenuity about it – a novel and distinctive element that inspires people to take ownership of that idea and participate in making it happen. This isn't about being different for the sake of it, but more about recognizing that game-changing strategies come about because they are fundamentally different from those chosen by everyone else – including your competitors.

Strategic thinking and the business analyst

The burden of the business analyst is a heavy one – bridging the unstable gap between technology and business, internal and external forces, or stakeholders and customers. Yet opening opportunities for capabilities that can unlock new market potential is a heady prize – along with the knowledge that the right insight and the ability to challenge appropriately can result in a sea change in organizational strategy.

The strategic challenges facing organizations in the 21st century are leading them to explore how to become more globally integrated, how to exploit digital technologies across their organization, how to drive better insight through analytics, how to understand customers better through social engagement and how to use the talents and skills of a geographically disparate workforce. Strategy is no longer the domain of a single department or something decided by senior management alone. Successful business analysts will influence strategy, implement solutions and of course monitor the resulting effects for later adjustment. They will have a direct impact on the direction of the project they are involved in, and will enjoy carrying out the investigation as much as providing the solution.

Developing new ways of thinking about how to compete and conduct business should not be left to fate. The role of business analysts is to discover the underlying issues that drive the organization. This, coupled with the ability to question existing ways of doing things in a methodical yet engaging way, is ultimately why organizations need business analysts to undertake and lead strategic thinking.

About the author

Dav Bisessar is a strategist and business architect in IBM's Global Business Services division. Dav is also head of the IBM UK business analysis community of practice.

References and further reading

Ackoff, RL (1987) Mission statements, *Planning Review*, **15** (4), pp 30–31

Checkland, P (1993) *Systems Thinking, Systems Practice*, John Wiley & Sons, Chichester

Grant, RM (2010) *Contemporary Strategy Analysis: Text only*, Wiley, Hoboken, NJ

Harding, S and Long, T (1998) *MBA Management Models*, Gower, Aldershot

Johnson, G (1988) Rethinking incrementalism, *Strategic Management Journal*, **9** (1), pp 75–91

Johnson, G and Scholes, K (1989) *Exploring Corporate Strategy*, Prentice Hall, London

Kahneman, D (2011) *Thinking, Fast and Slow*, Penguin, London

Kotler, P (1994) *Marketing Management: Analysis planning, implementation, and control*, 8th edn, Prentice Hall, New York

Lindblom, CE (1959) The science of 'muddling through', *Public Administration Review*, **19** (2), pp 79–88

Maister, D (2008) *Strategy and the Fat Smoker*, Spangle Press, Boston, MA

Minto, B (2009) *The Pyramid Principle: Logic in writing and thinking*, Pearson Education, Harlow

Mintzberg, H (1987) The strategy concept 1: five Ps for strategy, *California Management Review*, **30** (1), pp 11–24

Ohmae, K (1982) *The Mind of the Strategist*, McGraw-Hill, New York

PepsiCo [accessed 29 January 2013] PepsiCo's mission and vision [Online] www.pepsico.com/company/our-mission-and-vision.html

Peters, T and Waterman, R (1982) *In Search of Excellence: Lessons from America's best-run companies*, Harper & Row, New York

Porter, ME (1985) *Competitive Advantage: Creating and sustaining superior performance*, Free Press, New York

Quinn, JB (1980) *Strategies for Change: Logical incrementalism*, RD Irwin, Homewood, IL

Quinn, JB (1982) Managing strategies incrementally, *Omega*, **10** (6), pp 613–27

Rasiel, EM (1999) *The McKinsey Way*, McGraw-Hill, New York

Opinion piece
Leading from the middle – a business analyst in television

ROGER MAWLE

I came to business analysis at a large commercial broadcaster a couple of years ago, from a background in management consulting. I'd spent six years at Deloitte, where I was part of their media practice and involved in some big projects. When I moved into broadcasting, 'analysis' was almost a dirty word. Job titles were being changed away from 'business analyst'.

I joined as a business technology consultant. That was a problem, as no one really knew what it meant! After six months, I realized there were lots of people doing business analysis, but without clarity. Roles and responsibilities were confused, and some projects were started without much hope of being completed.

Over the last year, I've had the opportunity to rebrand the job of business analysis and put it in its rightful position, throughout the project life cycle. We are now clear about what business analysts do as well as what we don't do. We add rigour to what in the past was speculation. We provide tools and mechanisms to contribute to strategic as well as detailed operational conversations, in a way that other people are not able to.

I'm glad to say that business analysis is now becoming recognized and increasingly valued at the core of our organization.

Where does leadership fit?

Firstly, there are personal integrity and objectivity. Building credibility with business stakeholders comes right to the fore; my personal experience is that we only really get any leadership ability once we've built credibility.

It all starts with self and with examining personal motivations, being transparent with those around you. One of the pitfalls that business analysts can fall into is over-processing things and over-detailing. What I look for in business analysts when I'm recruiting, and what I encourage, is the ability to distil information into very high-level statements that tell me what I need to know. This shows they've thought about what I'm interested in and they're not just 'vomiting' everything that they know to try to impress me.

Other important skills for business analysts include grouping and mapping, the ability to see patterns in information, and restructure and reorganize information in a way that others may not see, and then critically apply narrative. A lot of what we do as business analysts is to communicate. Recently I was given a slide to look at. I ended up reworking it by imagining that I was standing in front of the individuals at the executive board and telling them the story. This approach meant we ended up with a very different outcome from the one we would have received had we gone in with a splurge of information on the page in lists and bullet points.

How do you develop leadership in other business analysts?

I'm really a consultant business analyst, but I need more than just consultant business analysts. I need people who will take a task and do it, with the substance and knowledge of their area to do the job well. This is important for building their personal credibility and confidence. I encourage people to step up into leadership and to feel confident in their own ability. The next step is to think about what other attributes and aspects of their career they should focus on.

I encourage people to develop their awareness of business context. This includes consideration of our position within our organization, as well as the position of our organization within the external environment. A pitfall for junior business analysts is that, when they're working on the detail of a project, they tend to think that it's the most important thing to everyone else too. As business analysts we sometimes make assumptions in our conversations with senior businesspeople that they really are going to care about what we're talking about. If we can start every conversation by, first of all, understanding where they're at, then it helps us to temper our conversations with them and the way that we offer our contribution. It also helps them to realize that we can see beyond our own small project. If we can offer some insight or observation about the broader context external to our organization then this adds even more weight to our 'pitch'.

While I can help by giving people context, it's critical to encourage them to build relationships with other people who can help too. One way to do this is to encourage a mentoring relationship. I'm constantly asking people at my level and more senior to mentor: to meet up formally or informally every month to give their perspective to my business analysts.

An example

We have a big project that's just kicking off. It's quite technical, focusing on replacing old legacy systems and infrastructure with more flexible systems that are scalable and more sustainable for a business unit going forward. We have some very clever engineers and developers who have been thinking about this for some time. They've already decided what the answer is and chosen the technology, and have ideas about how it's going to work together.

We've brought in three or four business analysts to do a short piece of work. They'll apply rigour to the project, forcing the business to ask themselves some questions that they might not otherwise have asked. So, instead of diving straight into the 'what' and the 'how' of solving this problem, the team members are spending time helping the business, perhaps forcing the business, to grapple with the 'why'. That's a fascinating journey! There are many differing opinions; there are lots of competing pressures; and the more you explore, the harder, the more complicated, the 'why' becomes.

To make it work, we have two streams. The first is doing a detailed 'as is' analysis, working out what boxes are where, what plugs into what, what the business processes are and how much all this costs. We're exposing the current complexity and uncovering the business case for what, ultimately, the project will deliver. The second stream, in parallel, is a principal business analyst working with senior stakeholders, walking alongside them and asking all the 'why' questions. This could result in a very different answer to the one our technical colleagues had previously anticipated.

This illustrates the importance of communication and asking questions, trying to be inquisitive. This is going to get us to the right answer for this broadcast organization.

We're seeing another trend too. Technology is so accessible and staff can search for and find products online very easily. We find that many of our business colleagues are choosing products before they've worked out the problem that they need to solve. We, as business analysts, then have to go back and ask them the 'why' questions when they've already decided the 'what'. That often reveals that the requirement can be answered with something we already have. This shows the other side of the same problem, where people act without business analysis providing leadership for change.

About the interviewee

Roger Mawle is a consultant business analyst working for a large commercial broadcaster in London, UK.

PART IV
Leadership in the wider world

Introduction to Part IV

Part IV, the final part of the book, explores how business analysis needs, and provides, leadership beyond the organization and across the wider world.

What do we mean by leadership in the wider world?

Business analysis is a global profession, with supporting bodies all over the world. As well as working within a specific organization, each business analyst has the opportunity to contribute in the wider world, whether that be as a volunteer with a professional body or as a thought leader, developing new ideas and methods.

All business analysts need to work out their own ethical basis for their work and will face dilemmas and pressure. Everyone who wants to become outstanding at business analysis will need to strive for excellence. Both ethics and excellence become more powerful when worked on within the context of a community of practice of business analysis. We call all this leadership in the wider world.

What does Part IV cover?

Part IV starts off in Chapter 23 by exploring the opportunities that exist to develop leadership within the professional community. Sharing ideas through thought leadership is just one of these, and is the focus of Chapter 24. Thought leadership can come in many different forms and, in addition to informing fellow practitioners, can reach beyond business analysis.

Chapter 25 gives an overview of professional ethics and challenges. It focuses on understanding ethics, morals and values and then applies this to business analysis work, especially when under pressure and facing dilemmas. It calls on business analysts to adopt approaches that support fair process and emotional commitment.

Chapter 26 argues that best practice *alone* is not enough for business analysis leadership and that there is no single 'silver bullet' for solving every problem. Business analysis is all about continuous growth and learning, supporting one another within the context of a community of practice.

Part IV is rounded off by an opinion piece written by a director of an international bank. He is responsible for one of the biggest global business analysis communities of practice, and he shares how business analysts can be seen as change agents.

As usual, there are resources at **www.baleadership.com** for business analysis in the wider world, including links to professional organizations, conferences and other reference material. Please join in the conversation about these topics there to help develop our profession.

In closing, we share a real-life story about how business analysis can make a difference well beyond its usual confines. We hope that this sums up the book for you, as it does for us editors, and gives you a glimpse of how much of a difference business analysis can make across the wider world.

Business analysis is a leadership role

23

KEVIN BRENNAN

Business analysis is a leadership role. Much of the time, people over-look that fact, because we confuse leadership and management. Business analysts may not manage many people in a formal sense, but we have to lead them. We lead them by influencing them to support a course of action, by encouraging them to consider ideas and alternatives they might otherwise have overlooked, and by provoking new insights and promoting new ways of doing things. Without leadership skills, business analysts are likely to find their insights overlooked, their contributions minimized, and their role viewed as little more than that of scribe or note-taker. Perhaps you recognize this. Leadership skills aren't just for people looking to move to management; they're a valuable and necessary skill for doing the job well. However, many business analysts are held back from developing their lead-ership skills in the workplace, as they encounter resistance from co-workers or low expectations from employers.

Fortunately, you have opportunities outside the workplace to build up your leadership skills and grow in your career. Professional associations such as the International Institute of Business Analysis (IIBA) – **www.iiba.org** – provide a number of ways you can practise these soft skills. Some opportunities to pursue include:

- self-education to build up your business analysis knowledge as well as teach it to others;
- mentoring junior people entering the profession;
- taking on leadership roles in local chapters or other volunteer groups, self-education and study groups.

Self-education

Business analysts who work as contractors, moving from project to project and often company to company, have to take responsibility for their own skills development and for keeping up with new developments in the profession. It can be difficult for the self-employed to attend courses or conferences, which are often priced for employers with training budgets to spend. These events can be expensive for the individual, never mind the lost income from taking time off work.

The big challenge with all self-education is that it requires you to really understand your personal learning styles and how best to exploit them. In a classroom, you're pushed along to study the material, given regular deadlines, and strongly encouraged to get through the course and learn from it, even if you forget all of it within a few months. Self-education requires personal discipline. Even with a virtual study group, it's very easy to drop out if you aren't committed to finishing the course.

While it might surprise you to learn this, getting involved in a study group for a virtual class can be a great opportunity to exercise your leadership skills. Many IIBA chapters run study groups for CCBA or CBAP certification, but you might also want to join an online group run through an online educational organization. One such is Coursera, a company that partners with the top universities in the world to offer courses online for anyone to take, free of charge, which can be found at **www.coursera.org**. The best way to make sure that you finish the course is to reach out to and organize a group of peers to work through the course material with you. You'll need to match up a group of people (giving you a chance to build a team), get them working together in a collaborative manner, and help them stay on track. Just as business analysts generally have to do, all of that will need to be accomplished without you holding any formal authority over anybody in the group. That sounds like a hard thing to do, but frankly most people in those courses will be happy to let anyone who wants to take on that extra work do so. If you're involved with your local IIBA chapter, consider starting up a study group yourself, or helping to lead one.

Branch out

Don't limit your professional education to topics that seem directly relevant to the job you do today. The workplace is always changing, and knowledge can prove useful in unexpected ways. While the history of the Roman empire may be unlikely to come up at work (although it did, once, in my job) there's no reason to limit your professional development to the kinds of projects you're working on or even to business analysis.

I spent a couple of years taking improv comedy classes at Second City, and it's one of the most useful professional development activities I ever did. Although my comedy talents are limited, improvisation taught me to relax and to think quickly when speaking in front of a crowd, a skill that has proven invaluable many times over. It can also be very helpful in developing your active listening skills and in learning to engage with stakeholders who go off on what appears to be a tangent from your discussion topic (which may sometimes lead to real, valuable insight into a problem).

An understanding of project management, software development, or testing can prove useful to you even if you have no intention of doing those things yourself. They're useful because, as a business analyst, you have to be concerned with the feasibility of any proposed solution. Understanding those topics will help you think of the kinds of questions and issues you need to raise with your stakeholders to assess a proposed change properly. For example, my knowledge of project management (and my experience with it) often proved useful when discussing possible scope changes with stakeholders. While I was always careful to avoid committing the project to a change, I could get a ballpark sense of the complexity, ask the right questions to assess how the change might affect our timelines, and perform a preliminary cost–benefit assessment without needing to distract the project team from their delivery work. Similarly, asking myself 'How would I test this?' generally led to writing better and more complete requirements.

I know some business analysts worry that, if they demonstrate knowledge in these skills, their employers might rope them into these other roles and prevent them from doing business analysis work. I'd suggest that the best way to make sure you keep doing business analysis is to be delivering so much value in your business analysis role that your employers don't want you doing anything else. If you find that people are discounting your knowledge, oddly enough, it can be more effective in turning that impression around for you to gain more knowledge of their job than to get better at your own.

Sharing what you know

One of the best ways to improve your knowledge of a subject is to teach it. It sounds counterintuitive, but having to teach a topic forces you to think about what you know in a different way and to structure it so that people can understand it.

A lot of people are intimidated by the thought of getting up in front of a group of their peers and giving a presentation. However, for a business analyst, this is a skill you use and develop every day, and the idea of doing it for your local IIBA chapter or other professional group shouldn't be scary. A presentation uses the same skills and places the same demands on you as a requirements walkthrough, something you've done many times before. While you may learn something from reading about effective presentation skills, or watching others do it, the best way to improve them is actually to get up there and talk about something you know about.

Don't be afraid that you have nothing to teach, either. A great way to educate people on business analysis skills is to enlist them in working through a problem, discussing the results, and sharing what they've learnt with one another. You may learn more from the people you're presenting to than they learn from you!

Volunteering

Last but definitely not least, there are many leadership opportunities available through volunteer work.

IIBA chapters

Most IIBA chapters are eager to find volunteers able and willing to work to keep the chapter operational. There are a lot of roles in any chapter that provide you with the opportunity to learn valuable governance skills. While each chapter has its own structure, here are some of the common roles you might consider and the leadership skills you can develop in those roles.

President

While this is not likely to be the first role you take on with your chapter, the top one does provide a great opportunity to learn. A strong chapter president has to focus on building a team to do what the chapter needs, and stay out of operational issues. Your first priority, and most important skill, is talent management. Find good people to take on the other roles and constantly keep an eye open for more people who can step into the role of one of your team members – or even your own.

As president, you also have the opportunity to learn about and apply good governance to an organization. This is harder and more important than it seems. Do people have clear roles and responsibilities? Do they know what's expected of them?

You'll also have lots of opportunities to practise your diplomatic skills as president. You might think that volunteers would work together more smoothly than the people in a typical office, but that's not a good assumption. Sometimes, because people are volunteering their time, the emotional stakes can be heightened.

Secretary

The secretary's job in most organizations is a vital one. The secretary has the critical but thankless task of ensuring that proper governance procedures are in place and that they are followed. That includes taking minutes, yes, and it includes documenting what is done at board meetings and enforcing Robert's Rules of Order. It also means dealing with legal issues and ensuring that taxes are filed, legal requirements are met, appropriate governance procedures are in place and the organization is in compliance with the law. A strong secretary should work proactively to make sure that the chapter would never fall afoul of an audit – and I've been on a few projects that would have benefited from someone on board who was willing to do that necessary role while knowing how not to alienate his or her co-workers.

Treasurer

This role presents an opportunity to learn the basics of small business finance, something that can be very helpful as you get engaged in enterprise analysis and the development of business cases. You'll need to develop a grasp of cash flow, revenue, accounting and budgeting, and ensuring that the revenue streams of the chapter are commensurate with its costs. You'll also be responsible for dealing with tax issues and compliance issues.

Events

The chapter vice-president (VP) of events is responsible for booking speakers, securing meeting space for the chapter membership, and organizing food, drinks and other necessities for events. The major opportunity in this role is to stay on top of interesting trends and ideas in the business analysis community and then to network with people who have something to say about them.

Sponsorship

Sponsors represent a major potential source of value to a chapter. Sponsors can provide funding, meeting space, speakers and other support to a chapter. As VP of sponsorship, you'll have the opportunity to negotiate agreements with sponsors, building up your negotiation and sales skills, and to find and design win–win solutions that benefit both your chapter and the sponsor without creating potential conflicts of interest.

Membership

The VP of membership has one of the most important jobs in any chapter, because without members there is no chapter. Your job will include maintaining the membership list, reconciling it against the international membership list, and figuring out how to increase your membership over time. Membership should be one of the most significant revenue streams for a chapter, and membership dues can go a long way to ensuring that a chapter is on a sound financial footing.

One of the key roles of a VP of membership is one that should come naturally to any business analyst: to be an advocate for the chapter's membership. You need to make sure that you are engaging with your members, understanding how well the mix of events and programmes is meeting their needs and how the chapter can improve the experience for them. Are they looking for other kinds of events? Are they having trouble finding employment? That information can and should be assessed and passed on to the rest of the board so that the board can consider the mix of programmes it has in place.

Marketing

Most of the other roles deliver value to a chapter's members after they join, but your job is to get them in the door. Participating in a marketing role will teach you a lot about what people are looking for. You may need to work with other VPs to design and communicate the chapter programmes that your members want and need, as well as reaching out to your members and keeping them informed.

Other non-profit organizations

Much as I encourage you to get involved in your local IIBA chapter, or other professional body, you don't have to limit your volunteer leadership activities to there. Many great charitable or other voluntary organizations could greatly benefit from the application of some business analysis skills. In addition to the roles outlined above, many of which have parallels elsewhere, you can help support their strategic planning activities, identify possible operational improvements, facilitate stakeholder meetings, or get involved in the operational daily work or management of the group.

This last has the potential to help your career more than you may realize. In my own case, working as an executive at IIBA, with day-to-day operational and management responsibilities, has given me an incredible appreciation for the other side of the fence. As change professionals, we tend to underestimate the impact of our work on others. I can now understand why stakeholders don't read the documents we produce, why they don't have time to engage properly in changes (even ones they wanted), why they have trouble articulating clear requirements, and other banes of a business analyst's existence. The problem is not that they don't care about what you're doing, but rather that they tend to have much more immediate problems on a daily basis that are far more urgent from their perspective. To an operational manager, a business analyst needs to be a problem solver, not just a facilitator.

In a real way, volunteering with a non-profit organization is a great introduction to a more agile mindset, as well as developing leadership skills. Since you're a volunteer yourself and probably working with other volunteers, you need to identify small, easily understood changes and improvements that can be made without too much difficulty. Cultivate small steps and ongoing measures of progress, and understand how to introduce change without interrupting the real work of the organization. Your stakeholders will thank you for it.

Conclusion

One of the most compelling reasons to develop leadership skills, at least for me, was the desire to be able to put forward my ideas about how things need to be done in practice. As a profession, we have frequently struggled to get our stakeholders and co-workers to see all the ways in which we can add value.

By engaging with your local business analysis community and finding ways to exercise your leadership skills, you will find opportunities to build on the knowledge and abilities you already have and learn a lot more about where and how you can increase the value you deliver to your employer.

Yes, it will demand some of your time and you may feel that you don't have a lot to spare. The point of volunteering and participating in the community isn't for it to become a major time sink. Figure out what you can do and what is reasonable for you to do while still maintaining your commitments to your family, your friends and your work. And then engage.

About the author

Kevin Brennan, CBAP, PMP, is the chief business analyst and executive vice president for IIBA.

24 Becoming a thought leader

PENNY PULLAN

In this chapter, we consider what a thought leader is. Who can become one? Why would anyone want to? What does it take to do so? How can people develop thought leadership? The chapter is illustrated by my own personal story of how I took up the challenge to become a business analysis thought leader. I hope this chapter inspires you to share your valuable expertise with others too.

What is a thought leader?

This is a book about 'leadership for change', and its message is that leadership in business analysis isn't about being a general leading the troops from the front. Instead, it is about being a leader without the formal power and authority of a general. This sort of leadership takes conscious decisions and effort, starting with the self and moving on to influencing your project, your organization and the wider world. Thought leadership is one of the ways that you as an individual in business analysis can provide leadership for the wider world.

Thought leadership is about sharing value with others, through ideas that merit attention and knowledge of how to get things done. It's about moving from being merely a person fulfilling a role in an organization, a commodity who could be replaced at any time, to becoming a unique, trusted source of knowledge and expertise.

Thought leadership is radically different from traditional leadership in many ways. It doesn't need any formal power or authority to spread. Thought leadership is not taken, but granted by others. While it may be top down, it can also come from the bottom up in organizations as well.

Thought leadership has also been taken on as a marketing strategy and has become an overused concept, often straying from the goal of sharing value to focusing on generating business. In this chapter, we will focus on the type of thought leadership that shares value with others involved in change and stays away from the marketing cliché.

Who can become a thought leader?

While organizations might prefer all the attention of thought leadership to focus on the organizations themselves, thought leaders tend to be individuals within organizations. Think of Seth Godin and Richard Branson. Think too of all the authors of this book. While a number of companies are represented, you're most likely to remember the name of the person who wrote the chapter that you found useful. I consider all the contributors to this book to be thought leaders in our field, most of them business analysts.

Thought leadership is about sharing value with others who can use it, so there is no reason why anyone involved in business analysis who has great ideas to share cannot and should not aim to develop this over time.

Why should I develop thought leadership?

If you're working in business analysis, you're likely to be focused on change and improving the future for your stakeholders. As this is a challenging task, people welcome hearing from people who have deep knowledge and inspiring ideas on how to make this work. Once you have the expertise to share with others, actually doing this can help you to become the trusted source in your area for your organization and beyond. It changes your position from one of a commodity to someone who is unique, who adds value in a particular area. In this way, it helps to build your own personal brand.

Another reason for developing thought leadership could be to fly the flag for business analysis and the difference it can make to projects and organizations. Yet another, for those working as contractors or consultants, is to help your business become known for the expertise that you deliver, and to help your firm grow.

What does it take?

The foundation must be deep expertise and knowledge, from experience and research carried out probably over many years. This should be in a tight, targeted area and should merit attention from others. Who determines if your ideas have value? Those who are likely to read them, your audience. Without followers, there is no thought leadership.

Just deciding that you'd like to give back to others by sharing your expertise is not enough. It takes courage to step up into the spotlight, to voice your view, to face up to possible rejection and to share your story with strangers. You'll need the commitment to deliver despite the hurdles in your way.

To succeed, expertise and commitment must be joined with compelling delivery. Ideas need to be presented in a way that inspires people to change their perspectives. Knowledge isn't enough on its own to do that.

How can I develop thought leadership?

The answer is that you probably have already taken the first steps. When you advocate new ideas or ways of doing things with your boss or colleagues, based on your expertise, that's thought leadership.

So what are the steps that go beyond your usual business analysis role? They fall into four categories: writing, speaking, media and awards.

Writing

Often the easiest way to start is to write an article to share within your project or your organization. Perhaps there is an internal blog or newsletter crying out for input.

Externally, there are many opportunities to share your knowledge through writing. White papers and articles give the space to cover an area in depth. Online articles tend to be shorter than print. Writing a guest blog post for an established blogger can be an easy way to give online writing a try. If you like it, why not set up your own blog? For inspiration see many of the blogs written by authors of this book, such as Adrian Reed's business analysis blog (**www.adrianreed.co.uk**).

As you become known as a writer, you may be approached to contribute a chapter to other people's books, perhaps moving on to your own book. Nowadays, there are so many options for writing books, from short self-published e-books through to traditionally published books with a world-wide reach, such as this one.

Speaking

Making presentations to groups of people is a central part of most business analysis roles. Speaking to develop thought leadership builds on this to share your knowledge, ideas and expertise in an inspiring way. The first step could be to give a talk or presentation to your project team or perhaps to your organization's business analysis community of practice, if you have one. Most organizations can support you as you develop your presentation skills. In addition there are groups such as Toastmasters International that offer a structured development programme for speakers.

The next step is speaking outside your organization. A good place to start is with your own professional body, such as the local chapter of the International Institute of Business Analysis (IIBA) and conferences such as Business Analysis Europe and Building Business Capability in North America. You might also consider webinars, which can reach wider audiences without you or your audience needing to travel at all.

Media

If you enjoy speaking and are becoming known for your ideas, the next step for you might be media. While business analysis doesn't usually come up in radio, TV and newspapers very much, there are now online equivalents that welcome such input. From podcasts to online video, there are opportunities for sharing value here.

Social media is growing. On Twitter, there is even a hashtag #baot representing business analysts. By using this hashtag, you can connect to people interested in business analysis and change from all over the world.

Awards

Another way to raise the profile of your work and that of your organization can be to enter awards. One such award is the Business Analyst of the Year award in the UK.

One winner of this award is my co-editor, James Archer, who won the award in 2009 for a ground-breaking piece of work that raised his profile as a thought leader. Here's what the judges said:

> James is an outstanding proponent for business analysis, an excellent role model who exemplifies his profession. James showed how by discovering and understanding the real business needs an IT solution was transformed from one designed to deliver financial benefits to one that also made significant improvement to the quality of home care delivered to some of the most vulnerable people in society.
>
> (AssistKD, 2009)

My story

So far, we have covered how to become a thought leader, giving some different approaches to take. To flesh this out, I'm going to tell my story as an example of how one individual was able to share her work and inspire others by building up thought leadership.

The story starts shortly after I set up my own business, Making Projects Work Ltd, in early 2007. The IIBA UK chapter had just been formed, and they invited me to speak on facilitation skills at a London meeting in May. When the Business Analysis Conference Europe was launched in 2009, I presented on virtual meetings and again, in 2010, on visual thinking. By now, I had shared my ideas and expertise with around a hundred business analysts through speaking. They were very supportive and asked for more, echoing the clients of my company. I was also an associate senior instructor with ESI International, working with business analysts all over the Middle East and Europe. As before, they gave me good feedback and encouraged me to share my work more widely.

At the conference in 2010, I discovered a problem. By speaking with a large number of business analysts, I found out that there were many more who were unable to attend. It seemed that each person I spoke to knew of at least 20 colleagues and friends who would like to be present but because of cost, availability or project constraints were not able to. This gave me an idea. Surely it would be possible to use the internet to provide all these business analysts with a chance to take part in a virtual conference, at a time to suit them and without charging anything. I was keen to make a difference, to share my own expertise and to encourage others to do so. I'd seen various self-help virtual summits from the United States and decided to adapt this idea for professional use.

So the Business Analyst Summit was born! Over two weeks in November 2010, I interviewed several thought leaders in the business analysis and change fields. We had almost a thousand participants who could listen in to the sessions at a time to suit them, as well as providing the questions I asked the speakers. By the end of two weeks, I had heard other people talking about me as a thought leader in business analysis. This hadn't happened before for me in the area of business analysis, although I was already well known in the project management field.

The summit is now an annual event at **www.basummit.com** and is self-funding through premium subscriptions. Less than two years after the first summit, I was approached to write this book. Through my experience, I've learnt that thought leadership is also about giving others the space to develop as thought leaders too. As a result, the book is better for the wide range of perspectives it includes than it would have been written by myself alone.

Has thought leadership helped my business? Yes, I'm sure it has, by people getting to know what I stand for and the knowledge and experience I share. For me, the best part about this journey has been receiving feedback from business analysts all over the world. They say that, through my work, they've been inspired to do things differently, to step up to leadership and to walk just a little bit taller as people involved in business analysis. Who could ask for a better reason to start on one's own journey? I wish you all the best!

Questions for consideration

How does thought leadership fit into your plans for your own leadership within business analysis? What is your own area of expertise that you'd like to share with others? How can you make it compelling enough to be able to change other people's perspectives? Are you willing to step up into the spotlight? How will you deal with the possibility of rejection?

What are the next steps for you to take as you develop your own thought leadership? What form will this take?

About the author

Penny Pullan is the co-editor of this book and holds the annual, virtual BA summit: **www.basummit.com**.

References and further reading

AssistKD (2009) *Business Analyst of the Year: Winner announced!*, http://www.assistkd.com/baofypresentation2009.php (accessed 1 December 2012)

Building Business Capability Conference in North America, http://www.buildingbusinesscapability.com

Business Analysis Europe Conference, http://www.irmuk.co.uk/ba2013/ (for future years, replace 2013 with the appropriate year)

Reed, A [Accessed 28 November 2012] *Adrian Reed's Blog* [Online] http://www.adrianreed.co.uk/

25 Ethics and fair process

JAMES ARCHER

Business ethics continue to grow in importance, as the handling of ethical issues in recent years has damaged many organizations, such as Enron, UBS, RBS, BP and Instagram, to name just a few. Ethical behaviour should not only be at the heart of the business analysis profession but applying ethical thinking to business analysis can create stronger and richer solutions. This chapter argues that seeing ethical issues solely as the responsibility of managers or leaders is a mistake and makes the case for positioning ethical thinking as a key part of the business analyst role.

The International Institute of Business Analysis (IIBA), the professional body for business analysts, has developed *The Guide to the Business Analysis Body of Knowledge*® (Brennan, 2009), or BABOK® Guide. The BABOK® Guide and the requirements of the range of qualifications in business analysis all help develop professional standards and codes of expected behaviour by people in the profession.

This chapter now examines ethics from two key perspectives. Firstly I hope to provide an understanding of why ethics are important for business analysis and how to identify and respond to ethical challenges. Secondly I will look at the importance of fair process and emotional meaning and suggest that how you reach a particular outcome can be more important than the outcome itself.

Understanding ethics, morals and values

This chapter is rightly towards the end of this book, because being an ethical business analyst draws together everything under discussion here. Start by understanding yourself; the same principle that applies to values (see Chapter 1) applies to morals and ethics as well. A starting point to recognizing ethical issues is to understand the difference between values, morals and ethics. Frank Navran (2013) gives simple but very useful definitions:

- Values are our fundamental beliefs.
- Morals are values that we attribute to a system of beliefs (usually a religious or political system) that have authority at a societal level.
- Ethics is about our actions and decisions.

We each have a personal code of ethics, morals and beliefs that we use to distinguish between right and wrong. Understanding your own values is important, because they may or may not be the same as those of other individuals you are working with or those of the organization as a whole. Organizations have both formal and informal cultures and behaviours; for example, the publicly pronounced code of conduct may or may not be followed in practice. As a business analyst you need to learn how to conduct yourself in an ethical manner that is acceptable to yourself, your projects, your organizations and the wider world. This raises some important questions:

- Are your values fundamentally different from the values of your organization?
- Do the actions and decisions you make in your organization clash with your values?
- Are you able to carry out business analysis in a way you find acceptable?

If the answer to any of these questions is no then you have hard decisions to make. The choices are stark: leave, try to change things or risk behaving unethically. However, what makes ethics even harder, and more interesting, is that there is often no simple right or wrong answer.

What ethical behaviour means for business analysts

The BABOK® Guide has an excellent short section on ethics as one of the underlying competencies required by business analysts. BABOK® states that 'Ethics requires an understanding of moral and immoral behaviour, the standards that should govern one's behaviour, and the willingness to act to ensure that one's behaviour is moral or meets those standards.' Going on to describe the purpose of the inclusion of ethics in the guide, it reasons: 'A business analyst must be able to behave ethically in order to earn the trust and respect of stakeholders, and be able to recognize when a proposed solution or requirement may present ethical difficulties.'

Occasionally an ethical issue is straightforward; often they are not, especially as many ethical issues can be right versus right. Here are three situations where tricky ethical issues may arise:

- prioritizing the benefits to a group or for the organization as a whole;
- prioritizing short-term or long-term benefits;
- the truth versus personal loyalty.

The five scenarios that are described below all have ethical dimensions that should be carefully considered. Some people will consider them straightforward, with a simple right or wrong answer; others will see them as more nuanced. The key is to consider how to respond to such challenges in a way that you would be happy to see on the front page of a newspaper or tell your mother about!

Scenarios

1 You work for the IT department and are expected to provide IT solutions to the business. Can you ensure the IT solutions really meet business needs and not the IT department needs?

2 You are asked by the finance department to propose a solution that automates a process to pay travel expenses. Staff used to send paper claim forms each month for the finance team to process. Your solution means staff claiming expenses will have to enter details of every item claimed online and scan all their receipts. You received all the requirements from the finance department, who were keen to reduce the amount of time their staff spend managing travel expenses.

3 You discover the best-performing team have discovered a short cut in the IT system that allows staff to move on to the next piece of work before a manager signs their work off. Other teams work to the rules, which sometimes creates a backlog of work that is waiting for managers' approval. In the best-performing team the managers retrospectively sign off the work.

4 You are asked to make a proposal to increase the amount of 'hidden extras' people purchasing flights from your company's website will pay. Your instructions are to ignore customer service and to include suggestions that are on the borderline of being legal.

5 You are asked to undertake a study into all the work a team does because the senior manager wishes to outsource the work. You are told that you cannot explain what you are doing.

Under pressure

There will sometimes be pressure on business analysts to view a situation from a particular perspective. This is a good indicator of a potential ethical dilemma. There may also be pressure to present findings in a particular manner or to make a particular option appear attractive.

Business analysts are sometimes the only people to have access to all the information about a particular situation. It is essential you remember the power that you can sometimes have in influencing decisions. The way information is presented can indicate different meanings to people or, as Mark Twain said, 'Figures often beguile me, particularly when I have the arranging of them myself; in which case the remark attributed to Disraeli would often apply with justice and force: "There are three kinds of lies: lies, damned lies and statistics"' (Twain, 2010).

There are important links to be made between credibility (Chapter 4) and ethics and between climate (Chapter 17) and ethics. Is it possible for you to be credible if you are not ethical? This may well depend on the climate in your organization. If someone or an organization is not ethical, there is unlikely to be a climate of trust. If challenging unethical behaviour is not encouraged then unethical behaviour becomes more likely (Ethics Resource Center, 2010).

Business analysts should develop an ethical radar, to become more aware of situations requiring an ethical response. Something as seemingly minor as who to invite to a workshop can sometimes take on far deeper meaning than the work the workshop will cover. This means recognizing that routine business analysis work, such as interviewing stakeholders, can have ethical dimensions. For example, if an interviewee makes an allegation that financial regulations have been broken but asks you not to repeat the allegations for fear of losing his or her job, what would you do?

Applying ethical thinking

Many managers will state that the hardest decisions they have to take are those that involve ethics. There is often little training or support available for managers to make such decisions. Decisions are often made either on gut instinct or by interpreting the organizational strategy. Making use of an ethical decision-making framework can often lead to more informed and satisfactory decision making.

The ethicist Rushworth Kidder (1995) developed a nine-step approach that can be used to understand complex ethical issues:

1 Recognize that there is a problem.
2 Consider problem ownership.
3 Gather the relevant facts.
4 Test for right-versus-wrong issues.
5 Test for right-versus-right values.
6 Apply the ethical standards or perspectives.
7 Look for a third way – creative solutions.
8 Make the decision – may not lead to action.
9 Revisit and reflect on the decision – learning process.

Try using this model the next time you face an ethical dilemma. Not only will it help you make more sense of a situation, but it shows how the skills of a business analyst can be applied to ethics.

Fair process – ethical approach for business analysis

Business analysts need to consider the impact that a proposed solution will have on all stakeholder groups and work to ensure that those groups are treated fairly. Fair treatment does not require that the outcome be beneficial to a particular stakeholder group, but it does require that the affected stakeholders understand the reasons for the decision, that they are not deceived about the outcome, and that decisions which are made are made in the best interest of the organization.

(Brennan, 2009)

The characteristics of ethical behaviour as described in the BABOK® Guide are an excellent description of fair process. Selected as one of *Harvard Business Review*'s top 10 articles on managing people, Kim and Mauborgne (2011) show that people care as much about the fairness of the process through which an outcome is produced as they do about the outcome itself. Kim and Mauborgne describe the profound impact adopting fair process can have: 'Fair process profoundly influences attitudes and behaviours critical to high performance. It builds trust and unlocks ideas. With it managers can achieve even the most painful and difficult goals while gaining the voluntary cooperation of the employees affected. Without fair process, even outcomes that employees might favour can be difficult to achieve.'

How do you get fair process?

Engagement, explanation and clarity of expectations are the three critical elements Kim and Mauborgne identified as essential for fair process. Taking each in turn:

Engagement

Engagement means involving individuals in the decisions that affect them by asking for their input and allowing them to refute the merits of one another's ideas and assumptions. Engagement communicates management's respect for individuals and their ideas. Encouraging refutation sharpens everyone's thinking and builds collective wisdom. Engagement results in better decisions by management and greater commitment from all involved in executing those decisions.

(Kim and Mauborgne, 2011)

Challenges and opportunities for business analysis include:

- engagement by business analysts that is not just asking stakeholders how they do their job, but encouraging debate and discussion about current practice and potential solutions;
- persuading managers of the benefits of genuine engagement;
- creating a trusting climate where people are able to engage honestly and openly.

Explanation

Explanation means that everyone involved and affected should understand why final decisions are made as they are. An explanation of the thinking that underlies decisions makes people confident that managers have considered their opinions and have made those decisions impartially in the overall interests of the company. An explanation allows employees to trust managers' intentions even if their own ideas have been rejected. It also serves as a powerful feedback loop that enhances learning.

(Kim and Mauborgne, 2011)

Challenges and opportunities for business analysis include:

- the need to produce information that is clear, in a language that is easy for all involved parties to understand;
- the importance of business analysts in producing alternative solutions;
- business analysts should be seen as honest brokers (linking to credibility).

Expectation

Expectation clarity requires that once a decision is made, managers state clearly the new rules of the game. Although the expectations may be demanding, employees should know up front by what standards they will be judged and the penalties for failure. What are the new targets and milestones? Who is responsible for what? To achieve fair process, it matters less what the new rules and policies are and more that they are clearly understood.

(Kim and Mauborgne, 2011)

Challenges and opportunities for business analysis include:

- thinking through and sharing the implications of a new solution;
- systemic thinking – the technical modelling skills of business analysis can be adapted to model policy and rules and show the connections with proposed solutions.

Fair process, engagement and commitment

The Effort Dividend: Driving employee performance and retention through engagement, a survey by the Corporate Leadership Council (2004) of 50,000 employees, found emotional commitment is four times more powerful than rational commitment (Table 25.1).

Fair process and emotional commitment are extremely important concepts for business analysts to grasp. They mean that you can come up with a brilliant solution that fails to be adopted because of the way you went about your work. There will usually be constraints on the amount of time and access there is to different groups of stakeholders, but that should never be used as an excuse to ignore their concerns or deceive them.

TABLE 25.1 Emotional commitment is four times more powerful than rational commitment

Rational commitment primarily relates to the outcome itself	Emotional commitment primarily relates to the process by which the outcome was achieved
People ask themselves: – Does the result make sense? – Is the outcome fair in the context? – Does it seem logical and rational?	People ask themselves: – Was the process by which the outcome was achieved fair? – Who was involved in reaching the outcome? – How was the process determined?

A common theme throughout this book is to adopt approaches that support fair process and emotional commitment. Design thinking, facilitative leadership and systems thinking all encourage wider thinking about how we solve business problems most effectively. Business analysis is, above all, a profession that deals with people in the context of their individual and collective complexity. This means that ethics and fair process are at the heart of everything we do.

About the author

James Archer is the co-editor of this book, a business analyst, consultant, trainer and associate partner at Perspectiv.

References

Brennan, K (2009) *The Guide to the Business Analysis Body of Knowledge*®
  (BABOK® Guide), International Institute of Business Analysis, Toronto
Corporate Leadership Council (2004) *The Effort Dividend: Driving employee
  performance and retention through engagement*, Corporate Executive Board,
  Washington, DC
Ethics Resource Center (2010) [accessed 23 January 2013] *The Importance of
  Ethical Culture: Increasing trust and driving down risks* [Online] www.ethics.
  org/resource/importance-ethical-culture-increasing-trust-and-driving-down-risks
Kidder, RM (1995) *How Good People Make Tough Choices: Resolving the
  dilemmas of ethical living*, Fireside, New York

Kim, WC and Mauborgne, R (2011) Fair process: managing in the knowledge economy, in *HBR's 10 Must Reads on Managing People*, Harvard Business Review, Harvard Business School Publishing, Boston, MA

Navran, F [accessed 23 January 2013] Defining morals, values and ethics, Navran Associates [Online] http://www.navran.com/article-values-morals-ethics.html

Twain, M (2010) *Mark Twain's Own Autobiography: The chapters from the North American Review*, 2nd edn, ed MJ Kiskis, University of Wisconsin Press, Madison

Professionalization and best practice

NICK DE VOIL

The business analysis profession is growing and maturing – the publication of this book is one sign of that. Practitioners can now demonstrate their commitment to a career in business analysis by joining the International Institute of Business Analysis (IIBA), a worldwide professional body with over 25,000 members. A range of professional qualifications is available, underpinned by *The Guide to the Business Analysis Body of Knowledge*® (BABOK® Guide) (Brennan, 2009), which codifies the areas of knowledge and skill that each of us needs to develop.

So far, so good. Yet I worry that there are two unfortunate side-effects of the now widespread perception of business analysis as a mature profession. These mutually related 'memes' crop up regularly in business analyst-related social media forums.

The first is the idea that there exists, independently of any context, a set of practices that define the best way of doing our job. According to this view, all we need to do is to strive to conform to this 'best practice' and we will have achieved excellence as business analysts.

The second is that there exists, again independently of any context, a 'role' that is known by the name 'business analyst'. This is somehow indivisible and has its own sovereign essence, which we must seek to define and preserve unadulterated; for example, a business analyst cannot and must not also be a project manager, a strategist or an IT specialist, and by doing so would forfeit the right to be considered a business analyst.

In this chapter I urge business analysts not to give these abstract concepts more weight than they deserve, but instead to have the courage to think for themselves, remaining open to challenges and opportunities, judging each situation on its own merits.

The silver bullet

It is a seductive myth that professionals have access to a set of techniques that will solve any problem they care to address. A quarter of a century after Fred

Brooks wrote 'there is no silver bullet' (Brooks, 1987), we continue to place unwarranted faith in pre-packaged techniques and methods. Zealous adherents of a method like to claim that, if it has not been swallowed whole, it will lose its effectiveness. Over the last few years the most striking example of this has been 'agile', some of whose proponents insist on the blanket application of a set of ideas with little obvious coherence, some of which may be useful in a given situation and some of which may not (Coplien and Harrison, 2004). In previous decades, the same was true of object-orientation and structured methods.

Seen in this way, techniques function as a kind of comfort blanket. As David Wastell (2008) writes, 'Methodology, whilst masquerading as the epitome of rationality, has the potential to operate as a ritual whose enactment provides individuals with a feeling of effectiveness but which in reality alienates them from their real task.' Can any of us say we have never come across this principle at work in an organization?

The map is not the territory

I must stress that I am absolutely not criticizing the BABOK® Guide. It serves an immeasurably valuable purpose in setting out the common areas of concern for business analysts, enumerating the most useful techniques and, above all, providing a common vocabulary for business analysts to communicate with each other about their work, both within an organization and in a wider context.

What I am objecting to is the careless attitude that can be glimpsed when people refer to 'the BABOK' when they mean 'the BABOK Guide'. We all do this, of course, but we shouldn't, because the difference matters. The book is what the title says: a guide to the body of knowledge. It is not itself the body of knowledge. That resides in the collective consciousness of members of the profession and can therefore never be fully articulated.

This distinction is exactly what Alfred Korzybski (1933) was referring to when he said 'the map is not the territory'. He was pointing out the importance of not mistaking the representation of a thing for the thing itself. He went on to describe how our human language constantly tricks us into doing this. Business analysts need to be aware of the problem, working as we generally do with representations of things and dealing with stakeholders who habitually mix up the two. Information technology has added another twist to this: now there is also the risk of confusing a thing's virtual surrogate with the thing itself.

The place of professional knowledge

In his seminal work *The Reflective Practitioner* (1984), Donald Schön describes the traditional image of a profession as a practice based on technical rationality, in other words the solving of well-defined problems on the basis of a systematic knowledge base that is specialized, firmly bounded, scientific and standardized. He also explains how this model was misleading and founded on an obsolete philosophy of science, and shows how the essence of a professional's work is an ongoing cycle of action and reflection. The professional's response to events is not a matter of applying cookbook recipes but is often guided by tacit knowledge – knowledge whose existence is unknown to its knower – together with experience, feelings and emotions. This is 'reflection-in-action'. The professional then reflects on what happened and learns from it. This is 'reflection-on-action'.

Schön's other key point is that professional practice is not primarily a process of problem *solving*, but often and far more importantly one of problem *setting*. In real life, problems do not come ready-packaged. As he says:

> When ends are confused and conflicting, there is as yet no 'problem' to solve. A conflict of ends cannot be resolved by the use of techniques derived from applied research. It is rather through the non-technical process of framing the problematic situation that we may organize and clarify both the ends to be achieved and the possible means of achieving them.
>
> (Schön, 1984)

Schön could almost have had business analysts in mind when he wrote this. At the same time, Peter Checkland was working on soft systems methodology to address exactly these issues (see Chapter 19).

In Schön's terms, we should not overestimate the importance of our technical knowledge base. Rather, we need to ensure that we give ourselves the opportunity to develop reflective practice. This is where social media forums, mentoring and coaching can help. Above all, local IIBA chapters and study groups can play a vital role in this.

As Schön's stress on reflection-in-action suggests, it is important to recognize the importance of applying knowledge intelligently. When it comes to developing our professional skills or those of others, a useful mental tool for thinking about the BABOK® knowledge areas is Bloom's Taxonomy of Educational Objectives (Bloom *et al*, 1956). This is a framework for educationalists which acknowledges that in each of three domains – cognitive, affective and psychomotor – there are several different 'levels' at which a learner can internalize an area of expertise. For the cognitive domain, the levels are:

- *knowledge:* the ability to recall facts;
- *understanding:* the ability to organize, compare, describe and interpret ideas;
- *application:* the ability to solve problems using knowledge and understanding;
- *analysis:* the ability to take ideas apart and identify relationships and principles amongst the parts;
- *synthesis:* the ability to recombine ideas in new ways;
- *evaluation:* the ability to make and defend reasoned judgements about ideas.

The designers of the IIBA certification examinations have done a good job of taking Bloom *et al*'s taxonomy into account and asking an appropriate mix of questions to test each of these levels. However, the very fact of having a printed guide to the body of knowledge can sometimes mislead us into placing far too much emphasis on the knowledge level and not nearly enough on the analysis, synthesis and evaluation levels. Yet it is only by mastering the ideas at these levels that we can really achieve reflection-in-action.

Static and dynamic worldviews

It seems to me that the issues discussed here can be illuminated by the research of Carol Dweck (eg Dweck and Leggett, 1988), a psychologist who has put forward a convincing case for the existence amongst people of two contrasting mindsets: the 'fixed' or 'entity' mindset, based on a deep-rooted belief that the attributes of people and the world are fixed or uncontrollable, and the 'growth' or 'incremental' mindset, based on the belief that those attributes can be changed. Individuals with a fixed mindset are oriented towards making positive or negative evaluations of other people and things. They exhibit rigid, oversimplified thinking and tend not to initiate or persist with change. People with a growth mindset tend to exhibit empathy with others and are oriented towards achieving goals by understanding and improving things, relationships and processes.

I think it is fairly clear which of these mindsets is more desirable for a business analyst. It is also clear that we all come across examples of the less desirable mindset more or less frequently, both in our own behaviour and in the behaviour of those we work with. Finally, it is clear that both the memes under discussion are examples of the first mindset.

Business analysis is a process of learning

In 'The fully functioning personality' (1963), Korzybski's pupil S.I. Hayakawa distinguishes between the 'extensional' individual, who is capable of responding both to similarities and to differences between things, and the 'intensional', who tends to ignore differences among things that have the same name. Intensional thinking is associated with an unreflective use of language, an insensitivity to the fact that words do not capture reality in an accurate way, and undesirable social phenomena such as stereotyping and prejudice. It can lead to conflict and insoluble problems. Extensional thinking, on the other hand, is associated with openness, flexibility, learning and self-actualization (Maslow, 1943) – very much like Dweck's growth mindset. I believe that business analysts can do good work only if they are capable of extensional thinking.

More than any professionals – except perhaps psychologists, with whom we have more in common than we may think – we need to cherish and develop our ability to 'think outside the box', see other people's worldviews, and learn. If business analysis does have a core or an essence, it is surely this: the insistence on looking situations squarely in the face while at the same time understanding that they present different faces to other people, and seeking to understand all of them.

Types of decision-making context

As researchers such as DiMaggio and Powell (1983) have noticed, with the increasing maturity and importance of professionalism within a field comes a phenomenon called 'institutional isomorphism'. This means that every organization employing people from a particular profession quickly starts to resemble every other organization that does so. Because the professionals all 'speak the same language', the resemblances are either not noticed at all, or dignified with the name 'best practices'. In the contemporary business environment I think we have to be very careful about assuming that something must be a good idea because everyone else does it.

Dave Snowden's Cynefin framework (Snowden and Boone, 2007) clarifies this admirably. Snowden points out that the decision-making context within which leaders may find themselves can be categorized as one of four kinds: simple, complicated, complex or chaotic (Figure 26.1). Simple contexts such as straightforward line-of-business operations 'are characterized by stability and clear cause-and-effect-relationships'. It is in these situations that best practice is indeed appropriate: leaders 'assess the facts of the situation, categorize them, and then base their response on established practice'. Complicated contexts 'may contain multiple right answers, and though there is a clear relationship between cause and effect, not everyone can see it'. Here, the use of classic business analysis techniques may come into its own: a leader must 'sense, analyze and respond'.

However, as Snowden says, much of contemporary business has now shifted to the unstable and unpredictable 'complex' domain, where there is no right answer and cause-and-effect is comprehensible only in retrospect. Here, 'instead of attempting to impose a course of action, leaders must patiently allow the path forward to reveal itself. They need to probe first, then sense, and then respond.' This is quite clearly a challenge for professionals who believe that their toolbox contains a ready-made tool for every problem.

A community of practice

I very often hear people saying that a business analyst cannot be a project manager, or that a business analyst cannot be an IT specialist, or that a

FIGURE 26.1 Decision-making contexts in the Cynefin framework

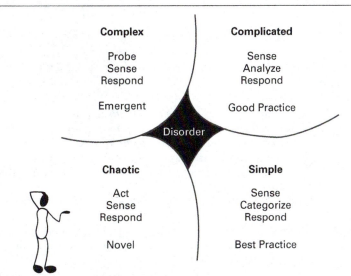

Snowden and Boone (2007). Used with the authors' permission.

business analyst cannot be a business strategist. The proponents of this idea would like to circumscribe the body of knowledge tightly using a lowest common denominator approach. This is simply nonsense. The label 'business analyst' does not have to dictate the totality of who we are as professional people. I believe that the reason for these attitudes, besides the problem of extensional thinking and fixed mindsets, is this: individuals fear that, if they cannot master the entire breadth and depth of the body of knowledge, they will have failed. There is no need for this fear.

There are no medical practitioners who claim to be experts on the whole spectrum of medical knowledge. Each operates within a relatively small area of the whole, yet they are all members of the same profession. The same is true of lawyers, educationalists and so on. A chartered accountant would be horrified at the idea of needing to remain current and active in every section of the syllabus covered by the professional examinations. Indeed, there are plenty of people who are qualified members of these professions, and who still regard themselves as members of them, but whose job titles are not directly related to their professional body of knowledge at all. Such people are often found in senior executive positions, for example. We do not need to be afraid of making it impossible for us individually to be experts in every area by drawing the boundaries of our profession widely.

What we need our profession to become is a 'community of practice' (Lave and Wenger, 1991), where we can all aspire to continuous growth and learning, and support each other along the way.

About the author

Nick de Voil is the founder and managing director of De Voil Consulting and a director of the IIBA's UK chapter.

References

Bloom, B *et al* (1956) *Taxonomy of Educational Objectives*, Handbook I: *Cognitive Domain*, David McKay, New York

Brennan, K (2009) *A Guide to the Business Analysis Body of Knowledge®* (BABOK® Guide), International Institute of Business Analysis, Toronto

Brooks, F (1987) No silver bullet: essence and accidents of software engineering, *IEEE Computer*, **20** (4), pp 10–19

Coplien, J and Harrison, N (2004) *Organizational Patterns of Agile Software Development*, Prentice Hall, New York

DiMaggio, P and Powell, W (1983) The iron cage revisited: institutional isomorphism and collective rationality in organizational fields, *American Sociological Review*, **48** (2), pp 147–60

Dweck, C and Leggett, E (1988) A social-cognitive approach to motivation and personality, *Psychological Review*, **95** (2), pp 256–73

Hayakawa, SI (1963) The fully functioning personality, in *Symbol, Status, and Personality*, pp 51–69, Harcourt Brace Jovanovich, New York

Korzybski, A (1933) A non-Aristotelian system and its necessity for rigour in mathematics and physics, in *Science and Sanity*, Institute of General Semantics, New York, pp 747–61

Lave, J and Wenger, E (1991) *Situated Learning: Legitimate peripheral participation*, Cambridge University Press, Cambridge

Maslow, A (1943) A theory of human motivation, *Psychological Review*, **50** (4), pp 370–96

Schön, D (1984) *The Reflective Practitioner: How professionals think in action*, Basic Books, New York

Snowden, D and Boone, M (2007) A leader's framework for decision making, *Harvard Business Review*, **85** (11), pp 68–76

Wastell, D (2008) The fetish of technique: methodology as a social defence, *Information Systems Journal*, **6** (1), pp 25–40

Opinion piece
Becoming the change agent

JAKE MARKHAM

The past couple of years' coverage on online blogs, forums, social networks and topics presented at business analysis conferences shows a growing awareness that business analysts are well placed within organizations to catalyse and facilitate change. Many large organizations recognize the benefits business analysis can bring. In some cases they have organized themselves around this, developing best practice, learning and development programmes, and developed consistency in their approach for engaging with clients and stakeholders.

This approach should yield significant benefit to large enterprises, where business analysts collaborate with one another to tackle systematically complex macro-challenges. In parallel there has been a debate around how to 'professionalize' the role of the business analyst and receive accreditation and recognition for analysts' valuable role in facilitating change. This is an area that it may take others some time to recognize. If the business analysis profession waits for recognition, it may prove a frustrating time.

When I think back to all the times I have met new sponsors and stakeholders when kicking off projects, I remember wondering how best to introduce the business analysis team and how to describe the way we go about collecting requirements and designing potential solutions. I recall one introduction to a senior banker. He was sponsoring an extensive research plan to improve how his teams operate both internally and externally. I started to explain the elicitation process that we would take and some of the techniques that the team thought would help uncover valuable improvements. As I described this, I started to lose him and saw his eyes glaze over. Ever since then, I have played down the formal process and terminology around the role and focused on the engagement – what to expect next and what we need to do as a team. While this may sound counter-productive to 'professionalizing' the business analysis role, it has proven to be very effective based on the referral projects we have received since. In several cases we have been introduced to peers of 'clients' who have claimed to enjoy the design process – often learning a fair amount about the business they run through working with us. These clients become sponsors – they championed the role of business analyst and endorsed the value we brought to the enterprise. Consider why a stakeholder would refer you to another – do yours enjoy the engagement enough to recommend you?

If you create an energetic and collaborative environment throughout projects, it is possible that stakeholders will enjoy discovering what their teams currently do and how that could evolve through innovation. If you were to ask a stakeholder or sponsor what role any of my team played, I am not convinced they would call it business engineering or analysis. They would probably say that we had helped them to understand what they needed, and what it could look and feel like. I'm not sure that this helps spread the word on business analysis as a profession, but it has proven effective in truly engaging clients and partners.

This style of engagement is nothing new for many. It is broadly user-centred design as used throughout business analysis, and it also applies the concept of collaborative design. The differentiator in my opinion is an analyst's soft skills and competences. These define someone's personal effectiveness. These skills are particularly important during high-touch engagements. These are the strategic engagements for which business analysts are airlifted in to lead and facilitate change rather than execute a research plan. For these engagements, having the ability to read between the lines, being an active listener and having strong street smarts really help. Business analysts need to provide the energy and motivation for teams to collaborate – this approach delivers results.

Given that this style of engagement has yielded results, are there certain skills that a business analyst needs in order to be effective during demanding projects? And which soft skills are most valuable to business analysts? This topic has been covered many times, and a number of these skills are discussed in this book. It is a topic that I focused on a couple of years ago when the organization invested in a learning and development curriculum for business analysts supporting development from career starters to senior leaders. We spent significant time as a team working closely with external companies and internal subject matter experts looking at the current industry models, and there were many opinions. Based on the type of engagements undertaken within financial services and the tightening of budgets, along with a requirement to rationalize technology across the available delivery channels, we defined a proprietary knowledge and skills model. The areas we supplemented over and above the industry-standard models were around modelling, specifically information architecture, requirements prototyping and human factors integration – these areas supported the increasing demand to collaboratively model requirements with stakeholders and iteratively design solutions. Additional personal effectiveness skills defined were creative thinking, leadership, influence and problem solving. With these skills and strong intrinsic skills, business analysts should be well positioned to drive engagements and act as vision owners within project teams, regardless of development methodology or domain.

I classify skills, when simplified, into two types: intrinsic and learnt. Arguably I think the business analyst role benefits from a number of these intrinsic skills, combined with learnt skills based on domain and context. When interviewing and recruiting business analysts, do you choose someone who has extremely strong practitioner skills around tools and techniques or the creative thinker who has highly developed listening, problem solving and street smarts. Ideally you would have a blend of the two, but where would you take the risk position? I would always take the intrinsic and teach the domain and techniques. This isn't to say that intrinsic and personal effectiveness skills cannot be developed over time, but more that they come naturally to some business analysts and that these individuals will probably feel more comfortable driving change and being the vision owners.

When there is organizational awareness backed up with a track record of innovation delivered by business analysis throughout an organization, then analysts are well placed to propose innovation opportunities for the enterprise proactively and to be listened to. Business analysts are among the very few groups that have access to and understanding of macro-requirements and capabilities across lines of business, regions and delivery channels. But how do business analysts justify spending time on innovation outside of core-funded projects? Some would agree that, given this knowledge base, business analysis functions are ideally placed to drive innovation across the organization, whether that is defining product differentiation, driving collaboration of enterprise opportunities or simply bringing to the surface thematic requirements not spotted within individual lines of business or teams that do not have access to the joined-up business intelligence.

When considering your role as a business analyst either as an independent consultant or as part of a professional practice, are you positioning yourself or the function to drive change or support change? I work within a large organization where there has been a lot of focus and investment in professional development, alignment of business analysis roles, institutionalization of knowledge and a focus on team collaboration. All of these activities have helped position the business analyst as a change agent, but there is still a need for the analyst to have the right blend of skills to be successful leading engagements and converting stakeholders into sponsors and champions of the business analysis role.

About the author

Jake Markham is a director at Credit Suisse and EMEA lead for Client Technology Solutions. Jake organizes Credit Suisse's Business Analysis Community events and training opportunities.

End piece
Integrating business analysis, creativity and play

ANDREW KENDALL

I am a business analyst with nearly 20 years' experience. While living in London and working for companies in the Square Mile, I led a team that developed a programme for London's Great Ormond Street Hospital for Children (GOSH). The programme allowed volunteers to visit children on the wards and bring with them play activities that could be completed at the bedside or in groups. Fortunately the job of understanding play was made easier because at age 15 I had become so good at building Lego that the Lego company hired me. I was able to combine my business analysis skills with my love of play and my desire to volunteer at children's hospitals.

In the development of the programme, the team really had to understand how play could be delivered to children on the wards with enough activities to keep them entertained but also to support the needs of the volunteers who had to provide the interactivity. Lots of business analysis skills were used here to understand 'the work of providing play'. Those skills were critical in understanding the needs of all kinds of stakeholders, not just children, but also parents and nursing staff, in what can sometimes be difficult circumstances. In 2009 I was honoured to accept an award from the Institute of Child Health in the UK recognizing my contribution to children's hospitals. This contribution could never have been made without the efforts of such a brilliant team of people.

Today I consult in business analysis techniques and teach alongside industry leaders James and Suzanne Robertson. Since the days at Great Ormond Street Hospital, I have partnered with Claire, a former member of my team, to create a social enterprise advising children's hospitals on establishing play programmes using child-led concepts. These concepts involve children in the design of their own programmes, which are facilitated by volunteers. After

INDEX

refining this in the development of a play programme for Sydney Children's Hospital, we recently worked with King's College London, where our programme design is being used to teach first-year medical students how to interact with children. It's great being part of something that has children teaching the doctors how to engage them through play, and that's got to be the ultimate in understanding user needs!

About the author

Andrew Kendall is a consultant and trainer, currently managing a creative problem-solving hub for the New South Wales government in Sydney, Australia.

CPSIA information can be obtained
at www.ICGtesting.com
Printed in the USA
LVOW13s0835260718
585014LV00019B/737/P